ROUTLEDGE LIBRARY EDITIONS:
EDUCATION IN ASIA

Volume 12

WOMEN, EDUCATION, AND DEVELOPMENT IN ASIA

WOMEN, EDUCATION, AND DEVELOPMENT IN ASIA

Cross-National Perspectives

Edited by
GRACE C. L. MAK

Routledge
Taylor & Francis Group
LONDON AND NEW YORK

First published in 1996 by Garland Publishing, Inc.

This edition first published in 2018
by Routledge
2 Park Square, Milton Park, Abingdon, Oxon OX14 4RN

and by Routledge
711 Third Avenue, New York, NY 10017

Routledge is an imprint of the Taylor & Francis Group, an informa business

© 1996 Grace C. L. Mak

All rights reserved. No part of this book may be reprinted or reproduced or utilised in any form or by any electronic, mechanical, or other means, now known or hereafter invented, including photocopying and recording, or in any information storage or retrieval system, without permission in writing from the publishers.

Trademark notice: Product or corporate names may be trademarks or registered trademarks, and are used only for identification and explanation without intent to infringe.

British Library Cataloguing in Publication Data
A catalogue record for this book is available from the British Library

ISBN: 978-1-138-30826-8 (Set)
ISBN: 978-1-315-14674-4 (Set) (ebk)
ISBN: 978-1-138-31013-1 (Volume 12) (hbk)
ISBN: 978-1-138-50586-5 (Volume 12) (pbk)
ISBN: 978-1-315-14396-5 (Volume 12) (ebk)

Publisher's Note
The publisher has gone to great lengths to ensure the quality of this reprint but points out that some imperfections in the original copies may be apparent.

Disclaimer
The publisher has made every effort to trace copyright holders and would welcome correspondence from those they have been unable to trace.

Women, Education, and Development in Asia
Cross-National Perspectives

Edited by
Grace C. L. Mak

Routledge
Taylor & Francis Group
LONDON AND NEW YORK

First published 1996
by Garland Publishing, Inc.

Published 2013 by Routledge
2 Park Square, Milton Park, Abingdon, Oxon OX14 4RN
711 Third Avenue, New York, NY, 10017, USA

Routledge is an imprint of the Taylor & Francis Group, an informa business

Copyright © 1996 by Grace C. L. Mak
All rights reserved

Library of Congress Cataloging-in-Publication Data

Women, education, and development in Asia : cross-national perspectives /
    edited by Grace C. L. Mak.
            p.   cm. — (Reference books in international education ; vol. 33.
    Garland reference library of social science ; v. 825)
        Includes bibliographical references and index.
        1. Women—Education—Asia.   2. Women in development—Asia.
    I. Mak, Grace C. L.   II. Series: Garland reference library of social
    science ; v. 825.   III. Series: Garland reference library of social
    science. Reference books in international education ; vol. 33.
    LC2302.W66   1996
    370'.82—dc20   96-16773
                                                                                    CIP

ISBN 13: 978-0-815-30795-2 (hbk)

Contents

VII   Series Editor's Foreword

IX   Preface

Part I East Asia

    Chapter 1
3   The People's Republic of China
    Grace C. L. Mak

    Chapter 2
29   Japan
    Machiko Matsui

    Chapter 3
51   South Korea
    Oksoon Kim

    Chapter 4
65   Taiwan, Republic of China
    Hsiao-chin Hsieh

Part II Southeast Asia

    Chapter 5
95   Indonesia
    Mayling Oey-Gardiner and Riga-Adiwoso Suprapto

Chapter 6
119 MALAYSIA
Robiah Sidin

Chapter 7
143 SINGAPORE
Guat Tin Low

PART III SOUTH ASIA

Chapter 8
165 INDIA
Ratna Ghosh and Abdulaziz Talbani

Chapter 9
187 PAKISTAN
Kowsar P. Chowdhury

Chapter 10
217 SRI LANKA
Swarna Jayaweera

245 BIBLIOGRAPHY

263 CONTRIBUTORS

267 INDEX

Series Editor's Foreword

This series of scholarly works in comparative and international education has grown well beyond the initial conception of a collection of reference books. Although retaining its original purpose of providing a resource to scholars, students, and a variety of other professionals who need to understand the role played by education in various societies or world regions, it also strives to provide accurate, relevant, and up-to-date information on a wide variety of selected educational issues, problems, and experiments within an international context.

Contributors to this series are well-known scholars who have devoted their professional lives to the study of their specializations. Without exception these men and women possess an intimate understanding of the subject of their research and writing. Without exception they have studied their subject not only in dusty archives, but have lived and traveled widely in their quest for knowledge. In short, they are "experts" in the best sense of that often overused word.

In our increasingly interdependent world, it is now widely understood that it is a matter of military, economic, and environmental survival that we not only understand better what makes other societies tick, but that we make a serious effort to understand how others, be they Japanese, Hungarian, South African, or Chilean, attempt to solve the same kinds of educational problems that we face in North America. As the late George Z.F. Bereday wrote more than three decades ago: "[E]ducation is a mirror held against the face of a people. Nations may put on blustering shows of strength to conceal public weakness, erect grand façades to conceal shabby backyards, and profess peace while secretly arming for conquest, but how they take care of their children tells unerringly who they are" (*Comparative Methods in Education*, New York: Holt, Rinehart and Winston, 1964, p. 5).

Perhaps equally important, however, is the valuable perspective that studying another education system (or its problems) provides us in understanding our own system (or its problems). When we step beyond our own limited experience and our commonly held assumptions about schools and learning in order to look back at our system in contrast to another, we see it in a very different light. To learn, for example, how China or Belgium handles the education of a multilingual society; how the French provide for the funding of public education; or how the Japanese control access to their universities enables us to better understand that there are reasonable alternatives to our own familiar way of doing things. Not that we can *borrow* directly from other societies. Indeed, educational arrangements are inevitably a reflection of deeply embedded political, economic, and cultural factors that are unique to a particular society. But a conscious recognition that there are other ways of doing things can serve to open our minds and provoke our imaginations in ways that can result in new experiments or approaches that we may not have otherwise considered.

Since this series is intended to be a useful research tool, the editor and contributors welcome suggestions for future volumes, as well as ways in which this series can be improved.

Edward R. Beauchamp
University of Hawaii

Preface

In 1970 Ester Boserup alerted us to the serious omission of women from the vast and ever-growing literature on economic development.[1] Basing her analysis on cross-national census data and other official statistics, she argued that the process of development would inevitably entail differential opportunities and different subsequent outcomes for the two sexes. The years that followed saw attempts to understand women's contribution to economic development,[2] as well as studies at the national level that called attention to the contradictions in the meaning of development to women and to men.[3] At the same time the focus of research attention has extended from women's roles in the private sphere to those in the public sphere.[4] In the policy arena, the UN Decade for Women (1976–1985) emphasized women's contribution to development. In recent years international development agencies have increasingly included women as beneficiaries in their planning. Nevertheless, gender planning, which has as its goal equality, equity, and empowerment, still has not attained legitimacy.[5]

Since the end of World War II we have witnessed a dramatic expansion of educational systems throughout the world. Education has been used as a vehicle for national economic development as well as for individual advancement.[6] By definition, the legislation of compulsory education includes both males and females as recipients. Considerable research has been devoted to identifying the contribution of educational expansion to the development of countries in what is commonly known as the Third World. Yet few authors have addressed this topic with women as the focus. While the experience of several decades has shown that educational systems continue to admit and treat males and females differently, still little is known about the effect of education on the subsequent lives of women.

Education for girls and women as a subject of study is relatively recent. It first appeared in compartmentalized forms: females' access to education, their schooling processes, and the effect of education on their subsequent paid employment and family life. Although the literature has helped us understand separate aspects of the subject, it has failed to explain how these various aspects relate to one another in a comprehensive manner. Much effort has been directed to the linkage between women's education and the labor force while ignoring the major factor of the family in shaping women's lives. Gail Kelly has proposed an integrative approach to understanding the influence on and consequences of women's education that takes into consideration women's lives in both the public and private spheres.[7]

This volume, which has been inspired by literature focusing on women in economic development and education, includes an additional theme: Asia's development experience. Quests for development in Asia are marked by contrasts and the routes vary. Some nations emphasize industrialization—Japan being the primary role model—and the newly industrialized and industrializing countries in the rest of Asia aspire to catch up. Others experiment with new political structures, as in the cases of China, North Korea, and Vietnam. The push for development has been complicated by clashes among regions, religions, ethnic groups, and social classes and castes. Surfacing amid the diversity, however, is the unifying theme of education as a tool for development.

Asia has been part of the global educational expansion since the end of World War II. How do its development strategies affect educational policies and women's status? In a continent largely patriarchal, how have women responded to the increase in educational opportunities? And how do education and development needs combine to affect women's chances in their subsequent lives?

This volume deals with four interrelated aspects of schooling for women in ten Asian countries. First, it examines the development experience of a country and how it affects education and women's status. Second, it reviews the types of educational opportunities available to women and investigates whether and how women have been able to take advantage of them. For women denied formal education, nonformal education may be an alternative route to a desired future. The third issue addressed is whether greater exposure to education has resulted in parallel participation in the public sphere, and, if not, how women's background characteristics and development needs can combine to shape it. Fourth, this volume examines the impact of education and economic participation on women's domestic status in terms of possible changes in marriage, fertility, and decision-making patterns at home and thus raises the question of whether society's definition of women's roles in the family acts to undermine the effect of schooling on women's public participation.

Nations in Asia have mixed experiences of economic development. Central to our investigation is the impact of development on women's lives and, conversely, women's contribution to it. Organized geographically, this volume includes chapters on countries in East Asia, Southeast Asia, and South Asia. Although the chapters rest on a common framework, the perspectives and emphases of the authors are not uniform. The variation among us precisely reflects the different social contexts in which we grew up and the ideological and material conditions in which we live today.

In September 1995 the United Nations held its fourth women's conference in Beijing, China. Although the conference attracted much media attention, feminist scholars are skeptical about the extent to which it succeeded in promoting women's rights. The struggle must continue at both the macro-societal and daily life levels.

Grace C. L. Mak

NOTES

1. Ester Boserup, *Women's Role in Economic Development* (New York: St. Martin's Press, 1970).

2. See, e.g., Irene Tinker, Michele Bo Bramsen, and Mayra Buvinic, eds., *Women and World Development* (Washington, DC: Overseas Development Council, 1976); Nadia Haggag Youssef, *Women and Work in Developing Societies* (Westport, CT: Greenwood, 1976); June Nash and Helen Safa, eds., *Women and Change in Latin America* (South Hadley, MA: Bergin & Garvey, 1986).

3. E.g., Judith Van Allen, "Modernization Means More Dependency," *The Center Magazine* (May/June 1974): 60–67; Nora S. Chinchilla, "Industrialization, Monopoly Capitalism, and Women's Work in Guatemala," *Signs* 3 (1977): 38–56; Gail Warshofsky Lapidus, *Women in Soviet Society* (Berkeley: University of California Press, 1978); Noeleen Heyzer, ed., *Women Farmers and Rural Change in Asia* (Kuala Lumpur: Asian and Pacific Development Centre, 1987).

4. E.g., Heleieth B. Saffioti, *Women in Capitalist Production* (New York: Monthly Review Press, 1978); June Nash and Maria Patricia Fernandez-Kelly, eds., *Women, Men, and the International Division of Labor* (Albany, NY: State University of New York Press, 1983); Susan Bullock, *Women and Work* (London: Zed Books, 1994).

5. Caroline O. N. Moser, *Gender Planning and Development* (London and New York: Routledge, 1993).

6. Robert Fiala and Audrey Gordon Lanford, "Educational Ideology and the World Educational Revolution, 1950–1970," *Comparative Education Review* 31, no. 2 (1987): 315–332.

7. Gail P. Kelly and Carolyn M. Elliott, eds., *Women's Education in the Third World: Comparative Perspectives* (Albany, NY: State University of New York Press, 1982); Gail P. Kelly, ed., *International Handbook of Women's Education* (Westport, CT: Greenwood, 1989).

Part I
East Asia

1   The People's Republic of China
Grace C. L. Mak

Introduction

A popular approach in assessing the status of women in China is to compare the present with the times before the Communist liberation in 1949; frequently the conclusion is that much progress has been made. Such an approach assumes a linear path of steady improvement, when in actuality the drive toward equality of the sexes has taken a wavering course at an uneven speed. In this chapter I propose an integrated, or spiral, approach to explaining the relationship between women's education, their family situations, and economic development. The spiral takes its shape from two sources. First, changes in policies affecting the status of women (education, marriage, population, and employment) have met mixed degrees of success in any time period. In general, education and population policies have met fewer difficulties than have employment and marriage/divorce policies, primarily because of men's resistance to or competition with the latter two. Thus any change in women's status is a result of the interplay of these four policy areas. Second, the situation of women varies in different time periods, as a result of the prevailing development strategies. However, in spite of a less favorable climate to women during a certain period, gains made in a previous period help women to continue the struggle from a new reality, and hence we see the spiral.

In the context of the spiral approach, I will argue that, first, the uncoordinated nature of the policies has had an uneven impact on women, which results in greater gains in education than in employment. Second, I will set forth that the degree to which opportunities are opened up to women has hinged on changing definitions of "gender appropriate" roles to fit development needs. Third, I will stress that women are not a passive group, that the ways they respond to policies have been crucial in their movement forward in the spiral course.

This chapter starts with a historical sketch of women's status in China. The main discussion focuses on two major phases of contemporary China: the years from 1949 to 1978, and the reform era that began in 1978 and continues today.

HISTORICAL SKETCH

Speculation has led to the notion that women in prehistoric China had a high degree of freedom.[1] The subordination of Chinese women as we know it is attributable to Confucianism, which sets a rigid hierarchy in social relations. The subordination of subject to ruler extended to that of sons to fathers, young to old, and females to males. An official ideology since the Han dynasty (207 B.C.–A.D. 220), Confucianism has dominated Chinese culture and society. State service, the ultimate achievement in life for Chinese in traditional China, was for males. The state selected talents through the imperial examination. This process excluded women from education. Nevertheless, women took part in economic life. Rural women helped in economic production, and some town women worked in the low strata of society.

Women's plight began to ease toward the end of the Qing dynasty (1644–1911) in the nineteenth century. The decline of the Qing spurred efforts toward national salvation. One such effort was to improve the Chinese stock through mothers. Education was given a pronounced role in enhancing women's, and subsequently the nation's, quality, and women began to be included. In the second half of the nineteenth century western missionaries gained entry to China and set up schools and hospitals. These were the first modern schools in China, and they admitted girls. Toward the end of that century, private Chinese schools followed suit. Some of the school graduates blazed the trail for professional women, who became doctors, teachers, and missionaries.[2] Education also enabled women to participate in politics. At the turn of the century revolutionaries from the Han majority group of the Chinese population tried to overthrow the Qing dynasty, which was ruled by the minority group of ethnic Manchus. A small number of these revolutionaries were women, mostly students and teachers.

In 1911 a new republican government was founded by the triumphant revolutionaries, who had renamed themselves the Guomindang (the Nationalist Party, hereafter the GMD). Among the new policies it devised was legislation of women's suffrage and rights, which subsequently proved to be rhetoric. In 1921 the Chinese Communist Party (hereafter the CCP) was founded. After initial years of collaboration, the GMD and the CCP split in 1927, a split that set the course of modern Chinese history. The following years saw two Chinas, with the GMD ruling most of the country and the

CCP occupying some rural bases. In GMD China, family ideology continued to center around women's fulfillment of their traditional roles. Only when women were sought to support government defense efforts in domestic warfare and in the face of external threats (the Japanese invasion in 1937–45) was there substance in the GMD's call for women to participate in economic production and service behind the lines. Even so, women were still told to fulfill their responsibilities in the national cause before demanding their rights.

Meanwhile, female participation in education had increased. A government system of schooling was established in 1902. It first admitted males, and from 1907 on it also admitted females. Female students accounted for 26% of national enrollment at the primary level in 1945 and for 20% at the secondary level and 18% at tertiary in 1946.[3] Schools were typically single-sex, and teaching became a major occupational outlet for educated women. Women made up 18% of all teaching and non-teaching staff in primary schools in 1945 and 12% of those in secondary schools in 1946.[4] Depending on their educational attainment, women also worked as clerks, salesladies, or professionals. However, in the 1920s to 1940s, the effect of education on women diminished with men's unemployment. Jobs were scarce, and men were hired first. The gender factor also limited women's length of employment. Often they left their employment upon marriage or at their first pregnancy. This leaving was sometimes arbitrary, however, because some posts were closed to married women. Nor was education always required for employment. Nascent industrialization, usually in light industries such as textiles, drew cheap labor from uneducated women.[5]

Industrialization weakened the economic function of marriage. Gainful employment postponed women's marriages and freed them from patriarchal and matrimonial yokes. Discontented daughters and daughters-in-law sought haven in factory employment.[6] Divorce, while relatively limited, became a social phenomenon.[7] Spinsterhood began to appear among the better educated women.

A multitude of women's groups had been formed to promote intellectual pursuits, national defense, and legal and other rights for women. Their members were the first generation of women feminists, in contrast to male reformists who had earlier advocated women's rights. With education and employment women had regained their voices. The Sino-Japanese war effort stimulated their growth.[8]

In CCP China (1927–1949), the liberation of women was on the agenda of party congresses. Education, free marriage, and political rights were promised. In reality the rights of women were neglected and sacrificed when they encountered male resistance.[9] Women were mobilized into the rural economy and guerilla warfare but were also told that their emancipation could come only out of a class struggle. This position resembled the GMD view on women's struggle.

Thus, as in the West during the two world wars, by the end of the 1940s warfare was crucial in drawing Chinese women into mainstream society. This new reality for women emerged from the interactive forces between national expediency, education, and economic demands. It was based on this reality that women entered the next phase of development.

National Reconstruction and Women's Status, 1949–1978

Attempts at raising women's status grew to a national scale with the success of the Communist revolution in 1949. The constitution stipulated equal rights for men and women, but as many studies on Chinese women in this period have noted, it was an unfinished revolution.[10] This section examines the degree to which these rights were translated into reality and what prevented them from full realization.

Marriage and the Family

The marriage law of 1950 aimed at protecting a woman's legal rights to choose her marriage partner and to apply for divorce when a marriage failed. The law was actively publicized, and women were quick to use this newly acquired right to quit unhappy marriages. Of all civil cases filed in the immediate period that followed, the majority were applications for divorce, an overwhelming percentage of which were submitted by women. Since Chinese women had been socialized into putting the family's well-being above their own, the surge of these cases revealed the extent of their conjugal discontent. In a society that condemned divorce as a personal and family failure, the law offended husbands, parents, and rural local authorities. Many women who filed divorce petitions were harassed or coerced into withdrawing them. As a result, large numbers of suicides and homicides occurred.[11] In 1953 a publicity campaign was staged to ensure that the law was implemented, but since then government effort has been scaled down and oriented toward reconciliation of marital conflicts. This is but one of repeated instances of male resistance to legislation designed to protect women and, more disappointingly, subsequent government compromise.

Other policies had varied impacts on women. The new government introduced a social security system that included sickness relief and postnatal and old age care. Eligible women workers were entitled to 56 days of paid maternity leave. However, this provision was mostly for urban employees, who made up 10% of the entire labor force in 1955.[12]

The population policy and public child care policy affected women's availability for economic participation. The active effort to control the birthrate in the mid-1950s was reversed a few years later when the government stressed that a large population would be an asset. In the mid- to late 1960s there was no definite population policy, although there were measures to help people plan and control births. Birth control was actively reinstated between 1972 and 1979. China's population policy in turn affected its marriage policy. Males were advised to marry after age 25 and females after age 23. Birth control became a top priority in 1979 with the introduction of the one-child-per-couple policy. Later marriage and lower fertility reduced women's maternal burdens and freed them for public participation. But women's receptiveness to birth control varied. In general, urban and/or educated women tended to have fewer children than rural and/or less educated women.[13] The setting up of child care centers and kindergartens in cities freed some women for employment.

The All-China Women's Federation was created shortly after the Communist Party came into power as part of the government. It was, in spirit, a continuation of the women's work committee in pre-liberation days. Its achievements have been mixed. While working for the advancement of women in broad terms, it is an extended arm of the government and, in the final analysis, tended to subsume women's interests to those of the government in cases of conflict. The earlier diversity of women's voices had vanished.

Education

In contemporary China formal education comprises three levels. Primary education lasts six years and lower secondary education three years. Upper secondary education is differentiated into general education and different types of vocational education which last from three to five years. Tertiary education comprises degree and non-degree courses. Graduate education, which includes master's and doctoral degrees, was dormant from the early 1950s on and reinstituted in the early 1980s. From the start, education was assigned a major role in development. It was to perform the twin functions of promoting social equity and nurturing talents.

The education system in general registered a spectacular increase between 1949 and 1990, during which period the population had approximately doubled (see Table 1.1). The decline since 1978 in absolute numbers at the primary and secondary levels reflects a drop in the birth rate. The enrollment rate had risen to 98% in 1992 for primary school-aged children, compared with 94% in 1978 and 49% in 1942.[14] The fluctuations in enrollment reflected political instability. The Great Leap Forward, a 1958–59 campaign to accelerate economic growth, had been accompanied by an upswing in enrollment. During the Cultural Revolution (roughly 1966–1976), the education system was disrupted and enrollment plunged. Education was again emphasized from 1978 on, when its role in economic development was realized.

Table 1.1 Enrollment Trends in China by Level of Education, 1949–1992 (in Thousands)

Year	Undergraduate	Secondary	Primary
1949	117	1,268	24,391
1957	441	7,081	64,283
1958	660	11,998	86,403
1960	962	14,873	93,791
1965	674	14,318	116,209
1970	48	26,483	105,280
1978	856	66,372	146,240
1988	2,066	53,628	125,358
1992	2,184	55,105	122,013

Source: 1949–79 figures from *Achievement of Education in China 1949–1983*, pp. 22–23; 1988 figures from *Achievement of Education in China 1986–1990*, p. 5; 1992 figures from *Educational Statistics Yearbook of China 1992*, p. 273.

Socialism had extended educational opportunities to previous underclasses. Women as a gendered class had made inroads (Table 1.2). The proportion of girls and women reached almost half of the total enrollment in primary and secondary education in 1992. As cross-national studies have shown, tertiary education limits women's access when it is scarce. Female students have never exceeded a third of tertiary enrollment in China. While women benefited as a group, they did so differently along geographic and social class lines. Expansion benefited sons and daughters of peasant-worker backgrounds the most. In 1952 they acounted for 80% of primary, 57% of secondary, and 22% of tertiary enrollment.[15] Stipends for children from poor families were a stimulus for females as well as males because their parents no longer needed to worry about educational costs. As is typical of developing countries, in China urban residence exerts a positive influence on women's access to education.

Table 1.2 Female Students as a Percentage of Enrollment by Level of Education, 1949–1992 (in %)

Year	Undergraduate	Secondary Technical	Teacher Training	General Secondary	Agricultural Vocational	Primary
1949	19.8	—*	—	—	—	—
1951	22.5	31.9	26.0	25.6	—	28.0
1957	23.3	25.4	28.4	30.8	—	34.5
1958	23.3	25.4	31.5	31.3	—	38.5
1960	24.5	31.3	31.3	31.2	—	39.1
1965	26.9	37.9	48.6	32.2	23.6	39.3
1974	33.8	38.3	—	38.1	—	43.7
1978	24.1	35.3	29.8	41.5	—	44.9
1985	29.9	38.3	39.3	40.2	41.6	44.8
1988	33.4	42.9	50.5	41.0	43.8	45.6
1992	33.7	42.7	55.0	43.1	46.1	46.6

* No such school in this year.
Source: 1949–1978 figures from *Achievement of Education in China 1949–1983*, pp. 39–40; 1985 figures from *Achievement of Education in China 1980–85*, pp. 39, 47, 59, 74, 77, 84; 1988 figures from *Achievement of Education in China 1986–1990*, pp. 39, 55, 69, 72, 78; 1992 figures from *Education Statistics Yearbook of China 1992*, p. 18.

China's development needs are reflected in the proportion of places allocated to fields of study in higher education. Engineering[16] has enjoyed the most emphasis (Table 1.3), reflecting an urgency to modernize and a belief in technological skills as the most effective means to do so. Medicine and teacher education are stressed, too, because both fields enhance the physical and intellectual qualities of the population. In contrast, disciplines that do not carry an immediate practical value, such as the humanities, are relatively small in size. The fields of finance and economics could offer few opportunities in a planned economy and, therefore, shrank in the three decades since 1949, but they have been making a comeback following China's recent espousal of market economics.

Available data suggest that sex-stereotypical division existed. For example, only 20% of all graduates from the polytechnical Qinghua University from 1949 to 1956 were women, compared with an average of about 25% women in higher education.[17] Sidel reported in the early 1970s that half of the medical students were women but that they were mostly in pedi-

Table 1.3 Percentage Distribution of Undergraduate Students by Field of Study, 1949–1992 (in %)

Year	Engineering	Agriculture	Forestry	Medicine & Pharmacy	Teacher Training	Humanities	Natural Sciences	Finance & Economics	Pol. Science & Law	Physical Education	Art
1949	26.0	8.4	0.5	13.1	10.3	10.2	6.0	16.6	6.3	0.2	2.4
1958	39.0	8.8	1.5	11.7	23.8	3.9	6.2	2.2	1.1	1.1	0.7
1966	43.0	8.3	1.5	12.1	13.8	7.3	9.2	2.9	0.7	0.6	0.6
1970	24.3	2.3	0.7	27.7	19.1	15.1	9.1	0.	—	—	1.5
1978	33.6	6.3	0.9	13.2	29.2	5.4	7.5	2.1	0.2	1.0	0.6
1988	35.2	4.5	1.0	9.3	25.7	5.4	5.3	10.0	2.1	0.7	0.8
1992	36.7	4.0	1.0	9.8	25.1	4.6	4.1	11.2	2.0	0.6	0.9

Source: 1949–1978 figures from *Achievement of Education in China 1949–1983*, p. 62; 1988–1992 figures from *Zhongguo tongji nianjian 1993*, p. 717.

atrics, psychiatry, internal medicine, and obstetrics/gynecology.[18] In general, half of the medical students were women but that they were mostly in pediatrics, psychiatry, internal medicine, and obstetrics/gynecology.[18] In general, fields of study that were perceived to be of higher direct value to modernization, such as engineering, tended to be less open to women than those that were not. This tendency is reflected in sex segregation in occupations today, which will be discussed later in this chapter.

Labor Force Participation

Although a reorganized economy was more willing to recruit women, urbanization was slow. Of the total labor force in 1952, only 12% was engaged in nonagricultural labor. This rose to 22% in 1978 and to 26% in 1992. The nonagricultural labor force—called workers (manual workers) and employees (nonmanual workers) in China—remains mostly urban.[19] Thus geography has always been a crucial factor in affecting women's employment prospects, but in urban areas education also exerts a significant influence.

URBAN WOMEN

Women as a proportion of workers and employees grew from 7.5% in 1949 to 33% in 1978 and about fiftyfold in absolute numbers between those two years (Table 1.4). However, this overall trend concealed a fickle attitude toward urban women's employment. Three related factors affected the pattern of female employment: ownership of production, development strategies, and degree of unemployment. In the 1950s the Chinese government took steps to nationalize private enterprises. The state became the largest and almost the sole employer. Centralization gave the state great control over the execution of equal employment policies toward women. The failure to realize such equality revealed a government ideology that in practice sacrificed women's interests to what it judged to be more important concerns.

The second factor was development strategies. Since 1949 the government had placed emphasis on heavy industry, which represented 26.4% of total industrial output in 1949 and 35.5% in 1952.[20] Such an emphasis intensified during the first five-year plan from 1953 to 1957. The increase in employment during this period was found mostly in heavy industry, which did not favor women.[21] Such lack of opportunity persisted. In a study of 35 industrial plants in China in 1966, women made up an average of 25% to 30% of all employees surveyed, but 60% to 70% of all workers in light industries such as textile and garment manufacturing and less than 30% in heavy industries.[22] Nevertheless, the emphasis on heavy industry did leave some mark on women. It stimulated a small number of women to study science and technology, as evidenced by the appearance of post-1949 women graduates in these fields who challenged occupational sex-role stereotyping. Whatever the industrial slant, a developing nation needed to improve its social infrastructure. Women took advantage of the acute shortage of teachers and health care workers in a new and aspiring people's republic. In 1952 they made up 18% of the teaching force, which was considerably higher than their overall representation in the entire nonagricultural work force.[23]

Table 1.4 Increase in Number and Percentage of Female Workers and Employees, 1949–1992

Year	Number (in Thousands)	% of total
1949	600	7.5
1952	1,848	11.7
1959	8,286	18.8
1966	8,260	16.6
1978	31,280	32.9
1988	50,360	37.0
1992	55,856	38.0

Source: 1949–1966 figures from John P. Emerson, "The Labor Force of China, 1957–80," in *China under the Four Modernizations, Part I, 1982* (Washington, DC: U.S. Government Printing Office, 1982): 259; 1978–1988 figures from *Statistics on Chinese Women*, p. 239; 1992 figures from *Zhongguo tongji nianjian 1993*, p. 111.

The third factor was the size of the labor market. Unemployment was pervasive at the beginning of the Communist regime, and government priority was to create jobs for unemployed men. Nonagricultural employment increased rapidly—25% a year on average—from 1949 to 1952.[24] New jobs were created and existing ones reshuffled. Women lost their jobs to men.

They were told that a housewife's work was an equally important contribution to nation-building. *Zhongguo funu* (Women of China), a monthly publication of the All-China Women's Federation, repeatedly conveyed this message. As in the two Chinas before 1949, the relative value of women's productive and reproductive work was manipulated to fit the larger employment situation.

Then came the Great Leap Forward campaign, which mobilized large numbers of men and women for agricultural and industrial production. State leaders recognized that China was behind industrialized nations in female labor force participation rate, which was to them an indicator of development,[25] and so they urged women to take up paid work. As a result of this policy, the number of female workers and employees more than doubled from 3.3 million in 1957 to 7.5 million in 1958. Small-scale street industries mushroomed, serving as feeders to large enterprises. These small industries had large numbers of vacancies in low-skill, low-pay positions and filled them with women. In 1959/1960 women constituted 85% of those employed in these industries.[26] Paid employment, a conventional yardstick of women's liberation, had the opposite meaning to these women. They were drawn into it not necessarily of their own free will. The meaning of paid employment thus has to be assessed in the context of how it happened. Expansion was followed by equally abrupt financial retrenchment from 1961 to 1965, during which many small local plants were closed. The number of women workers slumped after 1958.[27]

The next increase in women's employment occurred during the Cultural Revolution. Local cottage indurstries were again encouraged, and women and old people were recruited. On the surface this period witnessed a high degree of gender equality. Since the massive recruitment of women workers was only to meet the needs of industries, the Cultural Revolution provides a misleading yardstick of equality. Throughout the recent decades the expansions and contractions of the labor force were most drastic in unskilled jobs, and women with little or no education were more vulnerable to job loss than the educated ones.

Rural Women

As in the cities, ownership of production in rural regions changed after liberation from Guomindang (Nationalist) rule, starting in 1949. The land reform of 1950 to 1952 aimed at destroying the landlord class and redistributing land among poor peasants. Such redistribution blurred the differentiation between males and females. Unlike the cities, the government consistently encouraged rural women to participate in agricultural production, which had room for female labor. Campaigns were mounted to this end. The first one took place in 1956, when rural cooperatives were established across China and agriculture became collectivized. The second was the Great Leap Forward campaign (1958–1959). In rural areas men were drawn to farmland capital construction, and women to farming. Women were asked to take part regardless of their health or family situation. To free them from household responsibilities, child care facilities and communal kitchens were set up. They were staffed by women who were paid dismal wages. With the failure of the Great Leap Forward, the demand for labor dropped. In late 1959 communal canteens and child care centers collapsed, and with them women's employment.

The above account reveals that legislation was informed by mixed motives and was inadequate to engendering equal rights. The effectiveness of the drive for equality depended on processes of mediation between policy commitment and cultural norms for sex roles. However, despite ups and downs, women made inroads and, based on this new reality, continued the struggle for equality.

THE CURRENT ECONOMIC REFORM AND WOMEN'S STATUS, 1978 TO THE PRESENT

By the mid-1970s the damage to economic development caused by political movements was too serious to be ignored. Deng Xiaoping's return to power and the pragmatism he advocated ushered China into a new era of development that continues today. In 1978 the nation announced its pursuit of modernization in four arenas: the economy, education, science and technology, and national defense. Of these, the main focus would be on the economy, which would be fueled by improvements in education and science and technology. Economic development would in turn strengthen national defense. Individual productivity was to be unleashed in the transition to market forces. Efficiency was the order of the day. But women's role in the era since 1978 has been peripheral. In official communications addressed to women there is routine mention of their contribution to China's modernization, when in practice the impact of reform on women is mixed. This section examines this impact on women in the four areas of the family, education, the economy, and politics.

Marriage and the Family

Marriage and childbearing behaviors in China have changed in such a way as to further release women for economic participation. A woman's age at first marriage has been postponed from the former average of 18–19 years of age in 1949–1953 to 22.4 years in 1992.[28] Despite occasional fluctuations national birth rates declined from 37 per thousand people in 1950 to 18 per thousand in 1992.[29] Education and urban residence exert a markedly deterrent effect on women's desire to marry and to bear children. Compared with the national average, urban and/or educated women tend to marry later by 1 to 3 years, and to have fewer children. Average family size decreased from 4.33 persons per household in 1953 to 4.01 in 1991.[30] Divorce rates have risen from 0.66 divorces per thousand people in 1979 to 1.2 in 1988.[31] Relatively more women than before are unmarried; these are mostly urban dwellers with a third-level education. With increased earning power, educated women can opt for a route that excludes marriage. This echoes the early twentieth-century phenomenon mentioned earlier.

At the same time, some dimensions of women's oppression have persisted and intensified. The most widely reported is female infanticide, as reflected in the male/female sex ratio, which is 104:100 for the nation as a whole but 112:100 for the 0–4 age group.[32] Official media blame the poor education of village people for such behavior but it is actually economic in nature. Women marry into the husbands' families. A family that has no son is perceived to have terminated its line. Rural labor does not guarantee the same security and retirement benefits as does urban employment. Old people tend to invest their hopes in sons and daughters-in-law. When fertility is limited to one, a couple will choose a son even at the expense of getting rid of infant girls by brutal means. When traditional ideology prevails, as is often the case in rural China, a couple wants more children. An additional pregnancy is unlawful, and the state sends cadres to abort it, even by force. Ironically, the same state that has raised the status of women has also usurped women's control of their own bodies. Other forms of women's oppression—child betrothal, the abduction and selling of women, rape, and prostitution—crept back toward the end of the Cultural Revolution and incidences have increased with economic liberalization. The government condemns these practices as vice but has not taken firm measures to attack them. It has been so focused on the economic aspect of development that it has neglected the social aspect. What is different from the past is that some segments of the public, in particular women's groups, have actively criticized this trend. In response to this outcry and continual discrimination against women in education and employment, the state formulated a law in 1992 to protect women's and children's rights. While recognizing the state's responsibility, the document also emphasizes women's own responsibility to help themselves, thus identifying the victims as part of the source of the problem.[33]

Education

In the reform era the emphasis on educational development has been on basic education and vocational education. The compulsory education act was promulgated in 1986 and its importance reiterated in the "Outline on Education Reform and Development in China" issued in 1993. Nine-year basic education is believed to be most cost-effective for China's economic development, and vocational education is believed to be an answer to its needs for medium-level skilled workers. Since 1978 women have made further gains in educational participation, reaching 47% of the school population at the primary level in 1992, 43% at the secondary level, and 34% at the tertiary level (Table 1.2). However, these figures also indicated the persistence of gender gaps long after the founding of the People's Republic.

Illiteracy statistics in China fill out the incomplete picture presented by enrollment figures. In 1990 22% of the population aged 15 and over was literate or semiliterate; 70% of the illiterate ones were female.[34] In 1992, of 3.1 million school-aged children who had never been enrolled in school, 65% were girls; and of the 2.6 million who had dropped out from school, 80% were girls.[35] Discrimination within the family appears to have caused the inequality in access. A survey of reasons why children aged 6 to 14 were not enrolled in school showed that, while girls were 59% of the sample, they were 68% of those who cited "insufficient family finance" and 72% of those who cited "helping out the family in economic production" as reasons.[36] The problem is compounded by early marriages of girls from the minority groups who populate poor and remote areas.[37] Although scattered attempts have been made to improve girls' education,[38] the overall situation remains gloomy.

The degree of development in a nation of geographical contrasts also affects a girl's chance of receiving education. In 1992 the enrollment rate of school-aged girls in primary schools was 96.98% for the nation as a whole, 98.86% for Beijing, the national capital, and 99.26% for Guangdong, the most economically prosperous province, but 80.86% for the poor and remote province of Qinghai and 47.56% for Tibet (where the female and male combined rate was 55.43%).[39]

The distribution of girls in different types of secondary education varies, at times reflecting an obvious gender factor. Some urban vocational schools that promise good job prospects impose higher admission requirements for female applicants,[40] subsequently denying women equal contribution to development.[41] One of the means to redress the inequality has been to establish girls' vocational schools or postsecondary vocational institutes. They typically offer courses "suitable" for women, such as foreign languages, preschool education, and fashion design. Their graduates have little difficulty landing jobs. Ironically, these schools have been trapped into the conventional turf of gender-based knowledge and have undermined segregation as much as they have reinforced it.

A disproportionate number of females who leave secondary school are lost in the transition to tertiary education. Available data suggest that girls often outperform boys in secondary school, and so their attrition likely results from factors other than academic ability.[42] Educational authorities intervene by demanding higher exam scores from female applicants—in other words, granting preferential treatment to males. They justify their action with the unsupported assumption that intellectually boys bloom later than girls.

Nowhere is the discrimination more blatant and widespread than at the tertiary level. Admissions offices claim that their action is a response to work units (departments and enterprises in the state sector), which prefer to hire males. Such attitudes and actions incidents show that discrimination finds its way back once the state relaxes its enforcment of legislation. While legislation alone is inadequate, it is a necessary basic premise for the equality drive. In addition, government sponsorship of tertiary education is eroding. Places are held for self-funded students, and students who are recruited under the state quota are now charged some tuition and dormitory fees. This measure intended to remedy the fiscal constraints of the government ultimately has hurt women from poor families the most.

Graduate education is less competitive, since the attainment of a university education, or even less, places an individual among the knowledge elite. Even so there has been an attrition of female students from undergraduate to graduate education. In 1992 women constituted 27% of those enrolled in programs leading to a master's degree and 11% of those leading to a doctorate.[43] Again the degree of popularity of a field of study reflects its economic value. Programs in ancient history, linguistics, and the like failed to fill their quotas.[44] It will be interesting to watch the percentages of women in these fields if, or when, such data are released. Neither is the age limit imposed on applicants to graduate school in women's favor. Although it has been raised from 35 years of age to 40 for master's and to 45 for doctoral programs,[45] women in this age bracket are in the most hectic phase of their life cycle and therefore unlikely to go to graduate school. The higher percentage of men in higher education means that they are the major beneficiaries of public resources and in turn are better equipped to take a more active role in education and development.

Adult education constitutes a significant proportion of educational provision in China, representing 6% of the total enrollment in primary schools, 42% in secondary schools, and 40% in tertiary institutions. Because of their disadvantage in formal education, women tend to be the majority in adult basic education, in 1992 representing 59% of enrollment in adult primary schools and 61% in literacy classes for peasants but only 45% at the secondary level.[46] The needs of the new reforms have spurred the provision of nonformal agricultural skills courses in rural areas, and large numbers of women are reported to have taken part in them.

Labor Force Participation

In 1990 72% of all working persons in China were engaged in agriculture, forestry, stock farming, and fishing, compared with 13% in manufacturing and 15% in other nonagricultural employment (Table 1.5). These figures demonstate the agrarian nature of China's economy and the extent to which occupational segregation has persisted. Table 1.5 shows the percentage distribution of workers by industry and by sex. Modern employment benefits men more than women. A higher proportion (76%) of the female labor force was engaged in agricultural work compared with 69% for men. However, the current era of development has caused tremendous change in the patterns of women's labor force participation. This transition started in rural China and later extended to urban China.

Table 1.5 Sex-Specific Composition of Labor Force in China, by Industry, 1990

Industry	Labor Force		% Composition		% Distribution	
	No. in Thousands	% Total	Male	Female	Male	Female
Total	647,245	100	55	45	100	100
Agricultural, stock farming, forestry, and fishing	467,593	72	53	47	69	76
Manufacturing	86,579	13	57	43	14	13
Geological exploration	798	<1	75	25	<1	<1
Construction	11,643	2	84	16	3	<1
Transport and communications	11,751	2	81	19	3	<1
Wholesale/retail trade, restaurants, and storage	25,771	4	53	47	4	4
Housing management, public utilities, and community services	6,188	<1	55	45	<1	<1
Health, sports, and social services	5,168	<1	47	53	<1	<1
Education and cultural services	15,102	2	59	41	3	2
Natural and social sciences research and general technical services	1,451	<1	63	37	<1	<1
Finance and insurance	2,132	<1	60	40	<1	<1
National organizations, communist party, and other political groups	12,953	2	77	23	3	1
Others	116	<1	71	29	<1	<1

Source: *China Population Statistics Yearbook 1992*, pp. 164–77.

Rural Women

Reform of the rural economy is characterized by the family responsibility system. Instead of collective farming, a household now cultivates a plot under a contract with the local administration and can sell part of the crop on the free market. The family thus has more incentive to work. The value of total agricultural output grew 205% from 1980 to 1992.[47] Means of livelihood have diversified. We will first talk about traditional production, which ties people to the land, and then alternative means.

Households that practiced small-scale monoculture before have now diversified to various forms of commodity production. The press often reports success stories in agricultural innovations, and their heroines are dubbed "superwomen" *(nu nengren)*. These women's successes are often attributed to their educational attainments, which helped them to acquire new skills. Indeed, various surveys have concurred that education has a positive effect on the incomes rural women earn.[48]

However, rural prosperity has had an adverse effect on girls. Because increased labor brings immediate rewards, some parents tend to keep their children, mostly daughters, at home as additional farmhands. Sometimes young girls are sent to work in factories or to perform domestic service in nearby towns. Thus, despite the nondiscriminatory nature of universal basic education, economic restructuring and a culture of female subordination combine to contravene its spirit.

Higher individual productivity has unveiled the problem of surplus rural labor. According to one estimate, in 1984 30% of rural labor was redundant. The alternative is nonagricultural labor. In 1986, 80 million people from the rural labor force had moved to nonagricultural labor and, of this number, less than 30% were women.[49] Part of the reason is that the new employment channels favor men. The first channel is the transfer within rural areas. One can leave the field and work in small rural enterprises. These enterprises produce agricultural machinery, building materials, etc., and tend to hire men. The other channel is migration to towns and cities. Typically, men become traders, transport workers, or construction site workers, and women become factory workers. Generally the move favors better educated and/or young women rather than other kinds of women. Not bound to wedlock, these women become domestic helpers in towns and cities or unskilled workers in the foreign-invested factories that dot the coastal provinces. Women—with their "nimble hands"—are said to be suitable for the light industries. They are from poor provinces and are paid exploitive wages for long hours of work in substandard conditions. Many of them plan to work for a few years to save money and then to go back to their native place to marry and settle.

This pattern of labor mobility has upset rural demographics. Those who are unable to leave the village are mostly married and/or old women. According to a study of Guangdong province, 78% of the rural women who remained in the field were between the ages of 31 and 60, whereas 80% of those who had moved out were between the ages of 16 and 30.[50] Gender, lack of education, and family obligations have limited the movement of the former group and resulted in the feminization and aging of rural labor. However, the roles of women who remained have broadened. Because many men have left home, the women now shoulder major responsibilities in production and become de facto heads of households.

Since 1978 light industrial groups, called township enterprises, have mushroomed. These are located in areas that join cities and villages and act as a valve to absorb surplus rural labor without adding pressure to cities. Some of them are joint ventures with investment from Hong Kong and Taiwan, where production costs have become exorbitant. Thus the needs of outside economies to move to cheaper labor markets have interacted with China's development strategies and in turn created employment opportunities for rural women. In 1993 women made up 40% to 50% of those working in township enterprises,[51] but they were mostly at the bottom ranks. Women's labor mobility varies with the pace of economic development. Clusters of township enterprises in wealthy provinces like Guangdong, Jiangsu, and Zhejiang provide employment for married women with children. Proximity to them has facilitated these women's transfer to nonagricultural employment.

URBAN WOMEN

Economic reform has also changed the lives of urban dwellers. The value of total industrial output in 1992 had soared to 5.7 times the 1978 figures, at an average annual growth rate of 15% between 1986 and 1992.[52] In the nonagricultural sector, segregation is clear (Table 1.5). Women were underrepresented in industries that are perceived to be "musculine," such as geology, construction, communications, scientific research, finance, and government, but slightly overrepresented in the helping professions. A more in-depth examination of occupations shows the consequences of women's uneven participation in fields of study. Women were 44% of the total work force in 1982; they constituted 98% of early childhood teachers, 95% of nurses, 76% of textile workers, but only 12% of lawyers, 18% of engineers and technicians, and 17% of construction workers. They also tended to be concentrated in the lower ranks. For example, women comprised 6% of those in leadership ranks in party and government organizations but 84%

of those who headed neighborhood committees, which are the lowest level of public organization. Women also comprised 27%, 30%, and 42% of the teaching force at the tertiary, secondary, and primary levels respectively.[53]

The teaching profession merits discussion here because it illustrates the dilemma women are caught in. Abundant opportunities in the other markets, especially in cities, have diminished the attraction of teaching. The vacancies in teaching left by men are filled by women. Women make up a much higher percentage of the teaching force in major cities than the national average. Yet many educational administrators express cautious concern about the "detrimental effect" on children's personality formation of "too many" women teachers at the primary and secondary levels. They believe that at least 30% of teachers must be men so as to nurture such qualities as will power and perseverence in children, which by implication, women lack.[54] Of course, this alarm about one-sidedness, rooted in the bias of educators themselves, is never articulated at the tertiary level, which is heavily male.

The state continues to be a major employer, and in its urban sector educational attainment is an important avenue to jobs. According to a 1990 survey of women's status, education was crucial in the type of employment women landed: 78% of professionals and 70% of administrators in the state bureaucracy had ten years of education or more, compared with 27% of those employed in commerce and 26% of manufacturing and transportation workers.[55] More education has brought higher incomes for men and women, but wage differentiation remains; on average women in 1990 made 78% of men's income. The increase in amount of education, however, has helped to narrow the gap. The earnings ratios (F/M) of the urban employed women, by educational attainment, are as follows: 58% (little or no education); 72% (lower primary); 73% (upper primary); 80% (lower secondary); 86% (upper secondary); 90% (specialized secondary); 90% (non-degree tertiary); and 82% (degree and above).[56] The higher percentages are possible when the state is a major employer. As the non-state sector grows and the wage policy becomes less uniform, women may suffer more from lower wages in relative terms.

Urban economic reform is characterized by three aspects that have had a mixed impact on women—development strategies, an ensuing economic ideology, and liberalized ownership of production. The reform favors light industries. The prevalent ideology is rooted in efficiency, and individuals are in a rush to get rich quick. Social equity, while desirable, is no longer a priority. Changes in other policies may have a negative impact on women. A typical example is the abolition in 1989 of the central allocation system of all graduates from tertiary institutions. The first step is the bilateral choice system, which allows both the employer and the graduates discretion in choosing each other. Designed to allow some autonomy to both parties, the new measure has been used by many hiring organizations to screen out women. Many hiring units have a men-only policy. This problem was particularly acute in the mid- to late 1980s. In 1993, all graduates managed to obtain jobs,[57] for by this time the non-state sector had grown and could absorb women as well. However, this was no guarantee of future equality for women. When the labor market contracts women will likely be rejected again.

The ideology of efficiency has also seriously affected the size of organizations. China's employment policy in the past was to keep as many employed as possible, albeit at low wages, resulting in overstaffing. When organizations try to streamline, women are the hardest hit. Sex discrimination in employment is legitimized in the name of efficiency. Findings from a survey conducted in the late 1980s revealed that of those laid off, 63% were women.[58] The ways to eliminiate women vary. Some enterprises make it a rule for women workers to retire at the age of 44 or 45, regardless of their performance. What is usually seen as a mature age for men is considered too old for women. Other enterprises do not rehire women workers after their maternity leave.[59] To be fired at the age of 45 is particularly indicative of the conflict between women's productive and reproductive roles. Statistics of most developed countries show that women's age-specific labor force participation profile is marked by an M-shape curve showing highest participation rates of women in their early twenties and early forties, that is, before and after the busiest years of child rearing. Therefore the new rule in China means that women are deprived of the opportunity of active participation in development just when they are most available.

Unlike in previous periods, well-educated women feel the pinch, too. Although job performance is used as an excuse, often the discrimination is based on gender. For women who manage to keep their employment, the division of labor is biased in favor of men. For example, women academics are mostly assigned to teaching and men to research, when research performance is the major criterion in promotion. Thus a promotion mechanism that may appear fair is premised on unfairness to start with. Efficiency has been translated into elimination of women from employment opportunities and from employment itself.

Against this backdrop the view that women should go home has gained currency. While the government customarily boasts about China's degree of "women's liberation" by citing employment statistics, the idea that women should go back home points to the contrary, maintaining that economic participation is not always a necessary condition for women's liberation and that putting women into the labor market when there is no need for them may impede development. The blatant discrimination against women, when admitted, is attributed to their domestic responsibilities, which allegedly render them less committed to gainful work, and to their biological state, which allegedly renders them unsuitable for business trips. The problem has been aggravated at home. In addition to an increasingly hostile workplace and decline in child care support, women shoulder more domestic responsibilities than their husbands.

Political Participation

The formal political participation of women in China began when ten women were elected to the Guangdong provincial parliament in 1921.[60] However, after seven decades, women's influence in this sphere is still weak. In 1954 women made up 12% of the National People's Congress and in 1956 10% of Communist Party membership.[61] Their presence had increased to 14% of party membership and 21% of the National People's Congress by 1988[62] and to 31% of all cadres by 1991, but only 6.5% of all ministers and vice-ministers of the State Council and 6.3% of all governors and vice-governors of provinces in the same year were women. In some places women's representation at senior levels has actually dropped.[63]

The explanation for the low profile of women lies partly in that there has never been a strong women's movement on its own. While there have been activities to raise women's status, they came with a package of social and cultural reforms. This was true of the May Fourth Movement in 1919 and the Communist movement in the first half of the century. The assumption has been that the victory of mainstream social movements will trickle down to women. Feminism per se has not been able to establish itself as an independent movement.

Improving women's status has been the mandate of the All-China Women's Federation, which has little power or resources. It has a conservative family ideology and attempts to maintain the status quo by pursuading women to put the interests of the nation and the family above their own instead of challenging an unequal social framework. The irony is hardly surprising when Women's Federation cadres are sometimes trapped in sexist stereotyping that ranks male traits superior to female traits.[64]

Another crisis affecting the Women's Federation as it does other state-funded organizations is inadequate funding. To generate supplementary income, Women's Federation offices have engaged in profit-making businesses as diverse as counseling services to women, tourism, and manufacturing. In general they enjoy certain preferential treatment such as simplifed procedures in applying for bank loans. In return, part of the profits thus gained are set aside for Women's Federation operational funds. This strategy raises interesting questions about the judgment of the Women's Federation when its business interests conflict with its mandate. Also, it works at the beginning of a market economy, when the hitherto dormant market responds positively to new services. There will be more choice as the economy matures, but whether Women's Federation-operated businesses will continue to thrive is uncertain.

Women's Studies

Women's studies as a field of inquiry has emerged with the reform. New forms of discrimination against women and contact with feminist theories and scholars from the West have triggered its appearance. The Women's Federation and volunteer academic groups and individuals are active in this direction. In the case of the Women's Federation, since 1986 centers for research have been established; these focus mostly on contemporary women's history and surveys of women's status. Their publications often reflect a cconfusion between the concepts of fundamental women's rights and conventional social welfare for women. Another, more noticeable force, has come from academics. The first volunteer women's studies group was formed in Henan province in 1985 and led to the setting up of the first China women's studies center in 1987. Similar centers have since then appeared in a few other major universities. Scholars and students in this field are a very small minority, but they have been active in studying the nature of women's oppression in China.

CONCLUSION

This chapter has demonstrated the bumpy course of Chinese women's struggle for equality. An assessment of the strife hinges on one's criteria. Whereas women's status is far higher than before the Communist liberation of China, the improvement should be examined by phase. New measures toward equality that accompanied the victory of the revolution in the early 1950s marked a point of departure in national development. However, as these measures met resistance from different social groups in the process of implementation, their effectiveness weakened. In general, the first period (1949–1965) witnessed significant progress for women. The period since 1978 should be assessed on the premise of women's new reality rather than the pre-liberation era. As such it has shown little progress since the early 1950s. The Chinese experience shows the difficulty of sustaining equality.

The difficulty can be attributed in part to lack of power of women as a group. Equality measures vouchsafed from above can be taken back as easily. Women's employment history has demonstrated how vulnerable women are to economic fluctuations, and their access or lack of access to employment is justified by manipulating of the notion of what constitutes their contribution to national development. This explains the inadequacy of legislation to bring about equality. On the positive side, however, women are not a completely passive group. Education and economic participation equip them with the competence and will to endure despite hard times. Although it is an uphill climb, there is no return to where they started.

NOTES

I thank Philip G. Altbach and Karen Biraimah for their helpful comments on an earlier draft of this chapter.

1. Olga Lang, *Chinese Family and Society* (New Haven, CT: Yale University Press, 1946):42.

2. Margaret E. Burton, *Notable Women of China* (New York: Fleming H. Revell, 1912).

3. China Yearbook Publishers, *Zhonghua nianjian 1948*, Vol. 2. (Nanjing: Zhonghua nianjian she, 1948):1587, 1633, 1657.

4. Ibid., pp. 1634, 1660.

5. Emily Honig, *Sisters and Strangers: Women in the Shanghai Cotton Mills 1919–1949* (Stanford, CA: Stanford University Press, 1986).

6. Ta Chen, *Population in Modern China* (Chicago: University of Chicago Press, 1946).

7. For a pioneering analysis of divorce in four major cities in China during the late 1920s, see Tan Renjiu, *Zhongguo de lihun yanjiu* (A Study of Divorce in China) (Shanghai: Zhonghua jidujiao nu qingnian hui quanguo xiehui, 1932).

8. During the Sino-Japanese War there were 819 such groups. See Wang Mengmei, *Kangzhan shiqi de funu gongzuo* (Women Work during the Resistance War). Master's thesis, Donghai University (Taiwan), 1987.

9. Kay Ann Johnson, *Women, the Family and Peasant Revolution in China* (Chicago: University of Chicago Press, 1983).

10. E.g., Phyllis Andors, *The Unfinished Revolution of Chinese Women 1948–1980* (Bloomington: Indiana University Press, 1983); Margery Wolf, *Revolution Postponed: Women in Contemporary China* (Stanford, CA: Stanford University Press, 1985).

11. Ji Rong, *Zhongguo funu yundongshi* (History of Women's Movement in China) (Changsha: Hunan chubanshe, 1992):145–46.

12. State Statistical Bureau, *Zhongguo tonji nianjian 1993* (Statistical Yearbook of China 1993) (Beijing: Zhongguo tongji chubanshe, 1993):97.

13. Research Institute of All-China Women's Federation, et al., *Statistics on Chinese Women (1949–1989)* (Beijing: Zhongguo tongji chubanshe, 1991):404, 417–22.

14. Department of Planning and Construction, State Education Commission, PRC, *Educational Statistics Yearbook of China 1992* (Beijing: Renmin jiaoyu chubanshe, 1993):273.

15. People's Educational Press, *Jiaoyu shinian* (Ten Years of Education) (Beijing: Renmin jiaoyu chubanshe, 1960):1–16.

16. Engineering is a broad category that includes the subfields of mechanical

engineering, civil engineering, architecture, power engineering, chemical engineering, electrical machines and instruments, applied geology, mining, metallurgy, radio and electronics, grain processing and food industry, light industry, mapping/surveying/hydrology, transportation, and telecommunications.

17. Barry Richman, *Industrial Society in Communist China* (New York: Random House, 1969):303.

18. Ruth Sidel, *Women and Child Care in China* (New York: Hill and Wang, 1972):24.

19. A very small proportion (4%) of the total work force in 1952, 0.04% in 1978, and 1.4% in 1992, were self-employed persons in urban areas. *Zhongguo tongji nianjian 1993*, op. cit., p. 97.

20. Li Debiao, *Zhonghua renmin gongheguo jingjishi jianbian 1949–1985* (A Short Economic History of China 1949–1985) (Changsha: Hunan renmin chubanshe, 1987):143.

21. John Philip Emerson, "Sex, Age and Level of Skill of the Nonagricultural Labor Force of Mainland China." Washington, DC: Report by U.S. State Department of Commerce, June 1965, p. 5.

22. Richman, *Industrial Society in Communist China*, op. cit., pp. 304–5, 754–56.

23. Department of Planning, Ministry of Education, PRC, *Achievement of Education in China 1949–1983* (Beijing: People's Education Press, 1984):30, 41.

24. Emerson, "Sex, Age and Level of Skill," op. cit., ch. 5.

25. The urban female labor force participation rate in China was 14%, when it was 45% in the former USSR, 42% in the former East Germany, 27% in the United States, 35% in the United Kingdom, and 30% in Japan. Ji, *Zhongguo funu yundongshi*, op. cit., p. 172.

26. Emerson, "Sex, Age and Level of Skill," op. cit., pp. 6, 9.

27. Willy Kraus, *Economic Development and Social Change in China* (New York: Springer-Verlag, 1979):134.

28. Department of Population Statistics, State Statistical Bureau, PRC, *China Population Statistics Yearbook 1993* (Beijing: Zhongguo tongji chubanshe, 1994):19.

29. *China Populations Statistic Yearbook 1993*, op. cit., p. 4.

30. *Statistics on Chinese Women*, op. cit., pp. 9, 36, 240–55, 368.

31. *Statistics on Chinese Women*, op. cit, p. 10.

32. *Department of Population Statistics, Statistical Bureau, PRC, China Population Statistics Yearbook 1992* (Beijing: Zhongguo tongji chubanshe, 1993):8–10.

33. All-China Women's Federation, *Zhongguo funu falu shiyong quanshu* (Practical Guide to Law toward Women in China) (Beijing: Falu chubanshe, 1993).

34. *China Population Statistics Yearbook 1992*, op. cit., p. 141.

35. *Renmin ribao* (People's Daily) (overseas edition) (May 24, 1993):3.

36. *Statistics on Chinese Women*, op. cit., p. 219.

37. Center for Research on Educational Development, State Education Commission, PRC, *Yiwu jiaoyu xiaoyi yanjiu* (A Study of the Effectiveness of Compulsory Education) (Beijing: Renmin jiaoyu chubanshe, 1992):161, 221–22.

38. An example is the *chunlei* (spring bud) project, which aims to send girls from poor families to school. *Renmin ribao* (overseas edition) (May 23, 1993):3; *Zhongguo jiaoyubao* (Women of China Journal) (May 17, 1993):1.

39. *Educational Statistics Yearbook of China 1992*, op. cit., p. 275.

40. *Zhongguo funubao* (Women of China Journal) (June 20, 1990):1.

41. Beverley Hooper, "Gender and Education," in: Irving Epstein, ed., *Chinese Education* (New York: Garland Publishing, 1991).

42. See, e.g., Stig Thogersen, "China's Senior Middle Schools in a Social Perspective: A Survey of Yantai District, Shandong Province." *China Quarterly* no. 109 (March 1987):72–100; *Guangming ribao* (August 11, 1982).

43. *Educational Statistics Yearbook of China 1992*, op. cit., p. 38.

44. *Zhongguo jiaoyu bao* (July 19, 1993):1.
45. *Guangming ribao* (August 18, 1993):1.
46. *Educational Statistics Yearbook of China 1992*, op. cit., pp. 2–3, 112–13.
47. *Zhongguo tongji nianjian 1993*, op. cit., p. 21.
48. *Zhongguo funu bao* (January 11, 1988):2.
49. Jing Yihong, "The Status and Future Prospect of Rural Women in the Economic Reform," in: Li Xiaojiang and Tan Shen, eds., *Zhongguo funu fenceng yanjiu* (A Study of Chinese Women by Social Stratum) (Zhengzhou: Henan renmin chubanshe, 1991):33–41.
50. Miao Meixian et al., "An Analysis of Women's Employment in the Zhujiang Delta, in: Li et al., *Zhongguo funu fenceng yanjiu*, op. cit., p. 44.
51. *Renmin ribao* (overseas edition) (August 27, 1993):3; *Zhongguo funu bao* (August 18, 1993):1.
52. *Zhongguo tongji nianjian 1993*, op. cit., p. 21.
53. *Statistics on Chinese Women*, op. cit., pp. 260–69.
54. *Guangming ribao* (January 15, 1990):2; *Renmin ribao* (overseas edition) (July 1, 1993):8.
55. Research Team on the Status of Women in China, *Zhongguo funu shehui diwei gaiguan* (An Overview of the Status of Women in China) (Beijing: Zhongguo funu chubanshe, 1993):44.
56. Ibid., pp. 85–87.
57. *Renmin ribao* (overseas edition) (June 3, 1993):3.
58. *Zhongguo funu bao* (March 15, 1989):1.
59. *Zhongguo funu bao* (October 12, 1992):3.
60. *Zhongguo funu bao* (August 20, 1993):1.
61. State Statistical Bureau, *Zhongguo tongji nianjian 1989* (Statistical Yearbook of China 1989) (Beijing: Zhongguo tongji chubanshe, 1990):4.
62. *Statistics on Chinese Women*, op. cit., pp. 15–16.
63. *Zhongguo funu bao* (August 20, 1993):1, (October 16, 1992):1.
64. See, e.g., *Zhongguo funu bao* (July 28, 1993):3

2 JAPAN

Machiko Matsui

In 1868, Emperor Meiji was restored to power, marking an end to more than 200 years of rule by feudal lords. With the assistance of competent reformers, he ushered Japan into an era of industrialization and urbanization. The Meiji Period (1868–1912) thus laid the foundation of modern Japan. Education was charged with the mission of cultivating talents for national and economic development. The education of women was conceived in terms of a particular ideology. Mori Arinori, a member of the leading reformers of the Meiji Period and first Minister of Education, proclaimed in 1887:

> If I summarize the principle for the education of women, it is to train women for ryosai kenbo (good wives and wise mothers) who are capable enough to manage the household and to guide and edify their children. The foundation of our national strength and prosperity depends on education. The foundation of education depends on women's education. The stability of the nation depends on the success in women's education.[1]

From the time of the Meiji Restoration, the newly established nation-state placed the education of women at the center of its agenda for modernization.

The *ryosai kenbo* ideology that combined the traditional feminine virtues of Confucianism and the newly introduced ideal of Victorian womanhood became a leading principle for women's education.[2] Whereas Confucianism praised women's ignorance as a virtue, the new ideology envisioned a new dual role for women as "wise mothers" who educate their children to become loyal citizens and diligent workers and as efficient wives so that their husbands could devote themselves entirely to the nation's development. Ideal women were to dedicate themselves to their family's welfare in the spirit of Confucian womanhood, but in a modern manner. This ideology endowed women with the new prestige of full responsibility for their children's education but confined them to a prescribed sphere.

Whether the conservative or the modern aspect of the *ryosai kenbo* ideology was emphasized in women's education depended upon the political climate of the time. Despite such superficial changes, however, the core of the ideology—a rigid sexual division of labor based on "innate" gender differences—has persisted. Postwar Japanese society has recreated women as education-oriented mothers, welfare agents, and supplementary workers. Although the postwar educational reforms eliminated the legal barriers to educational access for women, considerable gender imbalance has persisted beyond the elementary level. Even today women are denied equal access to professional and advanced studies. They are streamed into gender-segregated institutions, where they study traditionally female-dominated subjects that lead them to occupations of lesser prestige and lower pay than are open to men. By limiting women's vocations to a domestic sphere, the *ryosai kenbo* ideology has contributed to the marginalization of female labor.

This chapter explores the interaction between women's education and economic development by defining the *ryosai kenbo* ideology as a key concept in women's education, as well as a crucial instrument in Japan's modernization since the Meiji Restoration. First, it gives a brief overview of the historical background of the ideology in relation to prewar women's education. Second, it examines how the ideology has revived in the context of postwar economic and educational development. Last, it attests the extent to which the Equal Employment Opportunity Law of 1986 has expanded women's access to education, particularly in nontraditional fields.

Prewar Women's Education

The Meiji government recognized the importance of basic education for all regardless of gender.[3] The Education Ordinance of 1872 declared the goal of achieving universal literacy through the establishment of four-year primary schools in every locality. Female attendance, however, lagged behind that of males, especially in rural areas. In 1873 only 15% of school-aged girls attended school compared with 40% of boys. In 1890 the rate for girls reached 31%, compared with 65% of boys. In 1907 compulsory education was extended to six years. In 1910 school attendance finally became universal for both sexes.[4]

This implementation of universal primary education equipped women with basic literacy and arithmetic needed for work in modern factories and trained them to work according to schedule. A sizable number of young women were recruited from the impoverished countryside to toil in flourishing spinning and textile industries as cheap replaceable labor. From 1894 to 1912, women constituted about 60% of Japan's industrial labor.[5] In modern spinning and textile mills they worked for 12 to 16 hours a day in poor conditions at half men's wages. Their cheap labor enabled the country to accumulate large capital to invest in heavy industries and to build a strong military.

Nevertheless, women's contribution to economic development was never recognized. Female industrial workers were seen as deviant since the social norm dictated women's place to be in the home. Most women quit work when they married. Although most women worked alongside their men in agriculture and family enterprises in preindustrial Japan, they were never considered a permanent work force in modern industries.

Instead of incorporating women into the labor force, the Meiji government instilled the *ryosai kenbo* ideology in women through its compulsory education system. The state expected women to contribute to national development through their devotion to their husbands and children. Given that the vast majority of women were then engaged in agrarian labor, this concept remained an unrealized ideal for the poor and thus was true only for upper-middle-class women who could afford to stay at home. Nevertheless, since the ideology successfully imposed the norm that women's vocation was in the home, women's employment and marriage were seen as incompatible. In this perspective women's labor was seens as temporary and merely a supplement to their family incomes.

Based on the *ryosai kenbo* ideology, the government considered elementary education sufficient for women. Consequently, secondary and tertiary schools for women were developed largely by private effort. In the early Meiji period, Christian missionary schools such as the Ferris Seminary (established in 1870) and Kobe Jogakuin (established in 1875) offered the only opportunities in secondary education for young women. In 1879 the government banned coeducation above the elementary level and made sewing a compulsory subject for girls. As the trend toward militarism gathered strength in the late Meiji period, the conservative aspect of the *ryosai kenbo* ideology was emphasized along with Confucian ethics, as witnessed in the Imperial Rescript of Education (1890) and the Meiji Civil Code (1898). The Women's High School Ordinance of 1899, aiming at tightening state control over women's education, requested local governments to open at least one high school for women in each prefecture. The law requested that female students receive domesticity training, with an emphasis on sewing and moral education. As a result, at the secondary level women attended four-year schools that were inferior to boys' five-year schools in content of teaching, quality of teachers, and facilities. Except in teacher-training courses, women's high schools prepared women for marriage rather than for study at a university.

At the turn of the twentieth century postsecondary education for women appeared in the private sector. Tsuda Umeko, one of five female students sent to the United States in 1871, founded Tsuda Women's College for English language training in 1900. Yoshioka Yayoi, one of the first female doctors in Japan, established Tokyo Women's Medical School in the same year. Japan Women's University opened in 1901. Prosperity in the post-World War I era expanded the urban middle class, who could afford to send their daughters to women's higher schools. In 1920 women's five-year high schools were introduced. Although only 10% of female elementary school graduates attended these high schools, the number of women's high schools and their enrollment exceeded the number of men's middle schools and their enrollment. Influenced by the first-wave feminist movement for women's suffrage, women began to demand access to higher education. By 1937, 42 private women's colleges offered three-year courses. Yet the Ministry of Education did not accredit these institutions as universities. Classified as *senmon gakko* (special schools), they could not award recognized degrees to their graduates.

The government was indifferent to public demand. There were only two national women's higher normal schools for the training of teachers for women's high schools and normal schools. One was opened in Tokyo in 1890 and the other in Nara in 1908, The first prefectural college for women opened in Fukuoka in 1922. Only five similar public institutions for women were established in prewar Japan. Except a few progressive institutions such as Tohoku Imperial University, almost all the prestigious imperial universities denied enrance to female candidates.

Since their options in fields of study were limited to the humanities, home economics, and education, the women who had finished postsecondary schools entered "feminine" occupations such as teaching, nursing, telephone operating, and retail and clerical jobs. Women's advancement in male-dominated professions was considered inappropriate and harmful to their "femininity." Therefore most private women's colleges functioned as finishing schools for women of the upper middle class rather than institutions that prepared them for professional work.

The Taisho liberalism was short-lived (1913–1925) and only an urban middle-class phenomenon. It excluded the vast majority of women living in the impoverished countryside. In the 1930s when patriotic motherhood was emphasized under accelerated nationalism and militarism, women's demand for higher education diminished. Toward the end of World War II, however, a great number of young women were mobilized into factories into fill the vacancies. To meet the new demand for female labor, the Education Policy for Wartime Emergency of 1944 promulgated that women's colleges and high schools be reformed to expand professional training courses such as commerce, technical education, and agriculture so as to train women for work previously performed by men. At the end of the war, 3.5 million female workers sustained Japanese industries.

In summary, women's access to schooling beyond the elementary level was extremely class-bound in prewar Japan because of the elitist system of education. The implementation of universal elementary education enabled young, poor women to leave home for modern factory employment. In contrast, higher levels of education, except in the fields of medicine and teacher education, served to train women of privileged classes to maintain their class culture. Women's educational attainment did not necessarily have a positive effect on their labor force participation. In the 1930s and 1940s the employment rate of the graduates from women's colleges was as low as 30% to 40%.[6] Women were denied access to universities because of the inferior content of gender-streamed secondary education. By World War II approximately 30,000 men but only 40 women were attending the most prestigious imperial universities.[7] In 1940 less than 1% of the relevant-age cohort of women was enrolled in postsecondary institutions, compared with 6.5% of men.[8]

POSTWAR REFORM

The U.S. Occupational Reform reorganized the entire education system. The new Constitution and the Fundamental Law of Education of 1947 granted women equal rights to pursue their educational goals. A series of reforms changed the elitism of the prewar system to a more egalitarian single-track structure. Compulsory education was prolonged from six to nine years, and a uniform 6–3–3–4 (elementary-junior high-senior high-university) system was implemented. Coeducation was established at all levels. Universities began to admit female applicants. Various post-secondary institutions for women were granted university status.

Education

Such democratic reforms dramatically expanded women's access to education, especially at higher levels (Table 2.1). By 1950 the percentage of female graduates from junior high schools entering senior high schools reached 37%, compared with 48% for male graduates. This figure increased steadily from 56% in 1960 to 83% in 1970 and reached 95% in 1979.[9] Dramatic growth in female enrollment at the secondary level occurred during the high economic development of the 1960s when Japan's education system transformed itself from an elitist to a mass system. Economic prosperity, accompanied by declining birth rates—at 4.11 per couple in 1940, 2.00 in 1960, 1.75 in 1980, and 1.53(the lowest ever) in 1990—created more middle-class families that could afford to educate their daughters.[10] Since 1969 women's enrollment in senior high schools has exceeded that of men.

Table 2.1 Enrollment Rates of Female and Male Students at Three Educational Levels, 1955–1990 (in %)

Year	Female			Male		
	High School	Junior College	Four-Year University	High School	Junior College	Four-Year University
1955	47.4	2.6	2.4	55.5	1.9	13.1
1960	55.9	3.0	2.5	59.6	1.2	13.7
1965	69.6	6.7	4.6	71.7	1.7	20.7
1970	82.7	11.2	6.5	81.6	2.0	27.3
1975	93.0	19.9	12.5	91.0	2.6	40.4
1980	95.4	21.0	12.3	93.1	2.0	39.3
1985	94.9	20.8	13.7	92.8	2.0	38.6
1990	95.3	22.2	15.2	93.0	1.7	33.5

Source: *Monbusho* (Ministry of Education) *Gakko Kihon Chosa* (Basic Survey on Schools), 1992.

Along with this dramatic increase in female enrollment, the proportion of female 18-year-olds entering colleges (including two-year junior colleges) and universities increased considerably from 5% in 1955 to 11% in 1965 and 18% in 1970.[11] Since 1975 the figure has exceeded 32%; and in 1986 the rate of 34% became comparable with that of male graduates. This remarkable quantitative growth, however, did not alter the essence of women's education. Gender differentiation by institution and by field of study has persisted in secondary and postsecondary education. Since the 1960s, 60% of women in the tertiary level have entered predominantly female two-year junior colleges, whereas more than 90% of men have entered four-year universities. Until 1989 the proportion of female students in four-year universities was approximately 20%, lagging far behind that of most industrialized countries. In prestigious national universities, notably Tokyo and Kyoto Universities, the female proportion has been less than 10%. In 1989 the percentage of women in the relevant-age-cohort entering universities was 14.7%, which was comparable with that of men 30 years before.[12]

In secondary schools, although more women have been enrolled in general academic programs, relatively fewer have taken rigorously academic courses for university preparation. In vocational high schools women have concentrated on commerce and home economics, while men took engineering courses. Even though a majority of public high schools are coeducational, 28% of students go to single-sex schools, most of which are women's schools.[13] Prestigious academic-oriented private high schools are exclusively for men. At the tertiary level, women are concentrated in traditional female subjects in sex-segregated institutions. In junior colleges, 80% of women major in home economics, arts and letters, education, and nursing. The pattern repeats itself in universities; 60% of all women enrolled in universities major in traditionally female-dominated fields. In contrast, nearly half of male students specialize in the social sciences and another quarter in engineering.[14]

Thus the postwar educational reforms failed to address the issue of gender equality. Instead a series of reforms in the 1960s instituted separate education for women based on gender streaming in secondary and postsecondary education. The changing economic structure during the high economic development period explains the institutionalization of junior colleges as a female track. Between 1960 and 1975 the proportion of the labor force engaged in primary industries declined from 32% to 13.9% while that in secondary and tertiary industries expanded from 56.4% to 85.9%.[15] Along with this rapid industrialization, industrial efficiency took priority. Women were regarded as incompetent workers because of their reproductive functions. From the late 1950s, based on the human capital theory, the higher education system was restructured to meet increasing demand from booming industries to train more qualified personnel in science and technology. Courses in secondary schools were differentiated according to one's ability, academic goal, and career path. Women were increasingly excluded from science education and required to take home economics courses. In 1966 the Central Education Committee, an advisory committee for curricular reform under the Ministry of Education, published a report entitled "The Image of Ideal Human Being." This document stressed a clear-cut sexual division of labor and became a guideline for educational reforms leading to economic development. The report defined the role of family as follows:

> Home is a place that provides people healthy joy and clean rest in today's busy life. People can recover themselves from the inhumane mass society in their own homes . . . If home is a place for healthy, clean, and pleasant rest, we can refresh our energy every day so as to increase productivity of our society and nation.[16] To create pleasant homes, "a foundation of the productive society," women were again expected to become *ryosai kenbo*.

Consequently, "education according to the special qualities of womanhood" was reemphasized throughout the recent period of high economic development. In 1958 gender streaming—home economics for females and technical education for men—first started in junior high schools. In 1962 the Central Education Committee recommended mandating home economics for women in senior high schools. In 1964 the two-year junior college system received full certification and became a permanent "women's track" in higher education. Modeled on the American community college, junior colleges were initially created under the Occupational Reform to provide opportunities in both liberal arts education and vocational training for adults and students from less privileged families.[17] They were regarded as a transition system that would at some point expand its facilities to meet the standards of four-year universities. During the 1960s, however, junior colleges became exclusively female and expanded to meet the social expectations of women's roles.[18]

Throughout the decades of educational expansion since the 1950s, female enrollment in prestigious national universities and coeducational private universities increased only marginally.[19] Increase in female enrollment in higher education occurred largely in the private sector, particularly in junior colleges. In the 1960s the government invested heavily in an expansion of facilities in science and technology at four-year national universities to meet the demand from growing industries. However, it was reluctant to provide low-cost public universities for the masses, particularly women. Although a limited number of *kotosenmon gakko* (national technical high schools) was established, they were exclusively for men. During the 1960s, when tremendous educational expansion occurred, approximately 200 new junior colleges were established, nearly all of which were private. As a result, today more than 90% of junior college students enroll in private institutions.[20] Furthermore, a third of the private universities founded in the same decade were exclusively for women. Women with little incentive to invest in their education, a result of limited career opportunities, have tended to avoid the intense competition through entrance examinations for the limited number of public universities. Instead they have been apt to choose less expensive—and less competitive—junior colleges. Women from more privileged families have tended to choose private women's universities affiliated with women's high schools.[21]

Because of the lack of government subsidies, junior colleges have suffered from deteriorating academic conditions. Between 1950 and 1988 the number of students at junior colleges increased 30 times from 15,000 to 450,000, yet the number of teachers increased only ninefold. The teacher-student ratio at junior colleges in 1989 was 1:23.4 compared with 1:16.8 at universities.[22] Inadequate finances made junior colleges and private women's universities unable to offer capital-intensive science and technical education. This resulted in the extremely low number of females majoring in engineering. In 1960 only 0.5% of all female students in universities took engineering. Although the figure increased to 2.4% in 1988, women were still a small minority among students of engineering. As competition for university entrance examinations accelerated in the 1960s, females in high school were increasingly streamed into a junior college track in which they were exempt from advanced math and science education. Finally, in 1970, home economics became compulsory for women in senior high schools. Consequently the majority of women were streamed into the female track as early as the secondary level and pursued traditional female subjects at junior colleges.

Labor Force Participation

Heavy female concentration in a few subjects in postsecondary education has created gender-segregation in the occupational structure. Women lacking adequate professional skills and advanced knowledge are likely to enter traditionally female-dominated occupations with less prestige and lower pay. Yet "special qualities of womanhood" such as patience, dexterity, and neatness were considered desirable for monotonous assembly work in growing manufacturing industries. Until 1989 female high school graduates maintained the highest employment rates (Table 2.2). Thirty percent of female graduates entered retail sales and another 30% went into manufacturing jobs.[23] In the 1960s and the early 1970s high economic development was sustained by young unmarried female workers who finished secondary education. In 1962, 55.2% of female employees were unmarried, again showing the incompatibility between paid work and the family.

Table 2.2 Employment Rates of Graduates by Level of Education, 1960–1991 (in %)

Year	Female				Male			
	Middle school	High school	Junior college	Four-year university	Middle school	High school	Junior college	Four-year university
1960	37.5	58.6	49.8	64.1	39.7	63.7	79.5	86.3
1970	16.1	61.2	68.8	59.9	16.5	55.4	80.5	82.8
1980	83.1	90.6	78.2	67.7	86.2	83.3	80.6	84.6
1985	78.0	90.0	83.1	75.4	88.3	88.3	82.4	86.6
1991	69.0	88.6	90.4	85.1	79.8	85.5	83.2	90.1

Source: *Monbusho*, 1991. From 1980, figures are given based on the following formula: the numbers of graduates employed/the number of graduates, excluding those who entered a higher level of education.

Educated women have had very few career options until recently. A majority studied traditionally female occupations such as clerical work, teaching, health care, nursing, social work, and retail sales. In 1975 only 2% of engineers, 5.3% of scientific researchers, 5.4% of managers, 2.8% of certified accountants, and 6.8% of jurists were women; 66.7% of health care workers and 40.9% of teachers were female.[24] Until 1975, as a result of the paucity of career opportunities coupled with *ryosai kenbo* ideology propagated by the mass media, the rate of women taking employment upon graduation from college or university was only 60 to 70%. Regardless of their educational attainment, most women quit work and stayed home upon marriage to support their corporate warrior husbands. Thus, throughout the high economic development period, the rising level of women's education never transformed gender-segregation in the occupational structure.

In postwar periods, with more than a sufficient supply of qualified male workers in a society infected with what Dore called "diploma disease," Japanese employers had no need to mobilize women into the professions.[25] Throughout the period of high economic growth, based on the human capital theory, the government stressed the importance of training personnel in science and technology for expanding industries. Yet women were totally excluded by virtue of their reproductive functions, which were considered a disadvantage in the labor market. Japanese capitalism chose to utilize women as cheap reserve labor in the workplace and as unpaid welfare agents in the family by effectively imposing the *ryosai kenbo* ideology.

Thus during rapid economic growth the sexual division of labor became pronounced. The average number of family members decreased from 4.97 in 1955 to 4.0 in 1965 (and to 3.23 in 1985).[26] A couple comprised of a *sararii man* (salaried worker) husband and a *sengyo shufu* (full-time housewife) became very common as rapid industrialization and urbanization proceeded. The terms *sengyo shufu* and *kyoiku mama* (education mom) first appeared in the 1960s. In this context the *ryosai kenbo,* which was once an ideal only for the upper-middle class, spread to the modern middle class nuclear family. According to a 1973 NHK (Nihon Hoso Kyokai—Japan Broadcasting) opinion poll, 74% of women believed that married women should devote themselves to their families and children and only 24% agreed that married women could combine family and work responsibilities.[27] In the same period a majority of parents began to envision a university education for sons and a junior college education for daughters.

In the late 1970s, when Japanese capitalism restructured itself from emphasizing manufacturing to emphazising information and technology, service industries in the tertiary sector expanded enormously (Table 2.3). Along with the demographic decline of youth, an unprecedented number of married women were mobilized into the work force, largely in the expanding service sectors. Technological change resulted in fragmentation of the work process in manufacturing sectors and created more work for semiskilled part-time workers. The labor shortage, together with increasing housing and education costs, pushed middle-aged housewives to work outside the home. In 1975 more than 60% of married women were engaged in paid employment.[28]

Table 2.3 Gender Composition in the Labor Force by Industry (in percent of total labor force)

Year	Primary Industry Female	Primary Industry Male	Secondary Industry Female	Secondary Industry Male	Tertiary Industry Female	Tertiary Industry Male
1960	16.9	15.7	7.9	21.3	14.4	23.8
1975	6.5	7.4	9.5	24.5	20.6	31.3
1985	4.3	5.0	10.2	22.9	24.2	33.1

Source: Based on *Somucho Tokei-kyoku* (Office of General Statistics), *Rodoryoky Chosa* (Survey on Labor Force) 1990.

The newly created jobs for women were mostly, despite long work hours, lower paying part-time positions in semiskilled sectors, often without social security or fringe benefits. In 1985 average female part-timers worked six to seven hours a day, five days a week, and received approximately 70% of the wage for full-time female workers.[29] As a result the average wage of female workers was approximately half that of male workers. (From 42.8% in 1960, it reached 55.8% in 1975 and again declined to 52.3% in 1987.[30]) This figure was significantly lower than that in other industrialized countries. The Japanese labor market closed its door to educated women who desired to return to professions after childrearing. According to a 1983 survey by the Prime Minister's Office, better educated women were less likely than less educated counterparts to return to employment, despite their higher career aspirations.[31] Although the female labor force became older, married, and better educated, most women still refrained from employment during the childrearing period. Therefore, the participation of Japanese women in the labor force was characterized as an M-shape with a sharp decline in the 30–34 age cohort (Table 2.4).

Table 2.4 Female Labor Force Participation Rate by Age Cohort in 1988 (in % of total female population)

	\multicolumn{11}{c}{Age Cohort}
	15–19	20–24	25–29	30–34	35–39	40–44	45–49	50–54	55–59	60–64	65+
LFP rate	17.3	74.3	59.6	51.1	62.4	68.8	70.7	64.2	52.2	39.2	15.8

Source: Based on Somucho, 1990.

At the same time the information-based industries created demand for office workers who had certain professional skills such as in the operation of word processors and computers. The majority of recent junior college graduates have found employment in these transformed clerical sectors. Since 1970 the employment rate of female junior college graduates has been higher than that of female four-year university graduates. By 1984 the employment rate of female junior college graduates (80%) exceeded that of male university students.[32] Despite their qualifications, however, college-educated women have been treated merely as temporary workers. From the beginning the seniority-based permanent employment system has excluded women and has tracked them into separate sectors for routine clerical work. Firms have seldom offered female office workers opportunities for more advanced training or promotion to administrative and managerial positions. Until 1986 most private firms considered female university graduates and female junior college graduates to be the same. Many companies even had policies not to recruit female four-year university graduates.

The establishment of junior colleges in the private sector as a women's track has been the most cost-effective way to incorporate women into the expected roles for women in corporate Japan. Women's primary vocation is in their homes. Temporary paid employment is allowed only if it does not interfere with family obligations. The "education mom" phenomenon in part contributes to maintaining the high academic achievement of Japanese children and therefore the high quality of Japanese workers.[33]

Such a clearcut division of labor has precisely met the demand of the rapidly growing Japanese economy. Restrained by the *ryosai kenbo* ideology, most women, regardless of educational level, refrain from work during the childrearing period and return to work only after their children have grown up. The mass mobilization of housewives into the labor force since the late 1970s has not changed this pattern. Rather, female labor has been further marginalized. In 1979 the Law for Fundamental Fulfillment of Family emphasized the "welfare state in Japanese style" by defining the family as the basic unit of welfare. Placing all the burdens of caring for children, the sick, the disabled, and the elderly on women's shoulders was the most effective way to reduce welfare costs for the government, which needed to invest more capital in industrial development.

Nonformal Education

The gap between the rising level of women's education and the paucity of career opportunities increased the demand for life-long education for women. Although formal education has been slow to respond, nonformal education, called social education in Japan, has become increasingly popular among middle-class housewives. In 1949 the government made a provision for social education for adults a mandate of local governments. Since the 1970s newspaper companies, department stores, the mass media, and private schools have started "cultural centers" to provide numerous courses on a commercial basis. In 1985 NHK launched the University of the Air for adults. In 1985, 250,000 courses were offered by public institutions at the national or local level. Nearly 10 million people participated, and over 60% of them were women.[34] In 1986, 40% of the women in Tokyo participated in some kind of social education, notably women in their forties after the childrearing period, who marked the highest participation rate of 49.7%.[35] Another research study shows a positive relation between women's participation rate and their level of formal education.[36] The International Women's Year (1975) created a new phase in social education. The National Women's Center opened in 1977 to encourage national and international exchange, research, and training for the enhancement of women's education. The number of local women's centers reached 100 in 1978.[37] These national and local women's centers have been serving as a core for collecting and distributing information regarding women's issues, organizing various community-based voluntary activities, and promoting life-long education for women.

The most remarkable recent change in the trend is the increase in courses on women's issues and women's history (from 4.3% of the total number of courses offered in 1978 to 24.5% in 1988) and a decrease in courses on leisure activities (from 22.2% in 1978 to 5.0% in 1988).[38] Women's studies courses organized by the National Women's Center every year have attracted many teachers, scholars, researchers, administrators, and members of local women's studies groups. This trend reflects the changing view toward the sexual division of labor among Japanese women.

The widespread social education courses, especially those oriented to women's issues, have created spontaneous study groups of women at the local level. Women collect, disseminate, and exchange information about issues concerning women and local facilities for women and build networks among various women's groups.[39] Such activities have formed a foundation of ever-increasing women's participation in community-based voluntary activities and grassroots social movements regarding consumer protection, the environment, and peace.

The prolonged life span of women (81.77 years in 1989, which was the longest in the world) and the rising level of women's educational attainment have made an unprecedented number of women pursue opportunities for self-improvement and social awareness. Nevertheless, most courses in social education still aim to provide middle-class housewives with opportunities for cultural enrichment. Very few courses offer vocational training for women who seek a career after childrearing. Moreover, even today, very few women are decision-makers. More than 90% of the social education leaders and planners at local governments are men.[40] Therefore, despite the significant growth of women's participation, social education courses still remain within the framework of *ryosai kenbo*.

CHANGES SINCE THE 1980S

Women's access to education has been closely linked to their opportunities in the occupational structure and therefore to the socioeconomic structure of postwar Japan. Without fundamental structural change, education alone could not enable women to surmount the various sociocultural restraints and to contribute directly to the process of economic development.

In the 1980s, however, various signs of positive changes emerged. In

1979 the total number of female graduates from universities and colleges in the postwar period reached one million.[41] The number of female researchers reached 14,000, enough to form a lobbying group.[42] The impact of the second-wave feminist movement, which started in the early 1970s, became visible in the establishment of Women's Studies courses at colleges and universities as well as at the community level throughout Japan.[43] Various scholarly journals began to publish articles on gender issues in education.[44] Gender asymmetry in educational content, curriculum, textbooks, classroom practices, and career guidance became a subject of great interest among concerned scholars and educators.

In 1985, under increasing domestic and international pressures, the Japanese government finally ratified the Convention on the Elimination of All Forms of Discrimination against Women. Article 10 specified the eradication of gender inequality in the curriculum, educational content, and quality of facilities and teachers. On this ground Japanese feminists launched a grassroots movement to abolish gender-streaming in secondary schools. They maintained that compulsory home economics for girls had created a premise for the clearcut sexual division of labor in Japanese society.[45] Consequently, in 1989 the Ministry of Education's new guidelines for educational reform, scheduled to come into effect in 1994, made both home economics and technical education compulsory for all secondary school students, irrespective of gender.

The passage of the Equal Employment Opportunity Bill in 1985 and enforcement of it as law (hereafter EEOL) since 1986 was another outcome of the Gender Equality Treaty.[46] Yet this law is deeply flawed. While prohibiting discriminatory practices in training, welfare benefits, retirement, and dismissal policies, it called on companies to try to treat women equally in recruitment and promotion, without risk of a penalty if they did not. A law without enforceable policies is futile. Further, the EEOL curtailed existing protective legislation such as menstrual leave and exemption of female workers from work during holidays and overtime after 10 p.m. It allowed employees to do overtime work for up to 24 hours in four weeks, in place of the former regulation of two hours per day. The protective regulations, with the exception of maternity leave, did not cover women in managerial posts. As feminists criticized, the law's purpose was to utilize women to overcome the serious shortage in the male labor force by forcing women to trade protection for equality. But this "equality" merely meant that female workers could work as ong as Japanese male workers, whose work hours were already notoriously longer than the international standard.

Since 1986 companies have offered *sogoshoku,* the permanent career track, with equal opportunities for training and promotion to managerial positions, to female four-year university graduates. Yet the number of women actually hired for *sogoshoku* has been extremely limited. For instance, in 1990 Tokyo Kaijo-Kasai, an insurance company that was ranked number one in recruiting female graduates, hired 294 male graduates but only 14 women for *sogoshoku*, while it hired 422 women and no men for *ippanshoku*, the routine clerical work track. Japan Airlines hired three women out of 142 for *sogoshoku*.[47] In the same year in Japan, 99% of male workers versus only 3.7% of female workers were in *sogoshoku*; thus 96.2% of female workers were concentrated in *ippanshoku*.[48] The new personnel control system has merely consolidated gender segregation in the workplace. The EEOL has divided female workers into two categories: a handful of elites who are forced to work as hard as male workers, versus the vast majority of female workers who continue to be at the bottom of the occupational structure.

Despite its obvious shortcomings, the EEOL did extend to female university graduates opportunities to compete with their male counterparts on equal footing. According to a Ministry of Labor survey, among 1,134 corporations, the percentage of companies that hired female university graduates increased from 55.3% in 1987 to 61.9% in 1989.[49] In 1990 for the first time the employment rate of female four-year university graduates reached a level comparable with that of males (81% for both sexes).

Reflecting this positive trend in employment, the percentage of women entering colleges and universities exceeded that of men in 1989 (36.8% of eligible females, versus 35.8% of males). The female ratio among four-year university entrants jumped from 27.9% in 1988 to 36.3% in 1989, while the percentage of women entering junior colleges correspondingly declined.[50] The ratio of women to men in four-year universities reached 30.2% (3:7) in 1990.[51] Change has also become apparent in women's choices of field of study. Since female graduates from the humanities, education, and home economics were not hired for *sogoshoku*, women began to choose subject areas more closely related to future career prospects. The percentage of female university students in the social sciences has increased from 14.7% in 1980 to 20.7% in 1990, compared to 7.4% in 1960.[52] The ratio of females among the entrants into the fields of law, economics, and commerce doubled in the past decade. During the same period the percentage of junior college students enrolled in home economics declined considerably, from 52% in 1965, 32.2% in 1975, to 27.5% in 1990.[53]

Along with this recent change in the character of female enrollment, coupled with the demographic decline of youth,[54] universities and colleges particularly in the private sector have begun to introduce nontraditional fields, including management, information science, architecture, and engineering, in order to attract more career-oriented female applicants and to offset the present financial crisis.[55] Several junior colleges have restructured themselves into coeducational four-year comprehensive universities. Together with structural and demographic changes in society, the higher education of women in Japan entered a new phase in the late 1980s.

Another promising trend is that women's studies courses have spread rapidly in colleges and universities across Japan. Between 1983 and 1988, the number of colleges and universities that offered women's studies courses increased from 75 to 135, and the total number of courses grew from 94 to 280.[56] According to a survey conducted by the National Women's Center, nearly a quarter of the universities and colleges throughout Japan offered women's studies courses in 1991.[57] This indicates a change toward increased gender-role awareness among the younger generation of Japanese women. Given the deeply rooted concept in Japanese society of the sexual division, a core of the *ryosai kenbo* ideology, it is crucial to raise the consciousness of women themselves toward more egalitarian views of gender roles. The role of women's studies courses should be important in helping to do this.

In spite of the positive trends in the late 1980s, marginalization of female labor persisted throughout the decade. During the 1980s part-time workers became increasingly married and female. In 1990, 75% of part-timers were female, compared to 43.6% in 1980. Also in 1990, one-third of female employees were part-timers. Of the female employees over age 30, 64% were part-timers.[58] Women's advancement in nontraditional professions is surprisingly slow. Although the total number of female professionals and technical workers doubled from 1.25 million to 2.55 million between 1970 and 1985, women were still heavily in traditional female professions.[59] In 1985, 69.7% of health-related workers, 65.4% of musicians and stage artists, 56.1% of clerical workers, 41.3% of teachers, and 37.1% of sales workers were women. This was a contrast to only 4.5% of engineers, 7.5% of scientific researchers, 7.3% of jurists, 3.8% of certified accountants, and 8.4% of managers.[60]

Inadequate provision of childcare leave and daycare facilities still makes it nearly impossible for women to continue work. Given the fact that only 19.2% of firms provided childcare leave for female workers in 1988, most women had no alternative but to quit work after childbirth. The M-shape curve of labor force participation has remained.[61] The return rate of female college and university graduates to paid employment after childrearing was still lower than that of their less educated counterparts. This reflects the limited career opportunities for educated women once they leave the labor force.

Cross-cultural studies on women's education have indicated that women will in fact pursue nontraditional fields and break cultural constraints when they find incentives for future employment.[62] The significant positive trend of the 1980s in female enrollment in higher education shows how important it is to link education to the widening of women's opportunities in the occupational structure. Yet the employment rate of female graduates again declined substantially in 1992 as the result of economic recession. It is evident that fundamental change is unlikely to occur in the absence of legislation enforcing gender equalization. It is also clear that women will continue to have difficulties in securing professional advancement unless the notoriously rigorous work schedule in Japanese workplaces becomes flexible enough to enable both sexes to meet obligations in the public as well as private spheres. Unless fundamental change takes place in the workplace, the education of Japanese women will continue to serve as "cultural enrichment" instead of as preparation for lifelong careers. Without educational and occupational reforms for gender equalization, Japanese women will continue to be incorporated into the process of economic development not as decision-makers and permanent workers but merely as wives, mothers, and temporary workers.

Notes

All Japanese names are written in the Japanese way: surname first and given name last.

1. Mori Arinori, "Speech upon Observation of Local Schools in Chugoku Area," in: Kanamori Toshie and Fujii Harue, eds., *Onna no kyoiku 100 nen* (Women's Education in the Past 100 Years) (Tokyo: Sansei-do, 1977):48–49.

2. There have been debates about the *ryosai kembo* ideology. Past studies focused on the pre-modern aspect of the ideology in relation to the *kazoku kokka kan*, family-state ideology, which functioned as an ideological instrument in the transfer of loyalty from the family to the emperor, thereby forming a foundation for imperial rule. See, for example, Fukaya Masashi, *Ryosai kembo shugi no kyoiku* (Education Based on Good Wife and Wise Mother Ideology) (Tokyo: Reimei, 1966) and Takamure Itsue, *Josei no rekishi* (History of Women) (1958: repr., Tokyo: Kodansha, 1972). Recently, Koyama Shizuko argued that the *ryosai kembo* ideology was created to impose and maintain a new concept of the public and private spheres, contemporary with industrialization. In her view, it was not a remnant of feudalism but a product of Japan's modernization. Koyama stresses the universality of this ideology by demonstrating that similar principles of women's education emerged in the early stages of nation-building and industrialization in other countries. See Koyama, *Ryosai kenbo toiu kihan* (The Norm, Good Wife and Wise Mother)(Tokyo: Keiso, 1990).

3. For a discussion of women's education in the prewar period see Kanamori and Fujii, *Onna no kyoiku 100 nen*; Mitsui Tametomo, *Nihon fujin-mondai shiryo shusei: kyoiku* (Source Book on Women's Issues: Education)(Tokyo: Domesu, 1977); Dorothy Robin-Mowry, *The Hidden Sun*, (Boulder, CO: Westview, 1983); Japan Wom-

en's University Research Center, ed., *Taisho no joshi kyoiku* (Women's Education in the Taisho Period) (Tokyo: Kokudosha, 1975) and *Meiji no joshi kyoiku* (Women's Education in the Meiji Period)(Tokyo: Kokudosha, 1967).

4. For a comparison of male and female school attendance rates from 1871, see Koyama Takashi, *The Changing Social Position of Women in Japan* (Paris: UNESCO, 1961):22.

5. Sharon Shievers, *Flowers in Salt: The Beginning of Feminist Consciousness in Modern Japan* (Stanford, CA: Stanford University Press, 1983):55.

6. Amano Masako, *Joshi koto kyoiku no zahyo* (The State of Female Higher Education) (Tokyo: Kakiuchi-shuppan, 1986):47.

7. Higuchi Keiko, "Japan," in: Robin Morgan, ed., *Sisterhood Is Global* (New York: Anchor Press, 1984):380.

8. Hara Kimi, "Joshi koto kyoiku no shakaigakuteki ikkosatsu (Sociological Thoughts on Higher Education of Women)," *Kyoiku shakaigaku kenkyu* 26, Table 3, p. 87.

9. Fujin Kyoiku Kenkyu Kai *(FKK), Tokei ni miur no genjo* (Statistics Concerning the Present Status of Women) (Tokyo: Kakiuchi, 1991), Table 37, p. 36.

10. Ibid., Table 6, p. 14.

11. Figures on female enrollment at the tertiary level are cited from Inoue Teruke and Ebara Yumiko, *Josei no deeta bukku* (Women's Data Book) (Tokyo: Yuhikaku, 1991), Table 47-1, p. 117.

12. *FKK*, Table 37, p. 37.

13. Monbusho, *Monbu Tokei-yoran* (Summary of Educational Statistics) (Toyko: Ministry of Education, 1987).

14. Rodosho Fujin-Kyoku, *Fujin rodo no jitsujo* (The Status of Women's Labor) 1991, Table 38, p. 45.

15. *FKK*, Table 59, p. 58.

16. Chuoo kyoiku shingikai, *Kitaisareru ningenzo* (The Image of Ideal Human Being) (Tokyo: Ministry of Education, 1966).

17. For a discussion of the development of the junior college and its negative impact on women's education, see Amano, *Joshi koto kyoiku no zahyo;* Fujii Harue, *Nihon no joshi kotoo kyoiku* (Higher Education of Women in Japan) (Tokyo: Domesu, 1973) and "Education for Women; The Personal and Social Damage of Anachronistic Policy," *Japan Quarterly,* xxix, no. 3:301–310; Kumiko Fujimura-Fanselow, "Women's Participation in Higher Education in Japan" *Comparative Education Review* 29, no.4(1985):471–489; Narumiya Chie, "Opportunity for Girls and Women in Japanese Education," *Comparative Education,* 22, no. 1:47–52.

18. In 1955, when the junior college system started, 54% of junior college students were female. In 1988, however, the figure rose to 90.8%. See *FKK,* Table 48, p. 119.

19. Even in 1975, after the period of educational expansion, female students were only about 10% of the enrollment in prestigious coeducational universities. Amano, Table 2–3, p. 66.

20. Inoue and Ebara, Table 48–1, p. 119.

21. According to a Ministry of Education survey, in the period of educational expansion (1965, 1968, 1972, and 1976), female students in private colleges and universities came from higher income families than did their male counterparts. Amano, pp. 74–75.

22. Inoue and Ebara, Table 48–3, p. 119.

23. Employment rates of female graduates from high school, college, and university are obtained from Fujin-kyoku, *Fujin rodo no jitsujo* (The State of Women's Labor), 1987, Tables 28 and 32, pp. 30–33.

24. *FKK,* Table 44–2, p. 105.

25. Ronald Dore, *Diploma Disease* (Berkeley: University of California Press, 1976):35–49.

26. Inoue and Ebara, Table 3–1, p. 7.

27. Ibid., Table 64–1, p. 161. In 1988, the percentage of women who believed that women could combine family and work responsibilities increased to 38%; the percentage of women who placed priority on the family decreased to 58%.

28. At present the figure is nearly 70%, compared to 45% in 1962. *FKK*, Table 63, p. 61.

29. Inoue and Ebara, p. 94.

30. *FKK*, Table 68, p. 63.

31. Prime Minister's Office, *Shakai seikatsu kihon chosa* (Basic Survey on Social Life), cited in Amano, pp. 169–172.

32. Rodosho, *Fujin rodo no jitsujo*, Table 33, pp. 38–39.

33. Joyce Lebra, "Motherhood and Education" in: *Japanese Women: Constraint and Fulfillment* (Honolulu: University of Hawaii Press, 1984):192–216; Merry White, *The Japanese Educational Challenge* (New York: Free Press, 1987).

34. Inoue and Ebara, Table 53–1, p. 129.

35. Ibid., Table 53–2, p. 129.

36. According to a Tokyo Board of Education survey on social education in 1986, nearly half the women who had had a post-secondary education participated in social education, while about 20% of female primary school graduates did so. Amano, pp. 172–177.

37. Nihon Fujin Dantai Rengokai (NFDR), *Fujin hakusho* (White Paper on Women, 1991) (Tokyo: Porupu-sha, 1991):212.

38. FKK, Table 41, p. 43.

39. Ueno Chizuko, *Joen ga yononaka o kaeru* (Women's Networking Will Change the Society) (Tokyo: Nihon Keizai Shinbun, 1988).

40. Inoue and Ebara, Table 53–3, p. 129.

41. Fujitani Atsuko and Uesugi Takemitsu, eds., *Daisotsu josei hyaku-mannin jidai* (The Age of One Million Female College Graduates) (Tokyo: Keiso, 1982).

42. Narumiya, p. 51.

43. Kuninobu Junko, "Nihon no joseigaku (Women's Studies in Japan)" *Annual Report of Women's Studies Society*, Vol. 10 (1988):1644.

44. Amano Masako, "Sei to kyoiku kenkyu no doko (Research Trends in Gender and Education)" *Shakaigaku hyoron*, Vol. 155 (1988); Kanda Michiko, "Josei to Kyoiku kenkyu no doko (Research Trends in Women and Education)" *Kyoiku Shakaigaku Kenkyu* Vol. 40 (1985).

45. Hara Bin and Koyama Masao, *Danjo byodo to gijutsu kyoiku* (Gender Equality and Technical Education) (Tokyo: Minshu sha, 1986); Handa Tatsuko, ed., *Kateika shinjidai* (The New Age for Home Economics Education) (Tokyo: We shobo, 1987).

46. For a general discussion on EEOL and its implications for women's work and education, see Takahashi Hisako, *Shinjidai no joshirodo* (Women's Work in the New Age) (Tokyo: Gakuyo shobo, 1989); *FKK*, 1991, pp. 2–80. For a feminist criticism of EEOL, see Nakajima Michiko, *Hataraku onna ga mirai o hiraku* (Working Women Open the Future) (Tokyo: Aki shobo, 1984).

47. NFDR, p. 208.

48. Ibid., p. 20.

49. Inoue and Ebara, 1991, Table 52–3, p. 127.

50. Inoue and Ebara, 1991, Table 47–1, p. 117.

51. NFDR, 1991, p. 203.

52. Rodosho, 1991, Table 38, p. 45.

53. Inoue and Ebara, 1991, Table 49–1, p. 121.

54. In 1960 nearly 40% of the Japanese population was under 19 years old. In 1985 the percentage declined to 30%. The Ministry of Health Demography Research Center estimated that the percentage would continue to decline and would become less than 25% in the year 2000. *FKK*, Table 2, p. 10.

55. For instance, Japan Women's University opened a faculty of social sciences called "Human Sociology" and is planning to develop a faculty of natural sciences, which would be the first among women's universities in Japan. Bunkyo Women's University, founded in 1991, opened the first school of management especially for women. Japan University opened an interior design course in the department of architectural engineering to attract female students. Hiroshima University of Economics has set a positive quota for women. Kumamoto University of Engineering opened a new women's dorm and aimed at raising the female ratio to 20%. NFDR, 1991, p. 205.

56. Inoue and Ebara, 1991, Table 51–1, p. 125.

57. *Kokuritsu fujin kaikan news* (National Women's Center newsletter), N. 53, April 15, 1991.

58. Rodosho, 1991, Table 60, p. 64.

59. Inoue and Ebara, Table 35–1, p. 87.

60. Ibid., Table 44–2, p. 105.

61. The percentage of firms providing childcare leave increased from 2.3% in 1971 to 19.2% in 1988. (Inoue and Ebara, Table 41–2, p. 99.) Yet, in big cities like Tokyo, more than 40% of children who need daycare are turned down by daycare centers because of the shortage of space. Ibid, Table 41–1, p. 99.

62. Nadia Youseff, "Education and Female Modernization in the Muslim World," *Journal of International Affairs* 30, no. 2 (1976/77):191–209; Katheleen Merrium, "Women's Education and Professions in Egypt," *Comparative Education Review* (1979):256–270; Afafeleis, et al., "Women, Modernization, and Education in Kuwait," *Comparative Education Review* 23 (1979):115–124.

3 SOUTH KOREA

Oksoon Kim

Despite the different meanings the term *development* carries,[1] in a newly industrialized society like South Korea national development is often treated as synonymous with economic development. Developing nations tend to put economic development plans at the top of their priorities. They assume that social and political *development* will follow as their economies develop. In this chapter, development refers primarily to economic growth. Proponents of the human capital theory argue that educational expansion is necessary for economic growth.[2] However, studies of the impact of education on development typically fail to differentiate females from males,[3] when in fact the effect is different for females. This chapter aims to investigate the extent to which female labor contributed to economic growth during the 25 years from 1960 to 1985 in the context of parallel rapid expansion of educational opportunities in Korea.

At the end of World War II, after Korea's liberation from the Japanese, more than half the children of elementary school age were able to attend school.[4] After the Korean War and subsequent economic reconstruction, elementary school enrollments increased slightly, but educational opportunities remained very limited until 1960.

Beginning in 1962 the first in a series of economic development plans was staged; this series of plans continued until after 1985, by which time Korea had achieved the status of a newly developed nation. The 25 years between 1960 and 1985 were the crucial years in the achievement of the so-called economic miracle. These two-and-a-half decades are the most significant time within which to investigate the effects of educational expansion on economic development and vice versa.

This study is based on three assumptions: that educational expansion in South Korea provided more educational opportunities for males than females; that female labor contributed to economic growth in Korea in characteristically different ways than did male labor; and that educational expansion did not lead to improvement in the economic circumstances of the female population during the years of rapid economic development.

EDUCATIONAL EXPANSION

From 1960 to 1985 there was massive educational expansion in South Korea. After 1960 the number of educational institutions, enrollment, and personnel employed steadily increased. By 1985 the number of secondary schools was 71 times greater than in 1960 and the postsecondary student population had increased eightfold (Table 3.1). When the low annual growth rate of population, at 2.64% from 1954 to 1961 and 2.11% from 1962 to 1975, was taken into account, these school figures indicated a great increase in the quantity of education provided in Korea.

Table 3.1 Number of Schools and Students in South Korea, 1961 and 1985

Level	Schools		Students	
	1961	1985	1961	1985
Elementary	5,317	130,750	4,089,152	4,856,752
Middle	1,122	64,057	655,123	2,782,173
High	621	60,408	323,594	2,152,802
University	85	234	125,797	931,884
Total	6,524	255,499	5,193,666	10,723,611

Source: Ministry of Education, *Statistical Yearbook of Education*, 1962 and 1986.

The overall age-specific enrollment rates between 1966 and 1980 also increased (Table 3.2). This increase was due mainly to the educational innovation introduced by the Korean government in the late 1960s which abolished the Secondary School Entrance Examination on the assumption that

Table 3.2 Enrollment Rates, 1966–1980 (in %)

	1966	1970	1975	1980
Elementary	96.8	100.7	107.8	102.9
Middle	42.1	51.2	72.0	95.1
High	26.8	28.1	41.0	63.5
University	—	8.8	9.5	16.0

Source: KEDI, *Educational Indicators in Korea*, 1991.

without this exam a larger number of students would receive education. Also, the student quota for each school was increased.

However, the continuous expansion of the education system at all levels was a result of private demand, rather than planned investment in education by government. According to the UNESCO Statistical Yearbook for 1974, the share of educational expenditure to GNP in Korea was lower than that for most developed countries. In 1973 it was 4.2% for Korea, which was lower than that of Canada (8.5%), the United States (6.7%), or Japan (4.3%).[5] Furthermore, according to Yungbong Kim, government investment in education has been decreasing in relative terms since 1969. He stated that the share of educational expenditures to GNP paid by government was only 3.3% in 1971 and 2.4% in 1975.[6] Ministry of Education statistics supported Kim's claims. As revealed in Table 3.3, the share of educational costs incurred by students increased substantially from 72% to 75% between 1967 and 1975.

Table 3.3 Educational Expenditures by Source of Finance and Level of School, 1967 and 1975 (in %)

Source	Year 1967	1975
Government	27.6	25.4
Students	72.4	74.6
Total	100.0	100.0

Source: Ministry of Education, *Statistical Year Book of Education, 1968* and *1976*.

In addition to this, Table 3.4 shows that about three-quarters of all government expenditure on education was allocated to elementary schools. Government investment in secondary and postsecondary education was neg-

Table 3.4 Percentage of Expenses for Compulsory Education (Elementary Schools) to Educational Budget

Year	Percentage
1960	80.9
1965	72.6
1970	76.6
1975	67.3
1980	62.2

Source: Ministry of Education, *Statistical Yearbook of Education, 1990*.

ligible in terms of providing the educated and skilled work force necessary for economic and technological development.

Taken as a whole, these statistics indicate that government investment in education during these years was minimal. In fact, during the crucial years of development, the expansion of education was financed predominantly by private interests and parents.

Popular Demand and Educational Opportunities

These private initiatives, which were instrumental in the expansion of the education system, only reinforced inequality in terms of the educational opportunities available to males and females. In Korean society parents have consistently made strong demands that readily available educational opportunities be open to their children. This is because, apart from the high value that was traditionally placed on learning, education has become the main channel for upward social mobility in modern Korean society.[7]

However, this strong popular demand for educational opportunities varies depending on the sex of children. A study by the Ministry of Economic Planning showed that while 56.3% of Korean parents were eager for their sons to have a higher education, only 33% wanted to send their daughters to university.[8] There were also group differences insofar as the educational demands of Korean parents were concerned. While highly educated parents made strong educational demands, parents with less education had weaker educational ambitions for their children.[9] These group differences in demands can be assumed to result from the different income levels between different social classes. Because highly educated parents had greater resources than those with less education, they could afford to make the most of educational opportunities for their children.

Table 3.5 Women as a Percentage of Total Enrollment by Level of Education, 1960–1980 (in %)

Level	Year				
	1960	1965	1970	1975	1980
Elementary	45.0	47.6	47.9	48.4	48.5
Middle	24.4	35.6	38.1	42.2	48.0
High	25.5	33.4	37.1	38.2	42.7
University	17.4	24.5	22.7	26.5	25.1

Source: *Statistical Yearbook of Education, 1961, 1971, 1976,* and *1981.*

These variations of socioeconomic status and gender in educational demands revealed an unequal distribution of educational opportunities. Although the overall percentage of female students has increased, the differences in the percentage of females to males have widened the higher the level of education, as shown in Table 3.5. Therefore, government innovations aimed toward expanded educational opportunities have affected fewer females than males.[10]

Besides gender differences in the distribution of educational opportunities, there was an unequal distribution between the sexes in disciplines at the college level. The majority of female students were concentrated in the liberal arts. While 27.7% of female students at college majored in education, 31.5% of male students majored in engineering. Table 3.6 shows the top five major fields that were studied by students at the college level in 1983. This uneven distribution of academic disciplines between male and female students at the college level can be attributed to the secondary school curriculum, which discriminated against female students. Whereas home economics was compulsory for female students, industry and technology were studied by male students in the secondary schools.

Table 3.6 Distribution of College Students in Academic Disciplines by Gender, 1983

	Female		Male
1.	Education (27.7%)	1.	Engineering (31.5%)
2.	Literature (19.7%)	2.	Social Science (27.6%)
3.	Science (15.1%)	3.	Literature (9.3%)
4.	Art (12.3%)	4.	Education (7.2%)
5.	Science of Art (5.1%)	5.	Agriculture (6.5%)

Source: Ministry of Education, *Statistical Yearbook of Education, 1983*.

The initiatives taken by the Korean government to expand educational opportunities, private-sector funding, and gender bias in the family and the education system all worked against equal opportunity between the sexes and prevented females from acquiring the skills, level of education, and specialization open to their male counterparts.

Economic Growth in Korea

South Korea's remarkable success in economic development started in the early 1960s with a sustained high growth rate. While real GNP per capita had grown only 1% in the year prior to 1962, it increased rapidly thereafter so that real GNP growth from 1962 to 1972 was 9.1% a year.[11]

The rapid growth of the Korean economy over the two decades 1962–1982 was largely the result of the adoption of an export-oriented industrialization strategy that had been implemented in the early sixties.[12] Merchandise exports amounted to only 55 million US dollars in 1962 but increased to $1,624 million by 1972, followed by an average annual growth rate of about 40% until 1982.[13] Table 3.7 shows that in the early 1960s primary

Table 3.7 Growth of Exports in Korea between 1962 and 1982 (in millions of U.S. dollars)

	Year		
Indicator	1962	1972	1982
Gross National Product	3,711	9,060	19,076
Primary Industry	1,711	2,645	3,661
(Share of GNP, %)	(45.3)	(29.2)	(19.2)
Manufacturing	343	1 892	6 524
(Share of GNP, %)	(9.1)	(20.9)	(34.2)
Social Overhead and Service	1 723	4 523	8 892
(Share of GNP, %)	(45.6)	(49.9)	(46.6)

Source: Bank of Korea, *Economic Statistic Yearbook*, 1973 and 1983.

(or agricultural) products rather than secondary (or manufacturing) products made up the bulk of Korean exports. This had changed by the early 1980s. The share of manufacturing in the GNP had more than tripled from 9.1% in 1962 to 34% in 1982.

Among the merchandise exports, manufactured goods such as clothing, electrical machinery, textile yarns and fabrics, footwear, rubber tires, tubes, and plywood together constituted only 27% of the nation's exports in 1962; and yet by 1982 they comprised 94% of the total (Table 3.8). Thus there is no doubt that the rapid expansion of exports contributed to the acceleration of GNP growth and the growth of the overall economy.

Therefore, in order to establish the extent to which education contributed to economic growth, it is essential to analyze the labor force in the manufacturing sectors in terms of its productivity and the educational background of its employees.

Employees in Manufacturing Sectors

Accompanying the promotion of manufacturing exports there was a noticeable expansion of employment in the manufacturing sectors, where the number of jobs rose from 610,000 in 1963 to 2.7 million in 1976. Over the same time period the employment share of the *primary* sector fell from 63.1% to 44.6%, and the employment share of the *secondary* sector rose from 8.7% to 21.8%.[14] The growth of employment in the manufacturing sector brought

Table 3.8 Economic Growth of Korea between 1962 and 1982 (in millions of U.S. dollars)

	Year		
	1962	1972	1982
Gross National Product	3,711	9,060	19,076
Commodity Exports	68	1,998	26,880
Commodity Imports	519	3,102	29,829
Share of Manufactured Exports in Total (%)	27.0%	87.7%	93.7%
Ratio of Commodity Exports to GNP (%)	2.0%	16.4%	31.8%

Source: Bank of Korea, *Economic Statistic Yearbook, 1973* and *1983*.

about an increase in the number of female workers. Statistics show that from 1962 to 1980 the number of female workers in the secondary sectors increased sixfold, and the percentage of female workers increased from 7.0% in 1963 to 22.3% in 1980 (Table 3.9).

The female workers in the secondary sector were almost totally employed in manufacturing. As is shown in Table 3.10, the proportion of the female labor force in manufacturing was over 80% in 1970 and this figure remained constant until the early 1980s.

Within the range of manufacturing, female labor was mainly centered in the textile and wearing apparel industries. The concentration of female workers in these areas led to them being called "female manufacturing industries."[15] The main reason for the concentration of female labor in these areas was low employment costs. Employers preferred to employ female workers, not because they were more skilled than male workers but because they could be paid much less. Table 3.11 shows the large wage differentiation between male and female workers in 1979. In fact, regardless of sectors, females were paid about half of what males received. And since manufacturing paid less than the other sectors, with the exception of construction, it can be assumed that the employment costs of female workers in manufacturing sectors were among the lowest of all industries.

Urbanization partly explains the concentration of low-paid female workers in these industries. There has been a continuous drift of population from the rural areas to the cities as a result of government-sponsored economic development plans. As a result, a large pool of newly urbanized

Table 3.9 Composition of Female Workers by Industrial Sector (in thousands and percentage)

Year	Industrial Sector			
	Primary	Secondary	Tertiary	Total
1963	1,837	186	651	2,674
	(68.7)	(7.0)	(24.3)	(100)
1976	2,388	1,031	1,401	4,820
	(49.5)	(21.4)	(29.1)	(100)
1980	2,034	1,166	2,022	5,222
	(39.0)	(22.3)	(38.7)	(100)

Source: Economic Planning Board, *Annual Report on the Economically Active Population Survey, 1981.*

women sought a relatively small number of positions open to females.[16] Because for them it was simply a matter of having a job, they continued to work for low wages in the manufacturing industries. Moreover, this situation perfectly matched the labor-intensive and export-oriented strategy implemented by the Korean government. All of these factors contributed to the employment of female workers as cheap labor in the manufacturing industries.

Employers could accumulate more capital by employing women at lower rates than men in this sector. And, as has been pointed out time and again, Korea's economic growth was heavily reliant on low-paid employees working in the manufacturing sectors.[17] Because the manufacturing sector has occupied such an important place in Korea's economic growth, low-paid female employees have contributed significantly to the accumulation of capital necessary for sustained economic growth.

EDUCATIONAL EXPANSION AND ECONOMIC GROWTH

Human capital theorists argue that educational expansion is a social investment that will bring national economic growth, since the main contribution of education to economic growth is to increase the level of cognitive skills possessed by the work force and consequently to improve their labor productivity.[18]

Table 3.10 Composition of Female Labor Force by Industry (in %)

Industry	1970	1974	1978	1982
Agriculture and Fisheries	0.3	0.6	0.4	0.1
Mining	0.6	0.4	0.3	0.3
Manufacturing	81.4	84.6	80.1	74.0
Electricity, Gas, and Water	0.3	0.1	0.2	0.2
Construction	1.4	0.6	1.7	1.5
Wholesale and Retail Trade and Restaurant and Hotel	3.2	2.3	6.6	7.9
Transport, Storage, and Communication	5.6	4.5	3.3	5.1
Financing, Insurance, Real Estate, and Business Service	3.8	3.7	3.7	4.7
Community, Social, and Personal Service	3.4	3.2	3.7	6.2
Total	100.0	100.0	100.0	100.0

Source: *Yearbook of Labour Statistics*, 1975 and 1983.

Attempts have been made in several studies to examine the relationship between the average educational level and labor productivity in South Korea.[19] For example, in his study concerning male labor productivity based on educational levels, Yeon concluded that education was the foundation for rapid economic growth in Korea. However, there has been no clear evidence that the same relationship between labor productivity and educational improvement existed in the female labor force. So while it can be argued that improved educational standards in the male population helped the economic growth of the nation, it would be problematic to conclude that this was the case in the female population.

Modeled after E. F. Denison's measurement of sources of economic growth, Yungbonk Kim studied the contribution of education to economic growth in Korea. He argued that increase in the educational attainment of the work force had enhanced the quality of labor, and in turn economic growth. However, he estimated that such a contribution of education was less significant than had commonly been thought.[20] During the period between 1960 and 1974, GNP grew by 9.17% per annum, whereas fixed capital formation, the number of persons employed, and the quality of labor caused by educational attainment increased by 7.19%, 3.55%, and 1.29% respectively. Kim concluded that the economic growth in this period of time was attributable to social and political stability, administrative efficiency, and entrepreneurship rather than to any improvement in labor productivity caused by educational expansion.

Table 3.11 Wage Differences Index between Male and Female Korean Workers in 1979

Sector	Sex	
	Male	Female
Manufacturing	100.0	45.5
Electricity, Gas, and Water	178.1	46.0
Financing, Insurance, and Real Estate	177.0	49.5
Construction	172.1	40.8

Source: *Survey Report on Circulation and Conditions of Labour Force, 1980.*

Table 3.12 shows that the educational level of female employees was possibly higher than was needed in manufacturing industries where the majority worked. Of female employees in the textile industries, 46.2% had graduated from middle school, and of those in electrical machinery industries, 70.3% had completed high school. But the kind of work that females were required to perform in these industries was only semi-skilled and non-skilled work.[21] Even with a moderately good educational background, females were able to earn only a very low wage. As was seen in Table 3.11, within the manufacturing sectors females earned only 45.5% of the wages earned by their male counterparts.

It becomes obvious, then, that the human capital theory does not apply to the female working population in the manufacturing sectors in Korea. If the human capital theory were applicable, then the educational background of female workers should have contributed to their earning capacity. But this has not been the case. Women continued to work under poor conditions for low wages, regardless of their educational background.

As has been previously stated, human capital theorists strongly believe that the productive capacity of labor can be improved through education. If the productive capacity of labor is interpreted largely as a "produced means" of production, the human capital theorists' assumption has been that human capital is the outcome of investments in which education forms a major part. But Table 3.12 argues that for female workers the outcome of educational investment has not been important in the labor market and that only women's cheap labor has been significant. Thus it cannot be claimed that educational expansion contributed to national economic growth through the improvement of both male and female productivity in the same way.

Table 3.12 Distribution of Female Labor Force in Manufacturing Industries by Educational Level (in %)

Industry	Elementary	Middle	High	University
Textiles	50.9	46.2	2.9	0.0
Electrical Machinery	3.3	26.2	70.3	0.1
Rubber Products	56.7	35.7	7.6	0.0
Food	61.6	30.1	8.2	0.1
Beverage	55.1	39.7	5.3	0.0
Printing, Publishing	80.0	6.7	13.0	0.0
Leather and Fur	47.4	46.8	5.7	0.2
Metal Products	30.6	32.4	36.9	0.0
Transport Equipment	68.5	26.4	5.2	0.0

Source: Association of Korean Labor Unions, 1978

On the basis of the statistics that have been used here, it is concluded that the relationship between the educational improvement of the female labor force and labor productivity is different from that of male workers. Male workers had been given more educational opportunities in secondary and higher education, skilled jobs with more pay, and consequently, more opportunities for advancement in the workplace as the economy prospered.

CONCLUSION

There was massive educational expansion during the key years of economic growth from 1960 to 1985. At no time during this period, when the Korean economy was rapidly modernized, did the government allocate sufficient expenditure to provide more educational opportunities at secondary and college levels. And as females came after males in a family in terms of opportunities available, fewer females could acquire the same level or type of education available to males. This was regardless of the parents' socio-economic status.

Since the Korean government's development strategy was primarily labor-intensive and export-oriented, women became the essential productive labor force for economic growth because of low employment costs. When the labor-intensive industries started to grow rapidly with the beginning of industrialization in the 1960s, the female population became significant contributors to economic growth because of their intensive labor. It is therefore possible to conclude that without the low-paid female workers, there would not have been such rapid economic growth. Korean women's contribution to economic development has been indeed greater than men's when it is considered in the context of educational background and payment for work done.

NOTES

1. For the political aspect, see, e.g., C. H. Dodd, *Political Development* (New York: Macmillan, 1972); S. P. Huntington and J. M. Nelson, *No Easy Choice: Political Participation in Developing Countries* (Cambridge, MA: Harvard University Press, 1976); Collin Leys, ed., *Politics and Change in Developing Countries* (Cambridge, MA: Cambridge University Press, 1969). For the economic aspect, see Everett E. Hagen, *The Economics of Development* (Homewood, IL: Richard D. Irwin, 1975). For the social aspect, see Irma Adelman and C. T. Morris, *Economic Growth and Social Equity in Developing Countries* (Stanford, CA: Stanford University Press, 1977); Hollis B. Chenery, editor, *Redistribution with Growth* (London: Oxford University Press, 1974).

2. See, e.g., Theodore W. Schultz, "Investment in Human Capital," *American Economic Review* 51, no. 1(March 1961):1–17; Gary S. Becker, *Human Capital* (New York: National Bureau of Economic Research, 1964).

3. See, e.g., Edward F. Denison, *Measuring the Contribution of Education to Economic Growth* (Paris: OECD, 1964); T. W. Schultz, *Education and Economic Growth* (Chicago: University of Chicago Press, 1961).

4. Horace G. Underwood, "Report of Education in South Korea," Records of the U.S Department of War, June 1947.

5. UNESCO, *Statistical Yearbook 1974* (Paris: UNESCO, 1974).

6. This was estimated on the basis of a survey conducted by the Manpower Development Research Institute in 1970. See Y. Kim, "Education and Economic Growth," in: Chongkee Park, ed., *Human Resources and Social Development in Korea* (Seoul: Korea Development Institute, 1980).

7. Chayoon Kim, *Study of Social Stratification in Korean Society* (Seoul: Moonjo, 1966); B. G. Moon, *Study of Occupational and Social Movement through the Educational Achievement* (Seoul: Seoul National University Press, 1984); Heeseup Lim, *Social Equality and Progress* (Seoul: Jungeumsa, 1983).

8. Data from the Report of Economic Planning (Seoul: Korean Government Printing Office, 1980).

9. Oksoon Kim, *The Role of Family Background on Educational and Occu-*

pational Attainment of Korean Adults (Ph.D. dissertation, University of Southern California, Los Angeles, 1988).

10. Korean Women's Development Institute, *Women Report* (Seoul: 1985).

11. During the two decades between 1962 and 1982, GNP in Korea grew at an average annual rate of 8.4%, which is higher than the average growth rate of 3.6% for the preceding period from 1954 to 1962. See Bank of Korea, *National Income in Korea* (Seoul: Bank of Korea, 1982).

12. See, e.g., J. E. Goldthorpe, *The Sociology of The Third World: Disparity and Development* (London: Cambridge University Press, 1984); Kwangsuk Kim, *Outward-Looking Industrialisation Strategy: The Case of Korea* (Seoul: Korea Development Institute, 1975).

13. Kwangsuk Kim and Joonkyung Park, *Source of Economic Growth in Korea: 1963–1982* (Seoul: Korea Development Institute, 1985).

14. Economic Planning Board, *Annual Report on the Economically Active Population Survey* (Seoul: Economic Planning Board, 1980).

15. See, e.g., Uhn Cho, "Industrialisation and Female Labor Absorption in Korea," *Women's Studies Forum* (Seoul: 1985).

16. Cho Hyoung, "Labour Force Participation of Women in Korea," in: Seiwha Chung, ed., *Challenges for Women: Women's Studies in Korea* (Seoul: Ewha Woman's University Press, 1986).

17. See, e.g., Kwangsuk Kim, *Sources of Economic Growth in Korea: 1966–1982* (Seoul: Korea Development Institute, 1985); Yoonhwan Kim, *Procedure of Korean Economic Growth* (Seoul: Dolbegae, 1981).

18. Neil J. Smelser, "Toward a Thoery of Modernization," in: Eva and Amitai Etzioni, *Social Change*, (New York: Basic Books, 1964); W. W. Rostow, *The Stages of Economic Growth* (Cambridge, MA: Cambridge University Press, 1960).

19. See, e.g., Hacheong Yeon, *Productivity, Labor Quality Indexes, and Labor Structure in Industry: 1962–76* (Seoul: Korea Development Institute, 1980); and Kwangsuk Kim and Joonkyoun Park, *Estimated Sources of Growth* (Seoul: Korea Development Institute, 1985).

20. Yungbong Kim, "Education and Economic Growth," in: Chongkee Park, ed., *Human Resources and Social Development in Korea* (Seoul: Korea Development Institute, 1980).

21. Hyoung Cho, "Labor Force Participation of Women in Korea," in: Seiwha Chung, ed:, *Challenges for Women*.

4 TAIWAN, REPUBLIC OF CHINA
Hsiao-chin Hsieh

During the past four decades Taiwan has undergone industrialization and urbanization processes characterized by remarkable economic growth and educational expansion. Not until recent years did the vast literature on Taiwan's "miracle" begin to deal with the gender aspect of these phenomena. Even less of this literature on Taiwan's economic development has touched on women's experiences and lives in relation to education and economic development.

Have the dynamics between education and economic development differed for men and women in Taiwan? What has been women's role in the process of Taiwan's development? And, have educational and economic growth bettered women's lives and raised their social status? This chapter addresses women's experiences in the context of Taiwan's development since the postwar era.

Following a brief review of Taiwan's history and its development in the past four decades, I shall describe and attempt to account for the characteristics of educational expansion in terms of gender and the relationship between women's educational attainment and their labor market participation. I argue that, with or without high levels of education, women have actively participated in Taiwan's economic development but not necessarily to their own benefit. In the second half of the chapter I shall examine women's roles and experiences during Taiwan's development process and the ways in which education and development have affected their lives.

A Brief Review of History and Social Change in Taiwan

Taiwan, an island off the southeastern coast of the Chinese mainland, has a complicated history of colonization. Before the European imperialists (Portuguese, Dutch, and Spaniards) discovered its agricultural and trade potentials in the seventeenth century, Taiwan had long been a Chinese settlement.

In the 1640s the Dutch ousted their European competitors and occupied Taiwan for 20 years until they were expelled by Cheng Ch'eng-kung, a Chinese loyalist. In the following two centuries under the rule of the Ch'ing Dynasty, increasing numbers of mainland Fukienese migrated across the strait to Taiwan, whose population reached 2.5 million by 1887.[1]

In 1895 Taiwan was ceded to Japan following China's defeat in the Sino-Japanese War. Fifty years later, as a result of Japan's loss in World War II, Taiwan once again fell under the jurisdiction of the Republic of China, which had replaced Imperial China in 1911. Before long, from 1945 to 1949, the Chinese civil war broke out. The Kuo-min-tang (KMT), then the ruling party of the Republic of China, was driven out of mainland China to Taiwan by the Communist Party and has maintained its rule over the island since 1949.

The people of Taiwan today come from a number of ethnic groups. Approximately 1.5% of the population is composed of aborigines who live primarily on reservations on the east coast of Taiwan. The rest of the population belongs to the Han majority and 85% percent are "Taiwanese," descendants of immigrants from coastal provinces of southeast China over the last three centuries. They Taiwanese comprise two ethnic groups of different cultural heritages and languages: the Fukienese (68%) and the Hakka (17%). The remaining 13.5% are "mainlanders," that is, the post-1949 migrants and their descendants. As inter-ethnic marriage is common, the boundaries between ethnic groups have blurred over time.

The population of Taiwan has exceeded 20 million as of the end of July, 1989. The island has a density of 2,300 persons per square kilometer of cultivated land—the highest in the world—and a sex ratio of 107.1 males to 100 females. The birth rate in the postwar period, which reached 46.6 per thousand in 1952, fell to 17 per thousand in 1990. This trend is expected to continue. The population growth rate, which dropped from 3.3% in 1952 to 1.2% in 1990, is predicted to reach zero in the year 2030. Because of improvements in public health, medical facilities, and standard of living, life expectancy rose from 62.6 years in 1961 to 71.3 years in 1990 for men and from 67.0 to 76.8 years for women in the same period.[2]

Over the last 30 years the economy of Taiwan has been transformed from predominantly agricultural to industrial. From 1952 to 1990 the proportion of the population employed in agriculture has decreased from 56% to 13%, while that in industry grew from 17% to 41% and that in service increased from 27% to 46%. The per capita gross national product soared from US$196 in 1952 to US$7,950 in 1990. Industrialization has been accompanied by brisk urbanization. It is estimated that the correlation between growth of the urban population and the ratio of nonagricultural employment in Taiwan is as high as 0.79.[3]

The socioeconomic changes have taken place under the strong leadership of the authoritarian KMT government as part of its ongoing nation-building program. Expansion of schooling has also been part of the program, serving the goals of political socialization and providing a supply of qualified workers to the labor market.

Gendered Educational Expansion in Taiwan

Education enjoys a high value in Chinese culture. Not only is being educated prestigious in itself, it is also a major means for upward social mobility. However, until this century education was a privilege available only to men.

Educational Expansion Before 1950

Education in Taiwan before the Japanese occupation (1895–1945) was similar to that in mainland China. Public education was not provided, but passing the imperial civil examination was the ultimate goal for the educated. In a migrant society such as that of Taiwan, women enjoyed a relatively higher degree of autonomy in comparison with their mainland counterparts, but education remained unavailable to them.

The Japanese colonial government established the first modern school system on Taiwan in 1922 and used it to politicize Taiwanese youngsters into loyal citizens. The implementation of compulsory elementary education in 1943 universalized basic education to school-aged children. At the secondary level, there were four-year and three-year grammar schools for boys and girls, respectively, as well as three-year and five-year vocational schools for Taiwanese and Japanese, respectively. In higher education only limited agricultural, business, and medical colleges were available to Taiwanese.

Discrimination against Taiwanese children in the colonial school system was apparent. They were segregated from their Japanese counterparts, and provided with an education of a lower quality and with fewer opportunities for advanced learning. In 1943, the elementary school attendance rates were 100% for Japanese school-age children yet only 70% for Taiwanese. Among the few Taiwanese children who went beyond basic education, most were channeled to vocational schools while the majority of Japanese children went on to grammar schools.

Among the Taiwanese girls and boys were entitled to equal access to elementary schools. Nevertheless, in 1943 the girls' enrollment rate was only 60% while that of boys was 80%. Girls' opportunities for secondary education decreased sharply. There were only two normal schools and one three-year grammar school, which could absorb less than 10% of female elementary graduates. Higher education was virtually not available to girls.[4]

Educational Expansion, 1950–1990

Having recovered Taiwan from Japan in 1945, the Kuo-min-tang government remodeled the education system and instilled its own political ideology into the practice and content of education. In addition to using it as a means of political control,[5] the government also viewed educational expansion as an investment in human capital and schooling as training of workers needed for economic development.[6]

The education structure now starts with a universal nine-year compulsory education (six-year elementary and three-year junior high schools). Upper secondary schools are highly stratified, and students are required to pass an entrance examination for admission to them. There are extremely selective three-year grammar schools that prepare students for higher education, as well as three-year vocational high schools and five-year colleges, both of which are vocationally oriented and provide very limited chances for continuing schooling. Higher education is offered by junior colleges, independent colleges, universities, and graduate schools. The most prestigious of them are four-year universities, some of which offer master's and doctoral programs. Independent colleges offer degree programs, whereas two-year colleges are designed for vocational high school graduates only.

The first wave of educational expansion in postwar Taiwan took place in 1968, when compulsory education was extended from six to nine years. It was followed in the 1970s by a rapid increase of vocational high schools and five-year colleges. Finally, expansion of higher education began in the mid-1980s and still continues. By 1990 the number of schools was nearly six times that in 1950, the number of teachers septupled, and that of students quintupled. There were 139.6 students per thousand people in 1950, and by 1990 there were 260.4 students per thousand people (Tables 4.1 and 4.2).

Two characteristics have been identified in Taiwan's educational expansion since the 1950s. First, despite the high growth rates of schooling, governmental investment in education remained relatively low.[7] Educational expenditure was 8.6% of the total government budget in 1950 and doubled to 17% in 1990, a growth rate far lower than the growth in number of places in school. This inexpensive growth in education was made possible by the swift expansion of private schools at postcompulsory levels. In 1950, 99% of Taiwan's schools were public, but in 1990 the percentage was only 66%. The proportion of students enrolled in postcompulsory public schools

Table 4.1 Numbers of Schools and Teachers by Level of Education, Selected Academic Years

	1950–51 Schools/Teachers		1970–71 Schools/Teachers		1989–90 Schools/Teachers	
Total	1,054	29,020	4,036	119,095	6,698	199,806
Kindergarten	28	144	570	2,293	2,548	13,446
Elementary	1,231	20,878	2,319	59,489	2,478	77,892
Junior High	128	3,777	553	27,282	683	48,195
Senior High	128	3,777	185	9,495	168	14,206
Vocational High	77	2,430	146	7,500	212	17,661
Junior College	3	95	70	4,720	70	10,524
University & Independent Colleges (4-year)	4	869	22	5,675	49	13,267

Source: *Educational Statistics of the Republic of China 1989*. Taipei: Ministry of Education.

Table 4.2 Numbers of Students by Level of Education, Selected Academic Years

	1950–51 Student	St/1,000*	1970–71 Student	St/1,000*	1989–90 Student	St/1,000*
Total	1,054,927	139.6	3,809,930	270.5	5,197,002	260.4
Kindergarten	17,111	2.3	91,984	6.2	248,498	12.5
Elementary	906,950	120.1	2,445,405	165.8	2,407,166	120.6
Junior High	61,082	8.1	799,233	54.2	1,088,890	54.6
Senior High	18,866	2.5	178,537	12.1	208,994	10.5
Vocational High	11,226	1.48	175,650	11.9	444,232	21.7
Junior College	1,286	0.2	108,328	7.3	203,894	13.6
University and Independent Colleges (4-year)	5,374	0.7	92,850	6.3	207,479	10.4
Master's	5	0	2,129	0.1	3,841	0.7
Doctoral	0	0	166	0.0	381	0.2

* Students per 1,000 population.
Source: *Educational Statistics of the Republic of China 1989*. Taipei: Ministry of Education.

dropped from 91% to 43% in the same time period;[8] yet the educational expenditure for public schools in 1991 was 1.8 times that for the private schools.[9]

The extremely uneven distribution of educational resources has resulted in a highly stratified school system. Public schools, relatively small in number but abundant in resources, enjoy higher prestige than their private counterparts. This advantage has attracted top students to public schools and, in turn, further enhanced their superior position. Severe competition for admission to public schools persists despite the increase in overall educational opportunities.[10]

Secondly, educational opportunities have increased unevenly across fields of study.[11] At the upper secondary level, the number of students enrolled in vocational schools increased 40 times between 1950 and 1990, much more than the increase in grammar schools, which was about 11 times. The ratio between students enrolled in grammar schools and in vocationally oriented schools at the senior level was 6:4 in 1950, which narrowed down to 1:1 in 1970, and went on reversely to 3:7 in 1989 (Table 4.2). Such a ratio, as Young correctly pointed out,[12] is a result of the government's forceful planning to accommodate and accelerate economic growth. This is evidenced by the closely coupled patterns of change in the student distribution in fields of vocational education and in the employment structure.[13] Students and their parents, influenced by traditional educational values, favor the grammar schools, which emphasize the liberal arts and prepare students for university. Vocational schools have become a second way out for students who fail the entrance examination to grammar schools.

As for higher education, expansion has taken place primarily in engineering and technology. In the humanities and social sciences, areas deemed to be nonproductive economically, provision for students has changed little.[14] It is not surprising to find that competition for admission has been much more intensive for humanities and social sciences than for engineering and technology. In 1982 the admission rate for natural sciences and technology was 40%, that for agriculture and medicine was 50%, and that for humanities and social sciences was 23%. The admission rates increased by 1989 to 56% and 65% for the first two areas and only 26% for the third area.[15]

The Gender Aspect of Educational Expansion

In the course of expansion women's opportunities for education have increased markedly and the gender gap in education has narrowed.[16] By 1980 the proportion of female students at the compulsory level had already reached 48%. At postcompulsory levels the vocational high schools have had the most rapid growth in female student population, rising from 16% in 1950 to 54% in 1989. Finally, the proportion of female students in college and above has also risen from 11% in 1950 to 44% in 1990.

Significant gender inequalities in educational opportunities nevertheless remain. As shown in Table 4.3, the higher the level of schooling, the lower

Table 4.3 Female Participation Rates by Educational Level Selected Years (in %)

	Public and Private Schools			Public Schools
	1950	1971	1989	1989
Kindergarten	44	45	48	49
Primary	39	48	48	49
Junior High	29	42	49	49
Senior High	27	37	47	46
Vocational High	16	44	54	48
5-year College			44	37
3-year College	11[a]	37[b]	51	36
2-year College			52	36
4-year College and University				
	NA	36	46	42
Master's	NA	NA	25	22
Doctoral	NA	NA	16	15

[a]11 = All colleges and universities
[b]37 = 5-year, 3-year, and 2-year colleges
Source: *Educational Indicators of the Republic of China, 1991*. Taipei: MOE 1991 p. 32; *Educational Statistics of Republic of China, 1991*. Taipei: Ministry of Education, p. 61.

the women's participation rates.

At the graduate level in 1989 women constituted less than a quarter of the student population. In the same year female students were more than 50% of the students enrolled in vocational high schools as well as in two- and three-year colleges. But they were underrepresented in the prestigious schools at the same educational level, that is, in senior-high schools and four-year universities. As recently as 1992 girls were underrepresented in public schools at all postcompulsory levels. In my study on the entrance examination to public senior high schools, I found that, despite increased opportunities to attend, the proportion of female students in grammar school enrollment has remained between 43% and 45% for the past 25 years.[17] Specifically, there have been approximately 10,000 fewer seats nationwide for girls than for boys in the admission capacity of public grammar schools.[18]

Vocational schools and colleges exhibit a clear pattern of gender segregation by field of study. In 1990 the proportions of female vocational high graduates in commerce, nursing, and home economics were 88%, 96%, and 99%, respectively, while the proportion of industry graduates was only 20% (Table 4.4). In colleges and universities, as Table 4.5 shows, women have clustered in humanities and social sciences, but have been underrepresented in science and technology. Since recent expansion in higher education has centered around science and technology, it is men, not women, that benefit more from the increased opportunities. Moreover, since the admission rates in "female-centered" areas are lower than those in "male-centered" areas, women have been confronted by much harsher competition than men.

Table 4.4 Proportion of Vocational High School Female Graduates by Field of Study, 1990 (in %)

Total	Agriculture	Industry	Commerce	Marine	Nursing	Home Eco.
53.7	48.6	20.4	88.2	41.0	96	99

Source: Calculated from *Educational Statistics of Republic of China, 1991*. Taipei: Ministry of Education, p. 91.

Table 4.5 Proportion of College Female Students by Field of Study and Level of Education, 1990 (in %)

	Humanities	Social Sciences	Science and Technology
5-year college	69.00	76.12	30.67
3-year college	54.54	58.57	35.70
2-year college	97.53	85.60	32.48
4-year college and university	66.53	61.09	22.19
Master's	55.60	35.23	14.39
Doctoral	38.39	18.81	11.05

Source: Calculated from *Educational Statistics of Republic of China, 1991*. Taipei: Ministry of Education, p. 61.

Gender Inequalities and Segregation in Education

Gender inequality in educational opportunity and segregation by field of study do not exist in Taiwan by chance. Rather, they are consequences of the interactive forces of strong state control and patriarchal values.

In Taiwan the state oversees not only the supply of public education but also school curricula, content of textbooks, and the subjects to be tested in entrance examinations. The standardized textbooks used in Taiwanese primary and secondary schools constantly present stereotypical gender roles and convey male-centered messages. For instance, in 12 volumes of elementary school social studies textbooks, 98% of the characters presented are males who play a wide variety of roles. The 2% female characters include three fictional figures, one empress portrayed negatively and one historical heroine of China.[19] The history textbooks also show overwhelmingly stronger representation of men than women. In the three-volume Chinese history textbook, except for Li Ch'ing-chao (a poet) and Ch'iu Chin (a revolutionary), women mentioned in the textbooks are all empresses and consorts of imperial rulers and are negatively portrayed. Only three of the 214 pictures in the Chinese history textbooks are of women. Similar phenomena exist in foreign history textbooks. Women are underrepresented, their roles restricted, and their images distorted in social studies and history textbooks because only men's activities in the public sphere and the histories of political rulers count as legitimate knowledge in Taiwanese schools. The very few women who involved themselves in activities in the public sphere in imperial China were either punished or blamed in the "official knowledge" defined in school textbooks. Although there is little evidence on the effects of such gender-biased textbook content, some suspected consequences can be identified: junior high school girls constantly perform significantly less well in history, and often in social studies, than their male counterparts.[20]

Moreover, the schooling process has been less friendly to girls than to boys. A study of teacher-pupil interaction in elementary school classrooms found that boys receive more attention than girls in math and science classes, while girls receive more encouragement in Chinese and social studies; overall, boys interact with teachers significantly more frequently than do girls.[21] Primary school teachers agree that they hold higher expectations for boys than for girls.[22] In junior high schools boys are significantly more likely to be placed in high-ability groups than girls at the same level of their fathers' education, their own IQ scores, and academic performance. The performance of girls is as high as, if not higher than, that of boys during the first year of junior high school. Girls, however, gradually fall behind and score significantly lower than boys by the last semester of junior high school.²³

Gender inequality in schools largely reflects that found in the family. A preference for sons remains strong in the patrilineal society Taiwan. The sayings "married daughter, spilt water" and "raising sons secures old-age lives" sum up the situation. Parents consider a son's education to be a worthwhile family investment, and would use all means to support it. In contrast, a daughter's education may often be viewed as nonproductive consumption or even a waste of family resources. Some researchers suggest that women's education will rise only if the familiy perceives an increased return from their investment in a daughter's education.²⁴

It is, therefore, not surprising to find that, according to the Social Change Survey 1991, more women than men report severe financial constraints as an obstacle in pursuing educational opportunities. The gender differential in perceived financial constraints is particularly salient for respondents born between 1947 and 1961,²⁵ during whose schooling years Taiwan underwent dramatic economic transformation and educational growth. It is only for the female respondents of the youngest cohort that factors such as effort and motivation are perceived as major factors resulting in insufficient educational attainment (Table 4.6). By the same token, only for the youngest cohort does the gender gap in educational attainment become insignificant.²⁶

Finally, traditional patriarchal values still prevail in modern Taiwan and support stereotypical gender roles. Respondents to the *Social Change Survey 1991* considered business, teacher education, and home economics to be the most suitable areas of study for women but considered technology, engineering, medicine, and the sciences as ideal fields for men.²⁷ The extent to which educational expansion helps to liberate modern Taiwanese women from their stereotypical roles thus comes into question. Tsai and Chiu found that even among students of Tai-ta (National Taiwan University), the most prestigious university in Taiwan, the average level of educational aspirations is significantly lower for females than for males.²⁸ While both men and women are likely to aspire to professional jobs, men are more likely to aspire to become employers.

Why do women hold lower levels of aspiration for advanced studies and for employment than their male counterparts? The schooling process in which girls grow up provides only a part of the answer to this question. The actual economic and social conditions that Taiwanese women face in adulthood, which shape girls' perceptions of the uses of education, may offer answers from a different perspective.

Table 4.6 Reasons Given by Male and Female Students for Insufficient Educational Attainment, by Birth Cohort Years (by % of male and female survey populations)

	Birth Cohort Years										Total	
	1927–1946		1947–1955		1956–1961		1962–1970		1977			
No. in Cohort Reason	567		604		419		387					
	M	F	M	F	M	F	M	F	M	F		
Effort	3.9	1.2	20.6	10.4	24.7	15.8	29.3	26.4	17.8	12.7		
Financial constraint	61.2	63.1	52.6	63.1	36.4	50.2	21.6	29.5	46.7	52.9		
Ability	3.9	3.8	5.2	5.0	11.6	7.2	9.0	5.9	6.7	5.4		
Motivation	6.8	5.4	17.3	11.4	18.2	17.6	24.0	25.5	15.3	14.3		
Other	24.1	26.5	4.2	10.1	9.1	9.0	16.2	12.7	13.5	14.7		

Source: Calculated from data in *Social Change Survey* 1991.

Women's Education and Labor Market Participation

As early as 1920, educated women in Taiwan entered the labor market and held salaried jobs. It is estimated that between 1924 and 1936 more than 50% of women with basic education were hired as domestic helpers, farm assistants, shop clerks, factory workers, nurses, and midwives and that 30% of those with a high school education worked as teachers and government employees.[29] The entire population of Taiwan was mobilized for war by the late 1930s. Women gradually took over production responsibilities as more and more men were drafted to, and died in, the battlefields, marking the peak of women's labor force participation in Taiwan. However, women retreated as the war ended in 1945.

During the postwar era, women's labor force participation rates fluctuated over the years but still increased from 42% to 45% between 1951 and 1989 (Table 4.7).[30] In 1989 labor force participation rates were 40%, 51%, and 60% for women holding basic education, high school education, and college education or above respectively.[31] The increased level of educational attainment also contributed to women's competitiveness in the labor market. In 1989, the average monthly earnings of women with a college education (New Taiwanese $21,981) were more than twice that of women with only a primary school education (New Taiwanese $10,650).[32]

Table 4.7 Labor Participation Rates by Sex, Selected Years (in %)

Year	Female	Male
1951	42	90
1956	38	80
1961	36	86
1966	33	81
1971	35	78
1973	42	77
1976	38	77
1981	39	77
1986	46	75
1989	45	75

Source: *Labor Statistics*. Taipei: Executive Yuan, 1990.

Increased levels of educational attainment, however, do not necessarily improve women's employment status in relation to men's. Empirical studies have found that women are required to have higher levels of education than men for entry into the same level of white-collar jobs, a phenomenon particularly conspicuous in clerical work[33] and in the public sector.[34]

The lower economic returns from educational investment for women are also revealed in their wage differences. In 1979 female workers earned an average of New Taiwanese $66 for every New Taiwanese $100 earned by male workers; the proportion even decreased to 65% in 1989.[35] This gender wage gap narrowed somewhat among those with higher levels of education. In 1989 the average wage for females with basic educational attainment was 56% of that of their male counterparts, while the wage ratio was 74% for those with at least a college education.[36]

Horizontal job segregation by gender in Taiwan's labor market is well documented.[37] Although jobs traditionally held by men are increasingly performed by women, statistics show that women workers continue to concentrate in manufacturing, commerce, and service work; these sectors constituted 39%, 23%, and 20%, respectively, of the overall female labor force in 1988 (Table 4.8). Except for manufacturing, none of these sectors is regulated by the Labor Standards Law.[38] Furthermore, the female/male wage ratios actually declined for manufacturing and service sectors during the 1980s, indicating deterioration in employment conditions for women in those sectors (Table 4.9).

Table 4.8 Percentage of All Employed Women in Specific Industries in Selected Years

	1966	1980	1988
Manufacturing	17.5	29.3	39.0
Commerce	13.7	15.0	22.5
Service	—	12.8	19.9

Source: Cheng and Hsiung, "Fu-nu ch'u-kuo tau-hsiang yu kuo-chia: yi tai-wan wei li" (1993):5.

Table 4.9 Average Wage Ratios of Women to Men in Specific Industries in Selected Years

	1973	1981	1989
Manufacturing	.55	.66	.61
Commerce	—	.51	.67
Service	.71	.85	.65

Wage Ratios: Average Monthly Wage of Females/Average Monthly Wage of Males
Source: Cheng and Hsiung, "Fu-nu, ch'u-kou tau-hsiang, yu kuo-chia: yi tai-wan wei li," op. cit., p.5.

Liao and Cheng reported in 1985 that discrepancies in pay between men and women are greater in the private sector than in the public sector.[39] The public sector, nevertheless, absorbed only 9% of the female labor force, though women working in the public sector have a higher average level of education than their male counterparts.

Vertical segregation by gender can also be seen in Taiwan's labor market. As reported in Table 4.10, women employees concentrate in middle (clerical) and lower (production) levels of the occupational hierarchy. Unfortunately, the female/male wage ratios were .62 for clerical and .48 for production work—the lowest in the occupations—although the average educational attainment is higher for women than for men in clerical work. Women holding clerical jobs thus face double discrimination by higher educational requirement for entry and lower wage in the workplace.

Table 4.10 Percentage and Wage Ratios of All Employed Women at Specific Levels of the Occupational Hierarchy, in Selected Years

	1966 Employment	1988 Employment	1988 Wage Ratio
Managerial and Administrative	1.4	0.2	.80
Professional	5.8	7.8	.69
Clerical	6.1	20.3	.62
Sales	12.4	15.1	.69
Service	—	11.8	.72
Production	16.6	34.2	.48
Agriculture	46.6	10.6	.57

Source: Cheng and Hsiung, "Fu-nu, ch'u-kou tau-hsiang, yu kuo-chia: yi tai-wan wei li," op. cit., p.48.

Furthermore, significantly more women than men perceive that there are serious discriminatory practices against women in promotion, salary increases, and in-service training.[40] Having investigated the wage structure for first-job holders, Lin contended that wage differential by gender is a direct consequence of structured unequal pay for equal work in Taiwan's labor market.[41]

With this review of available evidence, we arrive at several conclusions. Women's rising level of education may enhance their aspirations and human capital for paid work. Educational qualifications help women to gain access to certain desirable occupations, but they are far from sufficient in and of themselves for women to secure equal pay and treatment on the job. Moreover, fluctuations in women's labor market participation rates and steady increases in their educational attainment (compare Tables 4.3 and 4.7) suggest that the relationship between the two is by no means a simple, linear one. Let us further examine this issue from the perspective of development studies.

WOMEN'S ROLES IN TAIWAN'S ECONOMIC DEVELOPMENT

Taiwan's development story can be traced back to the time of the Japanese occupation. The colonial government utilized Taiwan as a major supplier of sugar and rice for its home base. To maximize productivity, the Japanese built a modern infrastructure on the island, mobilized its natural resources, and invested in human capital through the provision of basic education and agricultural and trades schools at the secondary level. All these paved the way for Taiwan's postwar industrialization.

After the war, with its austere control and American support, the KMT government first stabilized political order on Taiwan and then enforced land reforms and initiated Four-Year Economic Plans in the 1950s. The strategy of import substitution, adopted for the first stage of development, promoted agricultural production on the one hand, and on the other protected the island's infant industries in textiles, wood, and rubber products with measures such as import restrictions and tariffs.

When the domestic market became saturated, a labor-intensive, export-oriented policy was employed in the 1960s and 1970s. The highlight of the policy was the establishment of Export Processing Zones (EPZ), where foreign and local investment enterprises enjoyed tax incentives and avoided import duties as long as they exported all the goods they processed. Textiles, electronic appliances, and plastic products were the major categories processed in the EPZ, and the United States and Japan were the major trade partners.

These measures soon paid off in that, in spite of the end of U.S. aid in 1965 and the two global oil crises, Taiwan's economy continued to boom and foreign reserves rapidly accumulated. By 1980 Taiwan was the sixteenth largest exporter in the world, but challenges from other East Asian nations began to be strongly felt. Taiwan needed to upgrade its industries in order to stay competitive in the international market. To this end a technology-oriented, capital-intensive strategy was used for Taiwan's development in the 1980s and 1990s.

Numerous studies have attempted to account for the extraordinary economic growth in Taiwan, but women's contribution was not recognized until the mid-1980s. At the first Women's Studies conference ever held in Taiwan,[42] K. T. Li, one of the leading policy makers for Taiwan's economic planning, praised the female labor force for being abundant in supply, cheap in cost, and responsive to the ups and downs of market demands.[43] He accurately summed up women's contribution to Taiwan's labor-intensive development.

The Flexibility of the Women's Labor Force

The first wave of rapid growth in the female labor force during the postwar era took place between 1966 and 1973 at the beginning of Taiwan's most intensive period of industrialization. Large numbers of women were absorbed into factories to fill unskilled or semiskilled jobs that required a minimal level of training.[44] Their diligence, obedience, and willingness to accept low wages not only reduced production costs but also strengthened the competitiveness of Taiwanese products in international markets.[45]

When the oil crisis struck in the mid-1970s, women retreated from the labor market to minimize men's unemployment rates. They later returned as the economy recovered. The fluctuation of women's employment rates therefore corresponds to the vicissitudes of Taiwan's economy as a part of the global economy.

Women's employment status also varies by stages of the family lifecycle. Taiwan's traditional culture designates housekeeping and childrearing as women's primary responsibilities. When there is a conflict between careers and motherhood, women are inclined to give up their career in order to fulfill their maternal role.[46]

Moreover, the labor market has been unfriendly to women. Many women are forced by their employers to resign when they get married or become pregnant.[47] Others choose to return home because their wages are too low to induce them to keep the job.[48] In addition to unequal pay for equal work in the job market, employment discontinuity further hampers women's employment.

One thus observes an M-shape in the female employment pattern, highest in the 20–24 age group and then declining before rising again between the ages of 35 and 44.[49] Statistics compiled in 1990 show that 30% of women left their jobs when they married, and about 80% of them, it was estimated, will never return to job market because of the decidedly limited job opportunities.[50] Better education, however, helps married women to stay on the job. In 1990 the labor force participation rates were 43% for those with junior high education and 71% for those with at least a college education.[51]

Female Marginalization to Informal Employment

As in some developing countries, the female labor force in Taiwan has been marginalized in its industrialization process. In addition to the previously discussed gender segregation in the labor market, women in Taiwan tend to be employed in informal sectors. A significant portion of female laborers included in the statistics were in fact unpaid family-income-generating workers: 65%, 69%, 80%, and 78% for agriculture, manufacturing, commerce, and service sectors, respectively, in 1986.[52] This is because the bulk of Taiwan's industry is comprised of small-scale family enterprises (farm, shop, or factory)[53] that, regardless of women's contribution, are owned and inherited by men. Meanwhile, women whose families run private enterprises tend to be restricted to informal employment in the family business.[54]

Government policies also channel women into informal employment. The "Living Rooms as Factories (K'e-t'ing Chi Kung-ch'ang)" policy championed by the government in the early 1970s is a classic example. This measure was designed to mobilize the potential household laborers, especially women and children, without having to alter the patriarchal household structure. It at the same time made it possible to save employers' investment in facilities and expenses on regular employees. Thousands of housewives have turned into informally employed homeworkers, performing both low-waged (paid by piece) productive and nonwaged reproductive work at home.[55]

A few recent case studies have documented women's experiences in the small-scale family-centered factories. Hsiung noticed that, because of the subordinate position of wives in the family, their labor remained under the control of their husbands for multiple uses. In addition to rearing children, caring for elders, and running everyday errands for both the family and the factory, wives' of factory owners are also assigned the monitoring job in the production line.[56]

Li's study on family-run garment factories reported stories of exploitation of family members in small-scale family enterprises. She found that, within the family, women's status and power in the family decision-making processes have improved with their contribution to the family's economy. Outside the home, however, women are still treated as subordinates to their father, husband, and brother.[57] Both sons and daughters join the household labor force but for quite different purposes. The sons' work is considered as preparation for inheriting the family business. In contrast, daughters' work is considered as paying back the debt they owe parents, and, as Li suggests, marrying out of the family would be the way out of the daughter's obligation.[58]

Young Female Factory Workers and Student-Workers

Daughters from families who do not operate family enterprises tend to work in factories outside the home, more for the benefit of the family than for their personal autonomy. These daughters' choices of occupation and the particular firm to work in are strongly affected by parents' opinions, and their income is largely at the disposal of their parents,[59] often being used to pay school fees for brothers.[60] This, of course, accounts for the smaller financial constraints for men than for women in the schooling process, as was previously discussed. In terms of physical toll, more than ten hours' work on the production line per day easily exhausts these young female factory workers.

To these young women, such occupation is not a channel for upward mobility, nor is it a viable alternative to marriage. For them the most important consequence of making money, several studies have suggested, was the opportunity and ability to continue their education at night schools. A higher level of educational attainment would improve their future options: better jobs, higher income, a better husband, and higher status in his family.[61] In fact, females have been unequivocally the majority of students enrolled in all levels of supplementary education for adults.[62] For instance, in 1982 women constituted 95% and 59% of the students in basic and college-level supplementary education, respectively. Ten years later, the figures were 94%, 69%, and 61% for fundamental and college-level supplementary education and for the open university, respectively.[63]

The Factory-School Cooperative Education, a measure widely practiced since the late 1960s, has provided another attractive option for young women to combine work and study.[64] The program, promoted by the government, claims to offer its students efficient vocational training, but some researchers argue that it is the individual vocational schools and factories that benefit the most from it.[65] For a factory, schools help to attract and then instill a sense of discipline in young workers. For a school, factories help to pay for students' tuition, serving as a stable source of school income.

School and factory together program tight control over young student-workers. Hsia's study on female student-workers in a factory finds that, doubly burdened, the lives of these young women are extremely tedious and stressful.[66] The lack of connection between work in school and in factory gives them little inspiration in everyday life. Tension easily builds up among peers. Conflict between girls and their supervisors often results in high turnover rates. But the only alternative is in shifting from one factory to another, though so doing does nothing to improve the students' condition of being exploited. Again, for these young women, graduation and a high school diploma may be where future hope resides.

It is clear that socioeconomic changes in Taiwan have shaped the perception of people at large on women and education. It is now accepted, as pointed out by Gates,[67] that girls benefit from education and that their virtues will not be harmed by learning, as Chinese used to believe. And a continuously expanding economy in Taiwan has sustained such a faith, especially that of young factory women, in education, without having to change the gender relations in Taiwan. Consequently, given the upgrading of women's education and Taiwan's economy, women continue to serve the adjustment function in the labor market, remaining in inferior and marginal positions in relation to their male counterparts. A question that naturally follows is: How may other aspects of women's lives have changed in the course of Taiwan's development?

WOMEN'S STATUS IN TAIWAN

From a feminist perspective, Chen and Hsiung vigorously contend that Taiwan's economic advancement in a competitive world system has been built upon the exploitation of women as low-waged and unwaged income-generating workers and as unwaged domestic workers.[68] They further argue that such exploitation of women is promoted by the state, the family, and the factory as they are penetrated by the twin ideologies of capitalism and patriarchy. In other words, women have been actively integrated into Taiwan's development, without benefiting from it but rather sacrificing for its sake.

Using data from several women-related survey reports[69] and other materials, a 1992 women's rights report reflects a quite frustrating picture of the situation of women in Taiwan.[70] To delineate some basic facts:

1. Women have been victims of sexual violence. A survey of more than 1,000 high school girls indicates that 1.5% of the respondents had been raped and that 95% had experienced sexual harassment. Another survey reported that 11.5% of married women had been abused by their husbands.
2. Working women are doubly burdened with work and family responsibilities, working an average of more than nine hours per day. Among working women who needed childcare and public nurseries, 62% were denied access.
3. Women are deprived of property rights. A survey indicated that more than 80% of families share properties only with sons. The Family Law revised in 1985 endorses the joint ownership of property for husband and wife; however, only the husband is granted the right to manage and use the union property.

4. Divorced women face the most severe legal and social discrimination. According to the Family Law, in a divorce, the custody of the child goes to the husband unless otherwise agreed upon. No visitation rights are ensured for the mother, nor are there provisions of alimony in a divorce by consent.
5. Women are largely excluded from the society's decision-making primarily because of the above-reported factors, plus discrimination in the schooling system and the labor market. As of 1992 only two women held top-ranking official positions: the head of the Department of Health and that of The Council for Cultural Planning and Development. In the same year, female representatives constituted 14%, 10%, and 10.6% of the representatives in the National Assembly, the Control Yuan,[71] and the Legislature, respectively. It is of little surprise that women's interests have rarely been a concern in the decision-making regarding major public policies that affect them.

Different ethnic affiliation also makes a difference to women's status. Taiwan's development is basically "Han-centric." Over the past 40 years the social position of the aborigines has been further marginalized and their socioeconomic distance from the Han enlarged. Facing double discrimination against their race and gender, aboriginal women fall at the bottom of Taiwan's social strata. When their men are forced to take high-risk and low-pay jobs outside their own communities, married women often have to head their household alone in poverty. Prostitution has become a common practice among young aboriginal women.[72]

Among the Han women, mainlanders on average hold the highest level of education and job prestige. The Hakka are known for being hardworking and placing a high value on education. Using data from Social Change Survey 1991, Chang found that average educational attainment and first job prestige are both higher for Hakka than for Fukien women.[73] Fukien women, nevertheless, have greater power in domestic decision-making than their Hakka counterparts, suggesting the low family status of the latter.

Have women made any gains whatsoever in Taiwan's development? Surely the expanded opportunities for education and white-collar jobs have allowed women a chance for upward mobility and improved the material living conditions. While women from lower classes managed to zigzag their ways upward, their middle-class counterparts were able to unswervingly seize the new openings, attaining at least a college education, and transforming it into the human capital needed for securing desirable positions in the job market.

Compared with women at large in Taiwan, college-educated women tend to marry late, raise fewer children,[74] hold more satisfying jobs, and enjoy a more egalitarian mode of decision-making in domestic affairs.[75] They are the major female beneficiaries of Taiwan's industrialization. Small in number, these female beneficiaries may powerfully turn individual gains into social advancement when their feminist consciousness is raised. Western feminist ideologies have been introduced into Taiwan as part of the struggle for equality in all aspects of social life since the 1970s. The removal of the 40-year Martial Law in 1987 marked a new era for Taiwan's rapid democratization. Several women's organizations have emerged, striving for women's rights from various aspects.

Starting from the 1980s, against strong resistance from the patriarchal establishment, women lawyers and scholars began the reform of public policies that directly affected women's rights in Taiwan. The Eugenic Protection Law, passed in 1984, legalized abortion in Taiwan.[76] The revision of Family Laws has been advocated for the protection of women's rights in the family system. The Act of Gender Equity at Work has been drafted to be reviewed by the Legislature. Women's groups have formed women voters' coalitions to make women's voices heard in the major elections since 1989, and "Ten Major Women's Issues for the Legislature"[77] have been formulated for the betterment and well-being of all women.

WOMEN, EDUCATION, AND DEVELOPMENT IN TAIWAN

Under the forces of the state, the patriarchal family system, and industrialization, we see an intriguing dynamic between development and education with respect to women's experiences in Taiwan. On the one hand, as an integral part of Taiwan's economic growth, the gendered school expansion has made the increased educational opportunities less tangible for girls than for boys. Kept at a disadvantage, women still make good use of education to gain upward mobility and for occupying desirable positions in the labor market. On the other hand, Taiwan's industrialization has absorbed great numbers of women into the job market for waged work. Participation in waged work does not by itself improve women's lives; more often than not it may worsen women's lives, as much evidence has shown. Waged work may make a significant difference for young women when they use the money they earn to continue schooling. And a growing economy in Taiwan has helped maintain the expectation of upward mobility through education. Women in Taiwan thus have vigorously utilized new opportunities and options emerging from the development to enhance their lives.

It remains important to note that Taiwan's state policies of education and development are by no means meant for women's consciousness raising and empowerment. The Taiwan 1991 Social Change Survey shows that more than 90% of the respondents believe educational opportunities for men and women to be fair. Yet significantly more female than male respondents across birth cohorts thought that men should have more education than women. Only women with at least a college education held different attitudes. Why and in what ways a college education may contribute to the rise of women's consciousness will be worth studying in the future. The women's movement—initiated by highly educated women and recently emerged as a by-product of Taiwan's educational, economic, and social development—has produced the first steps toward the equal rights and empowerment of Taiwanese women.

NOTES

1. Ming Shih, *Tai-Wan-Jen Ssu-Pai-Nien Shih* (Four Hundred Years of the History of the Taiwanese People) (San Jose, CA: Paradise Culture Associates, 1980), p. 133.
2. Council for Economic Planning and Development, *An Analysis of the Utilization of Female Labor Force in Taiwan* (Taipei: The Executive Yuan, 1992).
3. Cheng-Hung Liao, "Urbanization in Taiwan." In: H. H. M. Hsiao, et al., ed., *Taiwan: A Newly Industralized State* (Taipei: National Taiwan University, 1989):345–378.
4. Chien-Ming You, *Tai-Wan Jih-Chih-Shih-Tai te Fu-Nu Chiao-Yu* (Taiwanese Women's Education Under the Japanese Reign)(Taipei: Department of History, National Taiwan Normal University, 1988).
5. Wilson, R., *Learning to Be Chinese: The Political Socialization of Children in Taiwan* (Cambridge, MA: The M.I.T. Press, 1970).
6. K. T. Li, *The Evolution of Policy Behind Taiwan's Development Success* (New Haven,CT: Yale University Press, 1988). See also Young, Yi-Rong, "Taiwan," in: Wielemans, W., and P. Chan, eds., *Education and Culture in Industrializing Asia* (Leuven, Belgium: Leuven University Press, 1992):327–378.
7. Hai-Yuan Chiu, "Education and Social Change in Taiwan." In: H. H. M. Hsiao et al., *Taiwan: A Newly Industrialized State*, pp. 187–206.
8. In 1950, 99% of all students were in the public system. Parallel figures were 92%, 71%, and 100% for vocational high schools, junior colleges, and four-year colleges and universities respectively. The proportion dropped to 78%, 40%, 16%, and 42% respectively in the same order in 1990. (Calculated from pp. 4–7 and 18–21, Ministry of Education: *Educational Statistics of the Republic of China, 1992*, Taipei.)
9. Ibid., p. 50.
10. Hsiao-Chin Hsieh, "Ability Stratification in Urban Taiwanese Secondary Schools," *Chung Yang Yen Chiu Yuan Min Tzu Hsueh Yen Chiu So Chi Kan* (Bulletin of the Institute of Ethnology, Academia Sinica) 64 (1987):205–252.
11. Hsiao-Chin Hsieh, "Chiao-yu chung te hsing-pie-yi-shih (Gender Ideology in School System)," *Jen-Pen Chiao-Yu Cha-Chi* (Humanistic Education) 7 (1989):30–35.
12. Yi-Rong Young, "Taiwan," in: Wielemans and Chan, *Education and Culture in Industrializing Asia*, op. cit.
13. Within the vocational sector, 37%, 22%, and 32% of the students enrolled in agriculture, industry, and commerce respectively in 1951. Four decades later, the proportion changed to 4%, 45%, and 36% in the same order. See Council for Economic Planning and Development, *Taiwan Statistical Data Book, 1992* (Taipei:

The Executive Yuan, 1992).

14. The number of students enrolled in humanities in 1990 was 1.3 times that in 1976, the ratio for social sciences was 1.7, and that for science and technology was as high as 2.3. See Ministry of Education, *Educational Statistics of the Republic of China,* 1991 (Taipei: Ministry of Education, 1991):44.

15. Ministry of Education, *Educational Indicators of the Republic of China 1992* (Taipei: Ministry of Education, 1991):35–6.

16. Hsiao-chin Hsieh, "Hsing-pie yu chiao-yu chi-hui: yi pei-shih liang-sso kuo-chung wei li" (Gender Differences in Educational Opportunities in Taiwan: Two Taipei Junior High Schools), *Kuo-chia K'e-Hsueh Wei-Yuan-Hui Hui-K'an: Jen-Wen Yu She-Hui K'e-Hsueh* (Proceedings of the National Science Council, Part C: Humanities and Social Sciences), Vol. 2 (1992): 179–201.

17. Ibid.

18. In the joint entrance examination to public grammar school, boys and girls do not compete with each other but only among themselves. The differential admission capacity by sex thus indicates as unequal supply of public grammar education for boys and girls.

19. Awakening, *Liang-Hsing P'ing-Teng Chiao-Yu Shou-Tse* (A Handbook for Equal Education for the Sexes) (Taipei: The Awakening Foundation, 1989). See also Yung-Sheng Ou, "Kuo-min hsueh-hsiao chiao-ke-shu chung te hsing-pie yi-shi hsing-tai (Gender Ideology in Elementary School Textbooks)," *Hsin-Chu Shih-Yuan Hsueh-Pao* (Bulletin of Hsin-Chu Normal College) 12 (1985).

20. Hsieh, 1992.

21. A Lo, and V. Shieh, "A Study from an educational perspective to investigate sex equity in the classroom between teacher and student at elementary school level in Kaohsiung" (Department of Psychology, Kaohsiung Medical College, 1992).

22. C. H. Chang and L. C. Chen, "Kuo-hsiao hseuh-sheng hsueh-yeh ch'eng-chi yu chiao-shih hsing-pieh kuang-hsi chih yen-chiu (The relation between academic performance of elementary school students and the sex of teachers)," *Chiao-Yu Hsin-Li Hsueh K'an* (Journal of Educational Psychology) 8 (1977):21–34.

23. Hsieh, "Chiao-yu chung ti hsing-pie-yi-shih," op. cit.

24. S. Greenhalgh, "Is inequality demographically induced? The family cycle and the distribution of income in Taiwan," *American Anthropologist* 87, no. 3 (1985):571–94; H. Gates, *Chinese Working-Class Lives: Getting By in Taiwan* (Ithaca, NY: Cornell University Press, 1987); and L. Cheng, and P. C. Hsiung, "Fu-nu, ch'u-kou tau-hsiang, yu kuo-chia: yi tai-wan wei li (Women, export-oriented growth and the state: The case of Taiwan)," *Tai-wan She-Hui Yen-Chiu Chi-K'an,* vol.14 (Taiwan: A Radical Quarterly in Social Sciences, 1993):39–76.

25. The *Social Change Survey 1991* is based upon a representative sample of the Taiwan civilian adult population. For the purpose of our analysis, the data are divided into four birth cohorts. Those who were born between 1927 and 1946 (N=711) mostly received their primary education under the Japanese regime; those born between 1947 and 1955 (N=722) received six-year compulsory education under the KMT regime. Those who were born after 1956 received nine-year compulsory education. Since this group is relatively large in number, I further divide it into two birth cohorts: 1956–1961 (N=539) and 1962–1970 (N=516). The former was born during the takeoff period of Taiwan's economy, and the latter after the economy had become fairly thriving.

26. Gender inequality respondents of the youngest cohort have decreased only in terms of levels of educational attainment, not in terms of the types of schools women and men attended at each level. Also, quite a few of the young respondents were still students at the time the survey was conducted. In other words, the levels of educational attainment reported by the youngest cohort in the survey may be lower than the levels of education they may attain eventually.

27. Institute of Ethnology, *1991 Tai-wan Ti-Ch'u She-Hui Pien-Ch'ien Chi-*

Pen Tiao-Ch'a Pao-Kao (Report on Social Change Survey 1991) (Taipei: Insitute of Ethnology, Academia Sinica, 1992).

28. S. L. Tsai, and H. Y. Chiu, "Hsing-pie yu cheng-chiu pao-fu:yi tai-ta hsueh-sheng wei li (Gender and achievement aspiration: The case of Tai-ta students)," *Chung-Kuo She-Hui Hsueh-Kan* (Chinese Journal of Sociology) (1988):125–168.

29. You, *Tai-Wan Jih-Chu-Shih-Tai te Fu-Nu Chiao-Yu,* op. cit., p.215.

30. I shall discuss this phenomenon in greater detail later. The high percentage in the early 1950s may be a legacy of the war. Men's participation rates, in contrast, declines steadily from 90% to 75% for the same period of time, largely because of postponed entry into the job market as a result of the lengthening of schooling years.

31. Labor Committee, *Liang-Hsing Lao-Tung Ch'ing-Shih T'ung-Chi* (Male and Female Labor Statistics, Taiwan Area, ROC) (Taipei: Labor Committee, 1990):6–7.

32. Ibid., pp. 22–23.

33. For example, in 1986 the mean number of years of schooling for female and male laborers in the clerical sector was 12.5 and 12, respectively; the difference is statistically significant.

34. Shu-Ling Tsai, "Occupational segregation and differential educational achievement: A Comparison between men and women," *Chung-Kuo She-Hui Hsueh-K'an* (Chinese Journal of Sociology) 11 (1987):61–91.

35. Labor Committee, 1990:39.

36. Ibid., pp. 24–25.

37. Tsai, 1987. See also Bih-eEr Chou, "Industralization and change in women's status: A reevaluation of some data from Taiwan," in: H. H. M. Hsiao, et al., *Taiwan: A Newly Industralized State,* op. cit., pp. 423–761.

38. Labor Committee, 1990:4.

39. Long-Li Liao, and Wei-yuan Cheng, "The contribution of female labor force to economic growth in Tiawan." Keynote speech delivered at the Conference on the Roles of Women in the National Development Process in Taiwan, March 14–16, 1985. Taipei: National Taiwan University, Population Studies Center, March 14–16, 1985.

40. H. Y. Yu, "Tai-wan ti-ch'u lao-tung shih-ch'ang te hsing-pie ch'i-shi (Sex discrimination in labor market in Taiwan)." Paper presented at the Conference on Sex Equality in the Workplace, Center for Population Studies and Women's Research Center (Taipei: National Taiwan University, 1991).

41. Chung-cheng Lin, "Sex differences in wage among first-job holders," *Economic Essays* 16 No.3 (1988) (The Graduate Institute of Economics, National Taiwan University):305–322.

42. Entitled "The role of women in the national development process in Taiwan," the conference was organized by the Population Studies Center at National Taiwan University in June 1985. A major accomplishment after the conference was the establishment of the first women's studies program in the country—Women's Research Program, Population Studies Center, National Taiwan University.

43. K. T. Li, "Fu-nu tzai tai-wan ching-chi fa-chan kuo-ch'eng chung te kung-hsien (The contribution of female labor force in Taiwan's economic development process)," in: N. Chiang, ed., *Kuo-Chia Fa-Chan Kuo-Ch'eng Chung te Nu-Hsing Chiao-Sse* (The Role of Women in the National Development Process in Taiwan) (Taipei: Population Studies Center, National Taiwan University, 1985):1–7.

44. As of 1989, more than 80% of the labor force in the Export Processing Zones was made up of women younger than 20 years old. Wages in the export industries were usually lower than those targeted at domestic markets primarily because of the nature of mass production practiced in the EPZs. Chi-Min Ho, "Chia-Kung Ch'u-K'ou Ch'u (The export process zone)," in: Kao Hsi-chun and Cheng Li, eds., *Tai-wan Ching-yen Ssu-shih Nien* (The Taiwan Experience 1949–89) (Taipei: Tien-hsia, 1991):380–409.

45. Y. Y. Bian, "Nu-hsing lao-kung tuei ching-chi fa-chan te kung-hsien: Taiwan te shih-cheng yen-chiu (The contribution of female workers to economic development: An empirical anaylsis of the case of Taiwan)," in: N. Chiang, ed., *Kuo-Chia Fa-Chan Kuo-Ch'eng Chung te Nu-Hsing Chiao-Se*, pp. 259–276.

46. Yu-Hsia Lu, "Women's informal employment in Taiwan." Paper presented at the conference on Gender and Society, National Tsing-Hua University, June 25–26, 1991.

47. A survey found that 7.6% of employers interviewed reported forced resignation of women upon marriage or childbirth in their firms, despite maternity protection regulated in the Labor Standard Law. See Yu, "Tai-wan ti-ch'u lao-tung shih-ch'ang to hsing-pie ch'i-shi," op. cit.

48. It was recently estimated that it was not worthwhile for a middle-class married woman to work outside unless she made at least New Taiwanese (NT) $18,620 to NT$36,620 per month. The average monthly earnings for a college-educated woman amounted only to NT$17,146 when the estimation was made. See Cheng and Hsiung, "Fu-nu, ch'u-kuo tau-hsiang, yu kuo-chia: yi tai-wan wei li," op. cit.

49. Ching-Hsi Chang, "A review of female labor force participation," *Economic Essays*, Vol. 8 (1978) (The Graduate Institute of Economics, National Taiwan University, 1978):275–284.

50. Executive Yuan, *Report on fertility and employment of married women, Taiwan Area, Republic of China*. (Taipei, Directorate-General of Budget, Accounting and Statistics, 1991).

51. Labor Committee, *Liang-Hsing Lao-Tung Ch'ing-Shih T'ung-Chi*, op.cit.

52. Chou, "Industrialization and change in women's status: A reevaluation of some data from Taiwan," op. cit.

53. For example, the 1990 Labor Statistics show that 53% of the labor force worked in enterprises with fewer than ten employees and 66% in those with fewer than 30 employees.

54. Yu-Hsia Lu, "Urban-rural economic development and employment of married women: An exploration of the theory of female marginalization," *Population Studies* (1992).

55. Cheng and Hsiung, "Fu-nu, ch'u-kuo tau-hsiang, yu kuo-chia: yi tai-wan wei li," op. cit., p. 36.

56. P. C. Hsiung, "The Social Construction of Paternalism: A Case Study of Taiwan's Satellite System." Occasional paper no. 6, Women's Research program, National Taiwan University, Population Studies Center, 1991.

57. Y. T. Li, *Chia-Hu Lao-Tung, Chia-T'ing yu Hsiao-Ch'i-Yeh: Yi Chia Tai-Pei Ch'eng-Yi-Ch'ang te Ke-An Yen-Chiu* (Household Labor, Family, and Small-Scale Entreprise: A Case Study of a Taipei Garment Manufactory Community). M. A. Thesis, Graduate Institute of Sociology and Anthropology, National Tsing-hua University, 1993.

58. Ibid. p. 51.

59. Based on her field study on industrialization of a Taiwanese village, Tai-Li Hu reported, in her novel *Daughter-in-Law Marries In* (Taipei: China Times, 1982), that many factories even pay the wage earned by these young women workers directly to their parents.

60. L. Kung, *Factory Women in Taiwan* (Ann Arbor, MI: UMI Research Press, 1978). See also N. Diamond, "Women and Industry in Taiwan," *Modern China 5*, no. 3 (1979):317–40.

61. Kung, *Factory Women in Taiwan*, op. cit., and Diamond, "Women and Industry in Taiwan", op. cit. See also Tai-Li Hu, "The influence of industrialization of Taiwan rural areas on the status of women," in: N. Chiang, ed., *Kou-Chia Fa-Chan Kuo-Ch'eng Chung te Nu-Hsing Chiao-Sse*, pp. 337–356.

62. Supplementary education is intended for people who have been denied regular school education. If passing the qualification examination conducted by the

government after a required period of education is passed, a supplementary school graduate is conferred with the diploma qualifying him/her as a graduate from the regular school at the appropriate level. With the diploma, he or she may pursue advanced regular education or seek employment. The National Open University was established in 1986. Students have to go through a screening process to be admitted. Whether or not graduates of the Open University deserve a bachelor's degree had been subject to hot debate and was finally agreed to as of the summer of 1992 (Ministry of Education, 1992:XXXIII-XXIV) [sic].

63. Ministry of Education, *Educational Statistics of the Republic of China, 1992* op. cit., pp. 120–123.

64. The program operates in various ways. The most popular form is called the rotation system. Students in the program usually rotate every three months between school for general education and factory for specific vocational training, or study and work in day-night shifts.

65. Lin-Ching Hsia, "Ts'ung hsueh-hsiao tao kung-ch'ang: kuo-chung pi-yeh nu-sheng kung-ch'ang sheng-huo chin-ju li-ch'eng chih miao-shu yu fen-hsi (From school to work: A description and analysis of the process of women junior high school graduates entering factory life)," *Chung-Hua Hsin-Li Wei-Sheng Hsueh K'an* (Chinese Mental Health) 5, no. 2 (1992):135–153.

66. Ibid.

67. Gates, *Chinese Working-Class Lives: Getting By in Taiwan*, op. cit.

68. Chen and Hsiung, "Fu-nu, ch'u-kuo tau-hsiang, yu kuo-chia: yi tai-wan wei li," op. cit.

69. These are: (1)*Report on The Minor Prostitute Survey, 1991* by the Li-Hsin Foundation; (2) *Report on The Sexual Harassment Survey, 1990,* by the Modern Women Foundation; (3)*Reports on The Life Situations of Women, 1989, 1990, 1991,* by the Taiwan Provincial Government; (4)*Report on Manpower Utilization Survey in Taiwan Area, 1991,* The Executive Yuan; (5)*Report on the Time Utilization Survey in Taiwan Area, 1990,* The Executive Yuan.

70. Yu-Hsiu Huang, "1992 Taiwan fu nu jen chuan pao kao (Women's rights report, Taiwan, 1992)," *Fu-Nu Hsin-Chih* (Awakening) 129 (1992):20–23.

71. The Control Yuan serves as a check and balance faculty in Taiwan's government system, exercising the power of impeachment, censure, and audit over the administrative sector.

72. According to one source, there are 210,000 women prostitutes in Taiwan, constituting 2.1% of the overall female population. Half of the female prostitutes are made up of aboriginal women, and many of them are adolescents (Ho, Chung-wen, 1988). In recent years the problem of minor prostitutes has become widely recognized in Taiwan. The Rainbow Coalition was formed to stop the spread of the problem, but only limited improvement has been achieved.

73. Wei-An Chang, *Ke-chia fu-nu ti-wei: yi min-nan tzu-chun wei tuei-chao te fen-hsi* (Status of Hakka women: An analysis using Fukien women as the reference group). Paper presented at the Conference on Hakka Culture, Council on Cultural Planning and Development (Miaoli, Taiwan, March 12–13, 1994).

74. In 1991 the average marriage age of female university graduates was 26 and the average number of children was 1.7. The figures for all Taiwan women were 1.9 and 3.2, respectively. See Executive Yuan, *Report on Fertility and Employment of Married Women, Taiwan Area, Republic of China,* op. cit.

75. Lu, "Women's Informal Employment in Taiwan," op. cit.

76. Ku argued that feminist groups, in order for the Eugenic Protection Law to pass, took a strategically compromising stand and did not appeal to women's "choice" or "right to body," but rather to the need and development of the society. Therefore, the law was passed without liberating women from the state's control over their bodies. For instance, the law mandates that a woman needs the husband's consent to carrying out an abortion; abortion is not covered by health insurance; and only

a limited number of doctors are allowed by the Health Bureau to perform legal abortion. See Yne-Ling Ku, "Fu-nu yun-tung yu kung-kung cheng-tse te hu-tung kuan-hsi: tuo-tai he-fa-hua yu p'ing-teng kung-tzuo-chuan te tse-lueh fen-hsi (The Dynamic between Women's Movement and Public Policy: An Analysis of Strategies for the Legalization of Abortion and Equal Right for Work." Paper presented at the Conference on State and Society in Taiwan's Democratization, March 7 and 8, 1992. Taipei: Chinese Society of Sociology, 1992.

77. The issues include: (1)the legislation of the Act of Gender Equity at Work; (2) the setting up of a Bureau For Women Laborers for their protection; (3) the wide provision of childcare to all those who are in need; (4) the employment of appropriate measures to protect women's safety and to free them from sexual harassment and violence; (5) the establishment of women's shelters in every county; (6) the institutionalization of a social security system to ensure the well-being of elderly women; (7) the revision of conjugal property laws to protect the rights of housewives; (8) the revision of divorce laws to protect women's rights over child custody, visiting, and property; (9) the promotion of gender-fair education; (10) the establishment of women's centers for provision of continuing education and systematic social support systems to women.

Part II
Southeast Asia

5 INDONESIA

Mayling Oey-Gardiner and Riga-Adiwoso Suprapto

INTRODUCTION

Even though the majority of Indonesians adhere to the Islamic faith, culturally Indonesia shares greater similarities with its neighbors than with other Islamic societies. Islam came to Indonesia with trade in the thirteenth century and became absorbed into already existing religions and cultures, which share at least one similar trait with East and Southeast Asian societies then in that women are active in the market. Throughout the archipelago, which is inhabited by some 300 different ethnic groups, Indonesian women are generally active members of the society and fairly visible in public life. As such, they are generally also financially independent. However, the ability to earn their own incomes does not automatically guarantee that women are treated the same way as men. Differences between men and women in rights and responsibilities as well as in activities are found in various domains. Women do not have the same access as men to education, jobs, and status positions in society.

This chapter presents a gender-based analysis of the educational conditions in Indonesia. The first part provides a description of education in Indonesia. The second part explores gender differences in employment resulting from rising education. The chapter concludes with an assessment of rising educational attainments of women and their position in the labor market.

THE EDUCATION SITUATION IN INDONESIA

The Education System

The basic structure of the current Indonesian education system has its origins in a system laid down by the former Dutch colonial government, which followed the structure prevailing in Holland. After independence, and as time went by, the demand for education expanded, and Indonesians were exposed to other systems as well. Continuous adaptations have been introduced, especially at higher levels, to become the current structure.

The formal education system in Indonesia consists of several levels: six grades of primary, three grades of lower secondary,[1] and three grades of upper secondary school. Some variations can be found at the tertiary level. Non-degree programs vary in length between one to three years. Undergraduate programs run for at least four years. Graduate programs comprise master's and doctoral levels.

The Ministry of Education and Culture defines the substance of the school system, in particular for primary and secondary schools. Religious schools, the majority of which are Islamic schools,[2] follow the secular curriculum, but a substantial proportion of their curriculum is religious instruction.[3] Regardless of the type of primary and secondary schools they are enrolled in, students are subjected to national examinations at the end of each level. These examinations, set yearly by the Department of Education and Culture, are held on the same dates throughout the nation.

Primary education is mostly provided for by public schools, but the higher the level the greater participation there is from the private sector. This is true of fully secular as well as religious schools. An array of vocational schools, initiated by various government and private agencies can also be found at the secondary level.

Prior to Indonesia's independence in 1945, only a thin upper segment of society attended school. Most of the students were trained to fill colonial civil service positions allocated to local people. Illiteracy among the general population was extremely high; even in 1961 illiteracy was still 47% among the population aged 10 years and over.

After independence, however, and in accordance with article 31(1) of the Indonesian Constitution, which states that "every citizen has the right to be educated," efforts to provide mass formal education for everyone were initiated across the archipelago.[4] This was facilitated by the favorable economic situation in Indonesia in the 1970s. Supported financially by oil revenues during the oil boom period between the years 1973 and 1982, the Indonesian government was able to invest large amounts of funds to improve and develop its infrastructure, including education. Although the largest expansions were made in education and health,[5] the percentage of the government's budget spent on education remained relatively small. Only 2.3% of its gross national product in 1986 was set aside for education, compared to 5.0% by Singapore, 7.9% by Malaysia, and 3.2% by Thailand.[6]

In 1974 the government launched a policy referred to as SD Inpres, a primary school special program, to make education compulsory for children aged 7 to 12. This was set as a target to be achieved during the Fourth

Five-Year Development Plan of 1984/85–1988/89. Since most of the population live in rural areas, the program design was village based, whereby each village is to have at least one public primary school.

It has been suggested that development programs, particularly the expansion of social infrastructure, have led to changes in the social fabric of Indonesia's society.[7] In particular, expansion of educational facilities in the 1970s has changed social values toward education. While in the past benefits from education were regarded as strictly for the elite to gain access to civil service positions, with the expansion of civil service jobs they were no longer open only to the elite and urbanites. Due to its extensive development activities, the government apparatus expanded rapidly, thereby resulting in high demands for civil servants. Between 1974 and 1984 the civil service expanded from 1.7 million to 2.8 million persons, showing an increase of 66% during the decade.[8] However, since formal education is the main route to positions in the civil service and the private sector, parents tend to be motivated to make sacrifices for their children to go to school. They regard education as a means to improve the children's economic and social well-being.

At the same time Indonesia was facing rapid increases in the working age population. However, the formal sector has only limited capacity to absorb large and rapidly growing numbers of graduates from the education system. This disparity between supply and demand has led the government and the private sector to conduct tighter and more competitive selection procedures for recruitment. Hence increases in the number of primary school graduates with limited access to employment along with rising expectations have created increasing demand for more education. It is understandable that in the Fifth Five-Year Development Plan of 1989/90–1994/95 the government extended compulsory education through lower secondary school, making schooling compulsory through ninth year.

Most of the schools in Indonesia are coeducational even though there is no law against sex segregation. Only a few schools, mainly religiously affiliated, remain segregated. This does not mean an absence of discriminatory practices against girls entering formal education, although a rapidly declining pattern of discrimination can be observed. The most probable explanation is that although legally there is no restriction for girls to gain formal education, when resources are limited parents tend to give preference for sons to attend school. On the other hand, the increase in female school attendance (Table 5.1) is an indication that as more education becomes accessible, in terms of proximity and cost, daughters are as, if not more, likely than sons to attend formal education. There is no cultural barrier as such against girls attending school, although an economic one does exist.

Table 5.1 Size of School Attending Population by Residence, Age, and Gender, 1971–1990 (in millions)

Residence and age	Females			Males			Total		
	1971	1980	1990	1971	1980	1990	1971	1980	1990
Urban									
7–12	1.2	2.2	3.6	1.2	2.3	3.8	2.4	4.5	7.5
13–15	.4	.8	1.5	.5	1.0	1.6	.9	1.8	3.0
16–18	.3	.6	1.2	.4	.8	1.3	.6	1.4	2.4
Rural									
7–12	4.6	7.6	8.6	5.2	8.1	9.1	9.7	15.8	17.7
13–15	1.0	1.7	2.3	1.5	2.3	2.7	2.5	4.0	5.0
16–18	.3	.6	1.0	.6	1.0	1.3	.9	1.6	2.2
Total									
7–12	5.7	9.8	12.3	6.4	10.5	13.0	12.1	20.3	25.3
13–15	1.4	2.6	2.6	2.0	3.3	4.2	3.4	5.8	8.0
16–18	.6	1.2	2.1	.9	1.8	2.5	1.5	3.0	4.7

Note: The numbers may not add up exactly as a result of rounding.
Sources: Biro Pusat Statistik, *Population Census of Indonesia, 1971 (Series D), 1980 and 1990 (Series S2)*

School Enrollment Patterns

In the last two decades increases in the numbers of children attending primary school have been substantial. The number of children between 7 and 12 years of age attending school increased from 12.1 million in 1971 to 20.3 million in 1980 and to 25.2 million in 1990 (Table 5.1). Between 1971 and 1990 the total number of children attending lower secondary level schools increased by 2.4 times. Higher increases occurred among the upper secondary school age (16–18 years), from 1.5 million in 1971 to 3.0 million in 1980 and to 4.7 million in 1990. Hence the number in this group more than tripled between 1971 and 1990.

Declining gender disparity in the school-attending population can be seen in the rising gender ratios, that is, the number of females for every 100 males (Table 5.2). Between 1971 and 1990 the gender ratios rose from 90 to 95 for those in the 7–12 age bracket, from 72 to 89 among those aged 13–15, from 59 to 84 for those between 16–18, from 41 to 69 for those in the 19–24 age bracket, and from 29 to 48 for those aged 25 years and over. The gender bias has basically disappeared among primary-school-aged children.

However, the gender bias does intensify with age or education level. Over

Table 5.2 Gender Ratios (F/100M) of the School Attending Population by Age and Residence, 1971–1990 (in %)

Age	Urban			Rural			Total		
	1971	1980	1990	1971	1980	1990	1971	1980	1990
7–12	94	95	95	88	94	95	90	94	95
13–15	83	86	93	68	76	86	72	79	89
16–18	70	77	91	51	58	77	59	66	84
19–24	49	54	74	32	45	59	41	50	69
25+	26	34	37	36	65	66	29	47	48

Sources: Biro Pusat Statistik, *Population Census of Indonesia, 1971 (Series D), 1980 and 1990 (Series S2).*

time female access to higher levels of education has increased, an indication that conditions for girls to attend school have become more favorable. Given that the government has already decided to make basic education compulsory, we can expect to see closer gender ratios among the 13–15 age bracket.

In comparing urban and rural areas, the rise in gender ratios is greater in rural than in urban areas; both areas reached 95% levels in 1990 for primary-school-aged children. In quantitative terms this is an indication of the positive impact of government policy for compulsory primary education on females in rural areas. Of interest is the similarity in gender ratios for primary, lower and upper secondary school-aged children between urban areas in 1980 and rural areas in 1990. Nonetheless, access to higher education for females in rural areas is still limited compared with that for males, and gender differences may continue for some time at the higher level. Rather striking are the substantially higher and rising gender ratios among the rural population aged 25 years and over. It is suggested that this phenomenon is a result of differential access to primary schooling. Of those at this age who attend school, many rural females tend to be in secondary schools, which, even though mostly located in urban centers, are still accessible to some rural residents. The males in this group, on the other hand, are more likely to be enrolled in postsecondary institutions, which tend to be concentrated in larger towns to which those men have moved.

School-enrollment ratios confirm the above observations (Table 5.3). There is no gender difference in enrollment ratios at the primary level. There has been a rapid rise in enrollment ratios during the last two decades among primary-school-aged children. From a situation in which six out of ten children were enrolled at the primary level, Indonesia in the 1990s has reached a level where nine out of ten children are attending primary school. When schooling is available and attainable in terms of proximity, parents are willing to send their children to school regardless of their gender. At the secondary level, substantial rises in enrollment ratios occurred among females, particularly in rural areas between 1971 and 1980. Enrollment of males aged 13–15 years remained practically constant between 1980 and 1990. This may well reflect a leveling-off. Since lower secondary schooling is planned to be made compulsory, the pattern probably will follow that of the primary school level. In rural areas enrollment ratios continue to rise both for males and females. This phenomenon has reflected a rising expectation that formal education will provide opportunities for better jobs, particularly in urban areas. It is not surprising to observe the rising migration of young, rural, educated youth to urban areas.

Table 5.3 School Enrollment Ratios by Residence, Age, and Gender, 1971–1990 (in % of total population)

Residence and age	Females			Males		
	1971	1980	1990	1971	1980	1990
Urban						
7–12	72	91	95	74	92	95
13–15	57	73	76	69	84	83
16–18	34	45	55	49	62	64
19–24	12	13	18	26	25	26
25+	1	1	1	3	2	2
Rural						
7–12	55	81	90	59	82	90
13–15	34	50	56	45	59	60
16–18	10	16	27	22	30	33
19–24	2	3	4	7	7	8
25+	*	*	*	*	*	*
Total						
7–12	58	83	92	62	84	91
13–15	39	56	62	49	65	67
16–18	15	24	37	28	38	44
19–24	4	5	9	12	12	15
25+	*	*	*	1	1	1

Note: * = less than 1%
Sources: Biro Pusat Statistik, *Population Census of Indonesia, 1971 (Series D), 1980 and 1990 (Series S2).*

The gender gap in enrollment ratios at the upper secondary level has been closing faster than at the lower secondary level. Even though the ratios are still low, gender differences continue to decline and may well disappear in the decade to come. The same patterns are also observable for enrollment ratios at tertiary level but with the expectation that gender differences may continue longer than the lower levels.

Of interest are the gender ratios of the population aged 10 and over by educational attainment (Table 5.4). Ratios of those with no schooling rose from 197 females in 1980 to 210 females in 1990 for every 100 males. In other words, the population that has never attended school is becoming increasingly more female over time. Feminization of this category of the population reflects past gender biases in access to any formal education. Lower ratios at the primary level and above are found in rural than in urban areas, indicating greater gender bias in rural areas. While the gender bias continues to decline, it is still prominent at higher education levels and more so in the rural areas. This means that preference continues to be given to male members of the family in completing their education.

Table 5.4 Gender Ratios (F/100 M) of the Population Aged 10+ by Educational Attainment and Residence, 1980 and 1990

Educational	Urban		Rural		Total	
	1980	1990	1980	1990	1980	1990
No school	276	283	189	199	197	210
Some Primary	106	113	87	97	90	100
Primary	92	106	75	88	79	93
Gen Lower Sec.	80	91	55	71	68	81
Voc Lower Sec.	61	70	50	63	55	66
Gen Upper Sec.	55	69	40	55	50	65
Voc Upper Sec.	65	78	47	62	56	71
Academy	39	69	28	48	36	63
University	31	45	26	37	24	43

Note: Academies are postsecondary schools offering diploma programs comparable to currently popular polytechnics.
Sources: Biro Pusat Statistik, Population Census of Indonesia, 1971 (Series D), 1980 and 1990 (Series S2).

In summary, during the last two decades rapid growth occurred at the primary and secondary levels. In absolute terms, the primary- and secondary-school-attending populations doubled, and in the upper secondary level the numbers even tripled. In other words, the higher the education level the faster the rate of growth. Second, growth appears to favor females. This was both a function of a lower starting base among females as well as a consequence of rising continuation rates from primary to lower secondary school. Education is increasingly valued as a means for economic improvement, resulting in higher aspirations and demands from females. Third, the higher the educational level the greater is the gender bias. This does not mean, however, that gender differences shall continue to persist at all levels. If the trend continues the absence of gender bias presently found at the primary level can soon be expected to appear at the lower secondary level, due to expansion of the education system. Fourth, educational attainment patterns of the population aged 10 and over differ from patterns in school attendance. In 1990 about 21 females for every ten males had never attended school; this resulted from the fact that more older females had never attended school. Since hardly any gender bias remains at the primary level, the same pattern of near-equality will soon be achieved among lower secondary graduates, provided that socioeconomic conditions continue to be conducive for females to attend school.

The patterns presented above are in quantitative terms. Questions are, however, being raised regarding the quality of the education and the returns from education.

Quality of Education

In spite of the quantitative progress made during the last two decades, Indonesia still faces problems of quality. Primary schools in rural areas often lack the necessary teaching equipment and materials as well as qualified teachers, and education there does not go beyond the very basic skills for literacy. Most of the government's routine budget is allocated for salaries and the development budget for new school buildings and equipment. Little is left for educational materials or maintenance. Even though children attending public primary school are exempted from tuition fees, parents have to bear the costs for uniforms, school materials, transportation, contributions and/ or supplements to teachers' salaries, and other incidentals. Most rural teachers live on rather low government salaries, making it necessary for them to seek second jobs, often at a cost to their quality of teaching. While urban conditions are relatively better, there remains great variation in the quality of education offered by schools throughout the archipelago. Both public and private schools suffer from quality diversity because not only private but also public schools are dependent on parents' contributions.

At the lower secondary level, many vocational and technical schools have been closed[9]—more than 800 vocational schools since 1976—and others were to follow.[10] Most of these schools have been converted into regular general schools. Many vocational schools are of poor quality, often teaching more theory than application, and their equipment is often outdated. Often qualified teachers are not available. Many vocational training institutions are gender-biased. Those related to technical know-how are attended more by male students, while those related to commerce (i.e., book-keeping) and home economics are almost exclusively female. The two latter types of vocational institution are basically adaptations of earlier finishing schools for girls, which were established in the early 1900s by Kartini, who aspired to provide education for girls at that time.[11]

It is often pointed out that education in Indonesia lacks the necessary subject streaming.[12] The main objective of primary schools is to prepare students for lower secondary education without any streaming. In turn, general lower secondary education prepares students to enter upper secondary schools, and the teaching at the upper secondary level is directed toward university education. Streaming occurs only in the second year of upper secondary school, when students are separated into four streams: mathematics, science, social science, and languages. While the rationale for streaming is to respond to variation in aptitude and interest, in practice it selects according to academic performance. Gender biases are observable in the streaming results. There are fewer female students in the mathematics and science streams than in the social sciences and languages.[13] Such a gender bias is often found in other countries and societies as well. At present it is still being debated in Indonesia whether such streaming is necessary at this level. Hakim argued that streaming should be directed toward differentiating those with an aptitude for academic study from those more inclined toward vocational training.[14] Under the current system, many upper secondary graduates aspire to continue to tertiary levels.

At the tertiary level, at least one public university is found in each of the 27 provinces in Indonesia. Although the government subsidizes these institutions heavily, only a few, and mostly the older ones, are of reasonable quality. These are the University of Indonesia in Jakarta, the Bogor Institute of Agriculture, the Bandung Institute of Technology, and Gadjah Mada University in Yogyakarta. All are located on the island of Java. Entrance into these universities is very competitive. National entrance examinations to public universities are held annually. Those who fail can retake the examination the following year, and in the meantime they can attend private institutions.

Private institutions outnumber public ones at this level. Many are of questionable quality, although some are quite reputable. The main problem faced by private institutions is the lack of permanent qualified staff, in contrast to public institutions. The Department of Education and Culture issues accreditation to private institutions, comparing them to public institutions in their respective provinces. They are ranked either as equal in status, acknowledged, registered, or licensed to operate. Only those with equal status may conduct their own examinations. Others have to submit to government examinations at various intervals. This is often seen as a constraint, as administration and examiners' fees have become a burden.

Although there is no policy of gender segregation at the tertiary level, due to high costs and distance from these institutions fewer females attend universities. In addition, females tend to have a lower academic performance rate than their male counterparts, and hence many attend vocational schools. Poor performance by females is a result of less time allocated to school work, since the traditional pattern still persists in which females are held responsible for household chores. In the socialization process girls often help their mothers take care of the household as well as their siblings. Hence, girls' studying is accomplished after or while such tasks are being done, while boys tend to be brought up free of such burdens and are being pressured to excel at school.

As a consequence of poor academic performance, many female students are barred from entering prestigious tertiary institutions and thus attend lesser ones or vocational schools which, in theory, should prepare them to enter the labor market. However, as indicated earlier, vocational institutions for females are often directed toward skills associated with femininity, such as sewing, hairdressing, handicrafts, and clerical work, which in turn leave many females with no option but to accept jobs that are traditionally considered feminine and often pay less. Female graduates from universities often face greater difficulties than men in obtaining jobs.[15] In education, and later in the labor market, gender discrimination continues.

The situation may be even worse in the future since it is projected that Indonesia will continue to have to wrestle with the problem of open as well as disguised unemployment caused by what Pangestu and Oey-Gardiner refer to as the mismatch between supply and demand for education and work.[16] While it is true that in general the Indonesian population is "better educated" in quantitative terms, the problem of quality and relevance is currently recognized and widely debated because many graduates do not have the necessary skills to enter the labor market. The next section describes the employment problems faced particularly by the female population.

Education and Work

The Impact of Education on the Labor Market

As mentioned earlier, during the oil boom of the 1970s employment opportunities in the public and private formal sector expanded rapidly.[17] At the same time infrastructure in education was widely developed by the government, making at least primary education accessible to most children in the relevant age bracket. Recognizing that education leads to employment opportunities in the formal sector, parents value it as an avenue to social mobility and economic gains. Hence the rise in demand for education continued throughout the 1980s regardless of the performance of the national economy. Yet the capacity of the formal sector economy to create employment opportunities sufficient for those seeking jobs remains limited. As a result of very rapid growth in the educational qualifications of the working-age population, open unemployment has risen, particularly among the better educated. This is often referred to as a mismatch between education and work. Projections prepared by the Human Resources Development Working Group showed that for the period 1989/90–1993/94 there would be 4.3 million people with primary education or less, 2.3 million with lower secondary education, 4.2 million with upper secondary education, and 1 million with tertiary education. In contrast, the projected demand was for 5.5 million people with primary or less education, 2.5 million with lower secondary, 3 million with upper secondary, and 517,000 with tertiary education. Hence the supply was expected to substantially exceed the demand for upper secondary and tertiary educated people, while the contrary situation of demand exceeding supply was expected to occur among those with primary or less and those with lower secondary education.

Comparisons of the last two population censuses show substantially higher labor force participation rates in 1990 (55%) than a decade earlier (50%, Table 5.5). The differences in rates between the two censuses were recorded for practically all education levels, in both urban and rural areas, and were higher for females than males. It is unlikely that all the intercensal differences in labor force participation can be attributed to macroeconomic performance during the census years. It has been suggested that the 1980 Census underenumerated the labor force relative to the 1990 Census results,[18] rendering the recorded rises partially a statistical artifact. The level of difference that can be attributed to differential levels of recording has not been ascertained, however. Very rapid economic growth did occur during the later 1980s[19] as a result of the introduction of various deregulatory measures. This led to substantial employment opportunities being created in both the formal and informal sectors of the economy. The introduction of deregulatory policies has especially boosted the export-oriented labor-intensive industries, which are very visible in and around larger metropolitan areas. Besides relaxation in the trade sector, financial institutions have also expanded their activities. Consequently not only the formal but also the informal sectors have expanded, thereby creating widespread employment opportunities, especially in salaried employment. However, in a nation as large as Indonesia, currently the fourth largest in the world in population, any real impact on the statistics has to be fairly massive. With that caveat in mind, the statistics should be considered with care.

As a result of differential economic and social pressures, urban labor force participation rates are generally lower than rural rates. Overall labor force participation for urban and rural areas rose by almost the same number of percentage points between 1980 and 1990; for urban areas it rose from 42% to 48% and for rural areas from 53% to 58% (Table 5.5). The urban-rural difference in labor force participation is, of course, due to differences in proportions involved in other activities. There is a higher concentration of the middle and upper classes in urban than in rural areas, and members of those classes can better afford to be involved in other activities besides joining the labor market, such as continuing schooling or being homemakers. In rural areas the pressures to join the labor market are stronger, and rural labor force participation rates are consistently higher among practically all education categories.

Table 5.5 Labor Force Participation Rates by Education, Residence, and Gender, 1980 and 1990

Residence and Attainment	Females 1980	Females 1990	Males 1980	Males 1990	Total 1980	Total 1990
Urban						
No school	33.0	35.1	71.9	72.4	43.3	44.8
Some Primary	20.3	24.7	48.2	48.3	33.9	35.8
Primary	19.0	29.0	60.4	63.6	40.6	45.8
Gen Lower Sec.	15.0	22.4	51.9	54.9	35.5	39.4
Voc Lower Sec.	23.1	28.0	68.4	74.8	51.2	55.6
Gen Upper Sec.	29.0	37.3	67.3	71.6	53.7	57.6
Voc Upper Sec.	54.3	60.5	81.4	89.3	70.8	76.7
Academy	58.8	71.0	87.6	90.5	79.6	82.5
University	69.3	76.0	94.0	93.4	88.2	88.0
Total	24.2	31.6	59.1	64.0	41.5	47.6
Standardized*		24.9		61.3		44.1

Residence and Attainment	Females 1980	Females 1990	Males 1980	Males 1990	Total 1980	Total 1990
Rural						
No school	41.0	48.1	82.1	85.4	55.2	60.6
Some Primary	30.2	37.3	64.6	65.2	48.6	51.5
Primary	32.5	42.1	74.3	78.9	56.4	61.6
Gen Lower Sec.	23.1	32.2	61.2	67.6	47.6	52.9
Voc Lower Sec.	31.5	38.6	74.8	78.0	60.4	62.7
Gen Upper Sec.	38.2	45.7	78.0	83.7	66.7	70.3
Voc Upper Sec.	66.7	71.2	87.8	92.6	81.0	84.4
Academy	60.7	78.1	90.6	93.2	83.8	88.3
University	56.0	69.9	91.7	92.9	84.2	86.7
Total	35.2	42.2	71.2	74.5	52.9	58.1
Standardized		34.7		71.8		54.0
TOTAL						
No school	39.9	45.8	81.1	83.7	53.8	58.0
Some Primary	28.3	34.3	61.9	61.6	46.0	47.9
Primary	28.2	37.9	70.4	74.6	51.7	56.9
Gen Lower Sec.	18.1	26.7	56.3	61.3	40.8	45.8
Voc Lower Sec.	27.3	33.3	71.9	76.5	56.1	59.3
Gen Upper Sec.	31.2	39.6	70.4	75.5	57.3	61.4
Voc Upper Sec.	59.7	64.8	84.7	90.8	75.7	80.0
Academy	59.2	72.7	88.4	91.3	80.6	84.1
University	66.8	75.0	93.5	93.3	87.4	87.8
Total	32.7	38.8	68.4	71.1	50.2	54.8
Standardized		31.8		68.8		51.2

Note: * = Standardized by the 1980 education-specific labor force participation. The standardized rate for 1990 shows what the total labor force participation rate would have been if there had been no change in the education-specific labor force participation rates.

Sources: Biro Pusat Statistik, *Population Census of Indonesia, 1971 (Series D), 1980 and 1990 (Series S2)*.

The gender differences are more striking. Labor force participation is substantially lower among females than males since not all women can be or are willing to join the labor market because of their reproductive responsibilities. More important, labor force participation rose faster among females than males, and this phenomenon occurred both in urban as well as rural areas. Total labor force participation among females rose by 6 percentage points (from 33% to 39%) from 1980 to 1990, while among males the rise was only 3 percentage points (from 68% to 71%). Similar patterns of differences by gender can be observed for practically all education categories.

The rise in labor force participation among urban females with all levels of education is consistent with rapidly expanding employment opportunities created in and around large metropolitan centers by export-oriented labor-intensive industries. Equally visible in large urban centers are jobs created in the formal trade sector by the expansion of supermarkets and shopping malls. Other service industries, such as finance and general public and social services, have also grown. Very rapid growth in these sectors occurred in response to various deregulation measures introduced in trade and finance starting in 1983. Moreover, rising incomes or the growth of the middle and upper classes, who are more likely to reside in urban areas, have also created employment opportunities for household helpers. In rural areas labor force participation rates have similarly risen because of expanding employment opportunities as well as household economic pressures. Among women this phenomenon occurred simultaneously with rising education and age at first marriage. While some women have benefited from expanding paid employment opportunities, economic pressures have driven many women from poor households to the labor market as unpaid family workers.

The relation between education and labor force participation is J-shaped, with the lowest levels recorded among those who completed general lower secondary education. This pattern can be observed among both females and males (Table 5.5). Consequently, the rising education levels of the labor force has had little or even a dampening effect on overall labor force participation rates, as about 80 percent of the labor force in 1990 had at the most completed primary schooling only. This observation is reflected by the negligible difference in the overall 1980 rates and the 1990 standardized rates, which assumes that education specific labor force participation rates remained constant at 1980 levels. Hence, the substantially higher actual rates for 1990 compared to 1980 are a result of rising participation among practically all education categories, for both females and males and also in both urban and rural areas.

Noteworthy are the gender differences between the recorded and standardized labor force participation rates, which are substantially higher for females than males (7% for females compared to only 2% for males). This differential is a result of females catching up with males in obtaining education, but the phenomenon is still limited to the lower levels of education.

This difference is also a function of the pattern of decline in labor force participation by education up to the lower secondary level being more consistent for females than males.

Furthermore, labor force participation rates are higher among those who completed vocational education than among those who followed the general stream. This pattern supports the idea that general education prepares students to continue their education toward ever higher levels while vocational education is directed to the world of work. In other words, lower labor force participation rates among those following the general stream are partially attributable to higher proportions of students continuing their education.

Because the majority of workers claimed to be actually working for at least one hour during the week preceding enumeration, comparisons of education-specific labor force participation with work force participation rates[20] show interesting and different changes in male and female patterns. Substantially higher work force participation rates were recorded in 1990 than in 1980 (overall 53% and 49% respectively; see Table 5.6). The levels are lower in urban than in rural areas, but both are rising (from 40% to 45% in urban areas and from 52% to 57% in rural areas). Of course, proportionately fewer females than males participate in the work force, but the rates rose more for females than males (for females from 32% to 37% and for males from 68% to 69%).

Higher rises in work force participation can be observed among primary and lower secondary levels, and more so in the rural than in the urban areas. It can be inferred here that this pattern reflects a condition in which those of lesser education have no choice but to work to fulfill the family needs. As in many other developing countries, the pattern is more prominent among females than males, and more so in the rural than in the urban areas.

The data also indicate a lower rise of female work force participation among lower- and upper-vocational graduates than among general education graduates. The differences between labor force and work force participation rates are less among those with lower secondary than those with upper secondary schooling. It is suggested that this is a function of overrepresentation of younger females in their late teens and early twenties who can afford to wait for the "appropriate job" to come along. A plausible reason is that those who can afford upper secondary education are better off than those who already have to join the labor market after completing their lower secondary schooling. As such the former group can also afford a longer waiting period before finally lowering their expectations.

Table 5.6 Work Force Participation Rates by Education, Residence, and Gender, 1980 and 1990

Residence and Education	Females		Males		Total	
	1980	1990	1980	1990	1980	1990
Urban						
No school	32.7	34.6	71.0	71.2	42.9	44.2
Some Primary	19.9	23.9	47.2	46.9	33.2	34.7
Primary	18.4	27.6	58.9	61.2	39.5	43.9
Gen Lower Sec.	14.2	20.2	50.3	51.6	34.2	36.7
Voc Lower Sec.	22.2	25.9	66.6	72.0	49.7	53.1
Gen Upper Sec.	26.8	30.4	64.6	64.2	34.2	36.7
Voc Upper Sec.	51.1	53.8	77.3	82.9	67.0	70.1
Academy	56.3	64.9	86.3	86.2	78.0	77.5
University	67.1	66.7	92.9	87.6	86.9	81.1
Total	23.5	29.3	57.5	60.5	40.4	44.7
Standardized*		24.0		59.5		42.7
Rural						
No school	40.2	47.5	81.4	84.9	54.5	60.2
Some Primary	29.6	36.7	64.0	64.3	48.0	50.7
Primary	31.7	40.8	73.4	77.6	55.5	60.4
Gen Lower Sec.	22.2	30.1	59.9	65.5	46.4	50.8
Voc Lower Sec.	30.7	36.8	73.6	76.4	59.3	61.1
Gen Upper Sec.	35.9	38.4	75.6	77.9	64.2	64.0
Voc Upper Sec.	64.0	65.3	85.8	89.0	78.8	79.9
Academy	57.9	71.8	89.2	90.4	82.2	84.3
University	54.1	60.1	90.7	87.3	83.1	79.9
Total	34.4	41.0	70.5	73.1	52.1	56.9
Standardized		33.9		70.4		53.2
Total						
No school	39.2	45.3	80.4	83.1	53.1	57.5
Some Primary	27.7	33.7	61.2	60.6	45.4	47.1
Primary	27.5	36.6	69.4	73.0	50.8	55.4
Gen Lower Sec.	17.3	24.6	54.9	58.6	39.6	43.4
Voc Lower Sec.	26.4	31.3	70.4	74.3	54.8	57.2
Gen Upper Sec.	28.9	32.6	67.8	68.6	54.8	57.2
Voc Upper Sec.	56.7	58.4	81.7	85.6	72.7	74.3
Academy	56.7	66.5	87.1	87.5	79.0	79.4

Residence and Education	Females		Males		Total	
	1980	1990	1980	1990	1980	1990
University	64.7	65.7	92.4	87.5	86.1	80.9
Total	31.9	37.3	67.5	69.1	49.4	53.0
Standardized		31.0		67.6		50.2

Note: * See Table 4.6.
Sources: Biro Pusat Statistik, Population Census of Indonesia, 1971 (Series D), 1980 and 1990 (Series S2).

Gender differences are observable in the rises of work force participation rates between 1980 and 1990 in favor of females in both rural and urban areas. This supports further the contention that education is seen by many women as a means to gain access to work and social mobility. In fact, the benefits of education for women are higher than for men, as the implied returns from education are higher for women than for men. This may well be seen as an increase in demand for female workers or as an increased ability of women to gain access to paid employment. The data also support the notion that given the chance and a conducive environment, women in Indonesia have little cultural constraint against work outside the household.

We have refrained from making any value judgment as to whether the trends in increased participation in the labor market are positive for women. If one were to take the position that women should be more involved in the labor market, then even in the absence of direct policies the phenomenon is already occurring. If, on the other hand, the question is not so much one of numbers but rather of the quality of the jobs—that is, women should have access to the same jobs as men with equal pay for equal work—then these data cannot tell us the story. Gender differential in wages controlled for education remains substantial. On average, women earn only between 50–70% of what men earn (Table 5.7). If, however, we consider these wages relative to a base set for those with little or no education, then we find that the ratios are substantially higher for females than males,[21] suggesting that if parents expect daughters to contribute to the household's maintenance, then investmenting in their daughters' education, and at ever higher levels, is a worthwhile effort. The substantial gender differences in the index values (more than five times for females with tertiary education compared to those with none, while for males the comparison is only three times as much) are indicative of the gender difference in the numbers of those with tertiary education.

Table 5.7 Average Monthly Wages by Educational Attainment and Gender, 1986 and 1989

	1986			1989			1986		1989	
Education	Females	Males	F/M	Females	Males	F/M	F	M	F	M
< Primary	22,740	44,657	51	22,727	54,930	50	100	100	100	100
Primary	29,638	58,361	51	34,970	69,333	50	130	131	125	126
Lower Secondary	50,743	82,652	61	57,296	95,003	60	223	185	207	173
Upper Secondary	71,648	103,850	69	90,531	122,274	74	315	232	326	223
Tertiary	117,762	167,064	71	141,115	205,563	69	518	374	509	374

*Currency in Rp. (Rupiah)
Source: Biro Pusat Statistik (1992), *Indikator Sosial Wanita Indonesia 1991*, Tables 3.3.1. and 3.1.2., pp. 62–63.

Open Unemployment

Returning to the data on labor force and work force participation by education (Tables 5.5 and 5.6), a closer examination of these rates controlled for education shows the following patterns. Either the differences are far greater in the more recent census, or the differences rose substantially during the last intercensal decade. Next, the differences in these rates are greater in urban than rural areas, and the higher the level of education the greater the difference between labor force and work force participation. Finally, among the better educated the differences between labor force and work force participation are greater among females than males.

As the labor force consists of those belonging to the work force and those seeking work, or otherwise also referred to as the openly unemployed, differences between the labor force and the work force are indicative of open unemployment. Even though overall open unemployment rates have risen during the last decade from 1.7% to 3.2%, they are lower than in many developed countries (Table 5.8).

As a developing society, Indonesia has no social security system. For most Indonesians who still rely on agricultural sources of livelihood and especially for the poor, open unemployment is not a very relevant concept because it is a "luxury" state they cannot afford. Thus even the 1990 Population Census recorded overall open unemployment rates of less than 3% for those with primary or less education.

Very rapid growth in educational qualifications of the labor force has,

Table 5.8 Open Unemployment Rates, by Education, Gender, and Residence, 1980 and 1990

Residence and Education	Females 1980	Females 1990	Males 1980	Males 1990	Total 1980	Total 1990
Urban						
No school	1.0	1.2	1.2	1.6	1.1	1.4
Some Primary	2.0	3.2	2.1	1.1	2.1	3.1
Primary	3.3	5.1	2.5	3.7	2.7	4.1
Gen Lower Sec.	5.7	9.6	3.1	6.0	3.6	7.0
Voc Lower Sec.	4.0	7.6	2.7	3.7	2.9	4.5
Gen Upper Sec.	7.7	18.4	4.0	10.4	4.7	12.5
Voc Upper Sec.	5.8	11.1	5.0	7.2	5.3	8.5
Academy	4.1	8.7	1.5	4.7	2.0	6.1
University	3.1	12.2	1.2	6.2	1.5	7.8
Total	3.0	7.3	2.7	5.5	2.8	6.1
Rural						
No school	1.8	1.1	0.8	0.6	1.3	0.9
Some Primary	2.1	1.7	0.9	1.4	1.2	1.5
Primary	2.5	3.1	1.2	1.6	1.5	2.1
Gen Lower Sec.	3.9	6.4	2.1	3.1	2.5	3.9
Voc Lower Sec.	2.7	4.6	1.6	2.0	1.8	2.6
Gen Upper Sec.	6.2	16.0	3.1	6.8	3.6	9.0
Voc Upper Sec.	4.0	8.2	2.3	3.9	2.7	5.3
Academy	4.6	8.1	1.5	3.0	2.0	4.5
University	3.3	14.0	1.1	6.0	1.4	7.8
Total	2.1	2.7	1.0	1.8	1.4	2.1
Total						
No school	1.7	1.1	0.8	0.7	1.3	0.9
Some Primary	2.1	1.9	1.0	1.7	1.3	1.8
Primary	2.7	3.6	1.5	2.1	1.8	2.6
Gen Lower Sec.	4.8	7.9	2.6	4.4	3.0	5.3
Voc Lower Sec.	3.3	5.9	2.1	2.8	2.3	3.5
Gen Upper Sec.	7.3	17.6	3.7	9.1	4.4	11.3
Voc Upper Sec.	4.9	9.8	3.6	5.7	3.9	7.1
Academy	4.2	8.5	1.5	4.2	2.0	5.6
University	3.1	12.5	1.1	6.2	1.5	7.8
Total	2.2	3.9	1.4	2.9	1.7	3.2

Sources: Biro Pusat Statistik, *Population Census of Indonesia, 1971 (Series D), 1980 and 1990 (Series S2).*

however, brought with it other problems of open unemployment, especially among females with a general upper secondary or university education. Those who continued their education beyond primary school expected access to formal sector employment similar to that of their brothers and sisters who entered the labor market only a decade earlier. At that time graduating classes were far smaller, and the government sector was expanding rapidly in the development of its social infrastructure, particularly in education and health. Hence, as Logsdon observed, this was the era when a disproportionate number of new entrants into the civil service were female.[22] Starting in the late 1980s, however, the public sector recruited ever fewer new employees into its bureaucracy.

Now there is a tendency to rely increasingly on the private and formal sector to create more employment opportunities. Notwithstanding the rapid economic growth that occurred during the late 1980s, the private sector is still limited in its ability to absorb as many graduates as the educational system produces at its accelerated pace since mass education is in place. Yet substantial numbers of women have found paid employment in export-oriented labor-intensive manufacturing industries and in a few service sectors. This situation is often referred to as the mismatch between education and work. Hence the 1990 Census recorded rather alarming double-digit open unemployment rates, particularly among those with a general upper secondary education. The overall rate was 11.3%, while the urban rate was 12.5% and the rural rate 9%. Women contributed a great deal to these rates, as 17.6% of the female labor force with general upper secondary education was openly unemployed compared with only 9.1% of males with similar education. Among this education category the urban-rural difference for females is not great, 18.4% for urban as compared to 16.0% among rural residents. Even more disturbing are the similar double-digit open unemployment rates among female university graduates recorded by the 1990 Census—12.2%, 14.0%, and 12.5%, respectively for urban, rural, and all females with university education. In contrast, for males the rates are substantially lower—6.2%, 6.0%, and 6.2%, respectively. It is suggested that the gender difference in this regard is partly attributable to past patterns of gender-differentiated access to occupations requiring this level of education.

In fact these rates are indicative of the count of the openly unemployed at the time of the census, which in the Indonesian case is October, a few months after graduation. The state of open unemployment or job seeking can be quite extensive, for some more than a year. It is usually among the new entrants into the labor force that extended open unemployment periods are experienced until an appropriate job comes along.

Table 5.9 Percentage of First-Time Job Seekers Among the Openly Unemployed by Education, Residence, and Gender, 1980 and 1990

Residence and Education	Females 1980	Females 1990	Males 1980	Males 1990	Total 1980	Total 1990
Urban						
< Primary	64.6	68.1	52.8	66.8	57.0	67.3
Primary	82.1	84.5	64.1	72.1	69.0	77.1
Gen Lower Sec	87.2	87.9	73.7	78.0	77.8	81.7
Voc Lower Sec	87.0	84.1	65.6	69.5	70.6	74.5
Gen Upper Sec	92.5	91.8	81.8	86.4	85.1	88.5
Voc Upper Sec	89.1	89.3	82.6	82.2	84.7	85.4
Academy	86.9	86.9	82.0	84.2	84.0	85.5
University	95.5	91.3	87.6	87.8	90.6	89.3
Total	80.8	86.8	68.7	79.5	72.5	82.5
Rural						
< Primary	34.7	44.3	32.9	59.7	33.9	51.5
Primary	52.8	72.8	50.4	71.6	51.4	72.2
Gen Lower Sec	72.7	83.6	60.7	75.1	64.0	78.6
Voc Lower Sec	75.9	81.8	57.2	75.4	62.2	78.1
Gen Upper Sec	84.9	89.6	75.5	83.6	78.1	86.1
Voc Upper Sec	85.9	89.1	79.2	81.7	81.8	85.4
Academy	91.2	91.3	71.0	88.0	78.7	89.7
University	76.0	91.6	78.5	85.0	77.7	87.6
Total	41.4	68.9	43.7	72.2	42.6	70.6
Total						
< Primary	37.7	49.9	37.1	62.1	37.4	56.1
Primary	60.6	76.9	55.9	71.8	57.6	74.1
Gen Lower Sec	81.4	86.0	68.2	76.9	72.0	80.4
Voc Lower Sec	81.8	83.0	62.0	71.8	66.9	76.0
Gen Upper Sec	90.7	91.2	80.0	85.6	83.3	87.8
Voc UpperSec	87.8	89.2	81.5	82.0	83.7	85.4
Academy	87.9	88.0	79.1	85.0	82.7	86.5
University	92.3	91.4	85.8	87.3	88.2	89.0
Total	50.2	77.7	53.5	76.3	52.1	76.9

Sources: Biro Pusat Statistik, *Population Census of Indonesia, 1971* (Series D), *1980 and 1990* (Series S2).

This assertion is supported by the data on the proportions of new entrants or first-time job seekers among the openly unemployed (Table 5.9). The percentages rose from 52% to 77% between 1980 and 1990. These percentages were substantially higher in urban areas, rising from 73% to 83%. A much higher jump, was however, recorded for rural areas, from 43% to 71%. Interestingly the gender differences are not consistent. Overall the percentage of new entrants among the openly unemployed was lower for females than males, in 1980, 50% as compared to 54%, but then reversed in 1990 to 78% and 76% respectively. In urban areas these percentages were always higher for females than males but in rural areas the reverse pattern can be observed, higher for males than females. These differences simply reflect different urban concentrations by gender among the better educated.

In summary, although education is seen as a means to attain social mobility and economic rewards, at least temporarily, education for women has also brought along with it problems related to unfulfilled rising expectations in the labor market. This may well result in a boomerang effect on women when experiences and perceptions fail to meet their rising expectations. On the other hand, the situation can also be avoided if the economy continues to perform as well as it has in the recent past, and widespread formal-sector employment opportunities can be created for increasingly better educated women.

In the meantime, as a recent World Bank report indicated, the East Asian miracle, which includes Indonesia as one of the high performing Asian economies, has been achieved through an emphasis on human resources development. In Indonesia there is growing concern about the size and quality of its human resources. Not only are the concerns in terms of quantities, but increasingly there is a realization that quality should be of greater concern for the future. There is also an awareness that in the future greater emphasis must be placed on science and technology. Within this debate, however, the gender issue is usually ignored. On the other hand, in other quarters the gender issues of the labor market are gaining prominence. Gender neutral—or gender blind—policies have, as shown in this chapter, not had gender neutral consequences.

NOTES

1. Primary and lower secondary will soon be combined to be a continuous level of nine years of basic education as part of the "compulsory education program" to be launched in the next planning period or REPELITA VI of 1994/5–1998/9.
2. They are the responsibility of the Ministry of Religion.
3. Religious schools, specifically Islamic schools, are defined as those allocating at least 30% of their class time to religious instruction. (See Biro Pusat Statistik,

Statistik Pendidikan di Bawah dan di Luar Lingkungan Departemen P dan K, 1988/ 1989, 1991:3). In 1988–89, 18% of all primary schools, 23% of lower secondary schools, and 19% of upper secondary schools were outside the governance of the Ministry of Education and Culture. (See Biro Pusat Statistik, op. cit., 1991:7).

4. In 1950 primary enrollment was just over 5 million children. See Lambert Kelabora and Kenneth Orr, "Stimulating the Appetite and Coping with the Consequences in Indonesia," in: Kenneth Orr, ed., *Appetite for Education in Contemporary Asia* (Canberra: The Australian National University, Development Studies Centre Monograph No.10, 1977):97. By 1971, 12.7 million or 5.2% of the children aged 6–12 years were attending school. See Biro Pusat Statistik, *Sensus Penduduk 1971*.

5. Martha G. Logsdon, "Women Civil Servants in Indonesia: Some Preliminary Observations," PRISMA, 37 (Sept. 1985): 77–87.

6. Mari Pangestu and Mayling Oey-Gardiner, "Indonesia," in: Wong Poh Kam and Ng Chee Yuen, eds., *Human Resource Development and Utilization in the Asia-Pacific: A Social Absorption Capacity Approach* (Singapore: Institute of Southeast Asian Studies, 1991): 61–79.

7. See, e.g., Pryosusilo, "Schooling in a Javanese Village: Some Observations," PRISMA, 38 (Dec. 1985): 95; and Mayling Oey-Gardiner, "Female School Attendance in Indonesia," unpublished paper prepared for the World Bank in Jakarta, 1989.

8. Oey-Gardiner, "Female School Attendance."

9. This policy was adopted during the Sukarno administration (1945–1966). Following the example of other developed societies, vocational and professional training, which are directed towards the labor market, become elevated and postponed to older ages. Under normal conditions children should complete their lower secondary education at age 15. At this age children are simply too young to start a career that limits their options in the future labor market, which becomes increasingly dictated by rapid changes in technology.

10. More recently, however, the new Minister of Education and Culture has decided to reinvigorate vocational schools at the lower secondary level. The main reason given is to deal with the large numbers of dropouts and to prepare them for the labor market.

11. Oey-Gardiner, "Female School Attendance."

12. Andi Hakim Nasoetion, "Indonesian Higher Education: Improving Input to Improve Output Quality," in: *Indonesia Assessment 1991*, Hal Hill, ed. (Canberra: Australian National University, Political and Social Change Monograph 13, 1991), 58–76.

13. Oey-Gardiner, "Female School Attendance."

14. Nasoetion, "Indonesian Higher Education."

15. Sudaryanti, "Persepsi Akuntan Publik Wanita Terhadap Penggunaan Jadwal Kerja Alternatif" (Perception of Female Public Accountants on Alternative Work Schedules), unpublished thesis, University of Indonesia, Jakarta, 1992.

16. Pangestu and Oey-Gardiner, "Indonesia," p. 68.

17. Logsdon, "Women Civil Servants;" Oey-Gardiner, "Female School Attendance."

18. Insan Harapan Sejahtera, *A Study of Women's Issues in Agricultural Transformation*. A study conducted for the World Bank, 1993.

19. For the period 1985–1990 average non-oil GDP at constant prices grew at 7.2% per annum. See Republik Indonesia, *Nota Keuangan dan Rancangan Anggaran Pendapatan dan Belanja Negara Tahun Anggaran 1993/94* [1993/94 National Annual Budget]. During the earlier half of the decade, the economy grew at only 4.7% per annum. See World Bank, *Indonesia: Adjustment, Growth and Sustainable Development*, Report No. 7222–IND, 1988, Statistical Annex Table 2.3 : 158.

20. The labor force consists of those working and those seeking work; the latter are also referred to as the openly unemployed. Thus, the work force consists of those actually recorded as working.

21. In the absence of more detailed analysis, it can be speculated that these implied gender differential returns to education are a function of the dynamism in the labor market and the gender differential supply and demand by education.

22. Logsdon, "Women Civil Servants."

6 MALAYSIA

Robiah Sidin

INTRODUCTION

The contribution of education to Malaysia's national development has long been recognized. Economists see in education a means to develop qualified manpower for economic needs. Politicians see in it a foundation for political stability and democracy. Malaysia comprises about 55% Malays and other indigenous groups, 30% Chinese, and 10% Indians. In this multiracial context, Malaysia's education policy functions as an important instrument for national unity. It comprises a common curriculum, a common language—Bahasa Malay—as the medium of instruction, and centrally trained teachers. In this way students are socialized and instilled with values that support the national ideology and visions of a united and progressive nation. Most schools teach in Bahasa Malay. A small number use either Mandarin or Tamil, the languages of ethnic Chinese and Indians, respectively, as a medium of instruction. Education in Malaysia is thus assigned the primary function of socializing children into accepted community values and behavior.

Like men, women contribute to development. It is difficult to ignore their contribution, partly because demographically they constitute about 50% of the total population. In 1991, there were 8.7 million women and nearly 8.9 million men in a total population of nearly 17.6 million.[1] The evidence of women's contribution is pervasive and obvious. Women are involved in all sectors of development, including education, health, public administration, politics, land development, welfare, transport, and business. Although women's labor force participation rate lags behind men's, it increased from 37% in 1970 to 47% in 1990. In comparison, men's rate decreased from 69% to 65%.[2] The rapid technological and social change taking place in Malaysia will call for more contributions from women. The economic boom, the shift from agriculture to manufacturing, and the economic boom, the shift from agriculture to manufacturing, and the government's effort to effectively incorporate women in the development process have created the space and a need for women's participation.

In Malaysia women are not all at the bottom of the employment structure. Their impact is felt at such decision-making ranks as political leaders, planners, and executives. Malaysia presently has two full ministers, three deputy ministers, 11 parlimentarians, and 10 senators who are women. In civil and diplomatic service the distribution of women in senior positions is also encouraging. A few women occupy positions as secretary general or deputy Secretary General at the Ministry Level. Seniority is indicated by rank and salary; women's share of senior ranks is shown in Table 6.1.

Table 6.1 Number of Men and Women in Senior Positions in Administrative and Diplomatic Services, 1992

Type of Post/Grade	Male	Female
Chief Secretary	1	—
Staff I	1	—
Staff II	7	—
Staff III	10	-
Superscale C	40	4
Superscale D and E	176	15
Superscale G and F	837	127
Total	1072	146
	(88%)	(12%)

Source: Compiled from Public Services Department, Senarai *Pegawai-Pegawai Persekutuan Malaysia* (Listing of Government Servants in Malaysia, 1992) (Kuala Lumpur: Government Printer, 1992), section on Administrative and Diplomatic Service.

Some research has shown that one of the major contributory factors to national development is education.[3] Education has equipped women with the relevant knowledge, skills, attitudes, and discipline for their roles as professionals, semiprofessionals, or production workers. It has also injected in some of them a sense of curiosity and courage to venture into male-dominated fields such as astronomy, physics, finance, and technology.

This chapter examines how the development of education in Malaysia has changed women's involvement in national development. It will discuss the different types of educational opportunities available to women and will then show the pattern of women's participation in the economic, social, and political arenas.

A Historical Account of Women's Education

In many ways, changes in the role and status of women are closely related to the development of education in Malaysia. Secular education for girls began after the arrival of the British in the eighteenth century. Informal education had a longer history and was given by parents and other members of the extended family.

Before independence in 1957, the status of Malay women's was lower than that of men's. Women were socialized early into subordination, and Malay girls had little freedom. They were confined to the house and trained to assist their mothers in domestic chores and caring for their younger siblings. Malay tradition and Islam required them to attend classes where they learned to read and recite the Koran. Girls were also taught skills considered appropriate for them, such as sewing, weaving, and mat making. In contrast, boys were required to go to school.

As in many other former colonies, Christian missionaries and private individuals were instrumental in setting up the first modern schools, both in the vernacular and in English. The first Malay school for girls was opened in 1884 with an enrollment of 60. It was, however, closed down in 1887 because of poor attendance. Another school that had been set up in Singapore in 1884 faced a similar problem. Although the number of Malay schools for girls had risen to five by 1916, the average attendance in each was only about 108 students.[4] The primary reasons for this low attendance were the distance between these schools and the girls' homes, parental bias against formal education for both girls and boys, and the Christian background of these schools, which led to fear of conversion to Christianity among some.[5] English schools for girls were built as an extension of boys' schools. This was the case with Penang Free school, the first English School in the Straits Settlement. These schools provided basic education for girls, including the teaching of crafts and domestic skills. The schools were subsequently taken over from the missionaries by the colonial government. The attendance at girls' schools continued to be poor for reasons already cited.

After World War II education for girls received a new impetus. The number of schools and their enrollment increased. In the Straits Settlement (early British settlements in Malacca, Penang, and Singapore) and the Federated Malay states (those States in which a British Resident was appointed to advise the rulers in administrative matters), the number of Malay schools

The number of English schools for girls increased from two in 1938 to six in 1948.[6] The increase of students from 1946 to 1950 was 192.5% for girls and 74.8% for boys.[7] Despite this, girls' enrollment lagged behind that of boys, especially at higher levels (Table 6.2).

Table 6.2 Enrollment by Standard Grade and by Sex in Government-Assisted Malay Medium Primary Schools in Peninsular Malaya, 1957

Standard Grade	Boys	Girls	Total
1	51,039	47,679	98,718
2	49,303	41,308	90,611
3	46,337	36,380	82,717
4	46,977	33,053	80,030
5	37,911	20,865	58,776
6	21,883	8,835	30,718

Source: Ministry of Education, *Education Statistics of Malaysia, 1938–1967* (Kuala Lumpur: Dewan Bahasa dan Pustaka, 1968), p. 32.

Educational expansion was related to various developments taking place after the war. The demand for education from all ethnic groups soared. Among the Malays particularly there was now a consciousness of their social position and a realization that they were far behind the other ethnic groups in social advancement. Education meant a chance for them to get jobs with the government, even if only as office boys, policemen, or junior clerks.

Also, in 1946 there was an attempt to unify all the Malay states under one sovereign government. This collection of states was to be called the Malayan Union. Under this arrangements the sultans were expected to surrender their sovereign rights to the king of England, and the state governments were to submit to the higher control of the central government. There was also to be provision of equal rights to all citizens regardless of race or religion. Immigrants could apply for citizenship after five years of uninterrupted residence in Malaya. Specific to education, the Malayan Union proposed that education for girls should be given as much emphasis as education for boys. However, the proposal gave rise to a storm of protests by the indigenous Malays. In any case, the British did not give real support to this scheme, and the proposal was therefore withdrawn.

scheme, and the proposal was therefore withdrawn.

After this failure there was a more concerted effort to plan and administer education to provide for better opportunities for both boys and girls. Many changes were brought about after the demise of the Malayan Union proposal and the formation of the United Malays National Organization (UMNO) in 1946. UMNO included a policy that made it compulsory for all children between the ages of six and twelve to attend school. The 1940s was thus a period of intense political activity. In 1949 the women's wing of the UMNO, commonly known as Kaum Ibu UMNO, was formed. The membership of this group, literally translated as the mother's group, was comprised mainly of educated women who were conscious of the need to increase women's community participation. One of its primary missions was to increase girls' access to education. Its leaders believed in education as a means to prepare girls for future public roles. Adult literacy classes as well as English classes were held, and more places for girls were demanded.[8]

The above provides a general overview of the educational opportunities available after World War II for indigenous Malay girls, most of whom resided in the rural areas.

As regards the Chinese and Indians, they came as laborers to Malaya at the beginning of British colonialism (1786–1957). The Chinese worked in the tin mines, the Indians as estate workers. These immigrant parents paid less attention to their daughters' education than to that of their sons. However, their daughters had more access to schooling than Malay daughters, as is evident from enrollment figures. Table 6.3 indicates the enrollment of girls in English schools in 1947. English schools were mainly found in towns and represented about 5% of the total number of schools then.

Table 6.3 Enrollment of Boys and Girls in English Schools, 1947

Ethnic Group	Boys	Girls	Girls % of Total
Malay	6,535	1,168	15
Chinese	16,979	9,339	36
Indian	9,253	4,224	31
Others (including Eurasians)	1,202	1,123	48

Source: Fatimah Hamid Don, "Opportunities for Women in Education." Paper presented at the Seminar Peranan Wanita dalam Bidang-Bidang Pelajaran Tinggi dan Implikasinya (The Role of Women in Higher Education and its Implications) at Universiti Malaya, Kuala Lumpur, Nov. 14–15, 1975, p. 20.

Better attendance among the non-Malays was related to religious and geographical factors. Fear of conversion to Christianity was not prevalent among non-Malays; most of the English schools were built in towns and village centers where the non-Malays, especially the Chinese, resided.

After independence in 1957, a national education policy was introduced through the Education Act of 1961. The government promised to provide a school place for every native-born child.[9] There was to be a national education system in which Bahasa Malay was to be the language of instruction. This was a departure from the colonial days when schools were grouped according to the various languages of instruction. Malay, Chinese, and Indian schools enrolled children from relevant ethnic groups; English schools enrolled mostly Eurasians and urban middle-class Chinese and Malay children. In the national system children were to follow a common curriculum locally oriented to meet national needs. Teachers were to be locally trained at national colleges or universities. The main objective was to promote national integration among the ethnic groups and to develop in them a sense of loyalty and pride in the newly formed federation.

A change in the structure and orgnization of schools took place with independence. All schools were to be classified as primary or secondary schools and were to be of two types: assisted or independent. Assisted schools received aid from public funds. Fully assisted schools, now called national schools, were those using Malay as the medium of instruction. Schools that used the ethnic mother tongue (Chinese or Tamil) or English as the medium of instruction also received aid, but only at the primary level. At the secondary level all assisted schools were required to use Bahasa Malay as the medium of instruction, although the transition from using other languages to Bahasa Malay could be gradual. It was only in 1982 that English ceased completely to be the medium of instruction in some schools and was taught as a second language.

By the early 1960s parents of all races were convinced of the value of education in securing jobs in the government service, which was a mobility route from work in the villages, estates, or tin mines. The United Nations Declaration on Human Rights in 1960, which included the right to education, also spurred the Malaysian government's effort to expand education. The secondary school entrance examination was abolished in 1960. Incentives were introduced in the form of scholarships and bursaries and hostel accommodation for students from villages. By 1970 a total of 672,898 girls, compared to 748,571 boys, were enrolled in all government primary schools. At the secondary level 192,113 girls as compared to 275,991 boys were enrolled. The enrollment rate of girls was 84.8% at the primary level,

43.6% at the lower secondary level, and 16.1% at the upper secondary level. The boys' figures were 91.6%, 60.6%, and 23.9% respectively.[10]

Thus significant expansion in education for girls took place after Independance. However, apart from school subjects common to all, girls were also taught domestic science. The public still regarded girls' education as inferior to boys' and education had the function of preparing girls to be good mothers and wives.

It was only with independence that Malay children were encouraged to attend school in large numbers. However, there were many cultural and economic barriers to girls' education. For example, for a long time most Malays were farmers and fishermen who were poor and so tended to send sons rather than daughters to school. There were also different role expectations for boys and girls; boys had to study so as to get jobs and become the main provider for the family.[11] Many Chinese also considered that sending girls to school was a waste of money, because they would eventually marry and follow their husbands.

Development in Malaysia

The Second Malaysia Plan (1971–75) demonstrated that the Malaysian concept of development evolved out of the Malaysian context, especially its sense of the unique importance of achieving equity and racial balance in the economy and of developing a common outlook among its multiracial population.[12] In many ways development was synonymous with nation-building, which aimed at a cohesive, progressive society.

A landmark policy announced in 1970 and embodied in the second and the third Malaysia Plans was the New Economic Policy (NEP). Although the plan was termed "economic," its objectives were also political and social. The NEP was a two-pronged effort to eradicate poverty irrespective of race and to reduce uneven access to occupations and places of residence among the races. Its emphasis was on assisting the indigenous Malays to increase their involvement in the modern industries, mining, manufacturing, and construction. Education and training, especially at the tertiary level, were deemed important. While research findings on the direct impact of the NEP on the target groups are not readily available, government documents have mentioned that much success has been achieved during the past twenty years since its implementation. It has promoted economic growth and has managed to redress some of the problems associated with poverty and imbalance in economic distribution among ethnic groups.[13]

Some aspects of the NEP had direct relevance to promoting the education of girls. The NEP highlighted the need for educating and training to be expanded irrespective of gender in order to meet national manpower needs, especially in science and technology. It also called for efforts to reduce waste in education and increase its effectiveness in nation-building. To assist more Malays to come out of their villages and participate in modern industries, the government embarked on strategies to provide more secondary schools in the rural areas, residential schools for bright students, and matriculation classes to prepare students for entry into the universities. It also implemented affirmative measures, namely a quota of 55 Malays to 45 non-Malays in the intake of new university students. Overall, the NEP has encouraged Malay boys and girls to receive more education and training in order to succeed in life.

Today, as Malaysia faces the twenty-first century, the main thrust of development is based on the National Development Policy (NDP), which is embodied in the Sixth Malaysia Plan (1991–1995). The policy is to sustain the current growth momentum and to bring about a more united and just society through balanced development.[14] Its major goals include reducing and ultimately eliminating social and economic inequalities, promoting national integration, developing a society in which all citizens enjoy greater material welfare and at the same time are imbued with positive social and spiritual values, promoting human resource development, and protecting the environment and ecology, along with the pursuit of economic development.[15]

Of direct relevance to further strengthening the role of Malaysian women in development are the following policies. First, education and training play a great role in producing high-quality labor. Second, the private sector is expected to play a much bigger role in the development process. Third, the development of human resources, particularly of the lower income groups, is emphasized. Finally, there is need to formulate specific strategies to effectively incorporate women in the development process.[16]

The stimulus to women's participation in national development does not come from the government alone. International events, particularly the United Nations' declaration of 1976–1985 as the Decade of Women and the subsequent resolution in Nairobi in 1985, led to a heightened interest in women's contributions. The National Advisory Council for the Integration of Women in Development (NACIWID) was established in Malaysia in 1976, its objective being to strengthen women's role in development. Other bodies have also been set up to improve various aspects of women's lives and distribute relevant data. Nonformal education has been used to develop women's potential and leadership. Among the most active of these nonformal education agencies are the Community Development Division of the Ministry of Rural Development (KEMAS); the Rubber Industry Smallholders

Development Authority (RISDA); the Federal Land Developemnt Authority (FELDA); and the Malaysian Fisheries Development Authority (LKIM). These organization mainly serve rural women. In the urban areas nonformal education focuses on occupational training and personal development. Examples of such organizations are the Muslim Women's Action Society (PERTIWI), The Malaysian Women Graduates Association (PSWM), and the Women for Women Association Malaysia (WOW).

In 1983 the government established the Secretariat for Women's Affairs (abbreviated in Malay as HAWA) in the Prime Minister's Department. In 1990 this was put under the jurisdiction of the Ministry of National Unity and Community Development. This division functions as a monitoring body; it will also evaluate projects and services for women undertaken by public and private agencies and the nongovernment organizations (NGO's) and oversees the activities of NACIWID.

To ensure that all the activities for women are well planned, comprehensive, and of far-reaching effect, a National Policy on Women (NPW) was formulated and announced in 1989. This policy is considered testimony of the government's commitment to optimize the potential of women in the social and economic development of the country. The policy has two main objectives. First, it aims to ensure equitable sharing of resources, information, opportunities, and benefits of development between both men and women. Second, it aims to integrate women into all sectors of national development in line with their abilities and needs.[17]

To summarize, during the last two decades certain events and policy changes have boosted women's participation in Malaysian national development. In spite of that, women in Malaysia are still underrepresented in particular sectors and levels of development activities. Consequently, various calls have been made for more systematic and comprehensive programs to overcome existing shortfalls. There is a particular need to increase women's involvement in planning, decision-making, and implementation processes at all levels.

OPPORTUNITIES IN EDUCATION
Primary and Secondary Education

Since 1956 education at the primary and secondary school levels in Malaysia has been provided free to all children irrespective of sex, class, or ethnicity. The government regards education as part and parcel of economic development and national unity. Toward this end it states that the broad objective of the development of education is: "to mould individuals to become better Malaysians with the right attitude toward life and work, and to equip them with the knowledge and skills necessary to make Malaysia a developed nation by the year 2020."[18]

As Table 6.4 shows, girls make increasing use of the new opportunities.

Table 6.4 Female Students as a Percentage of Enrollment by Level and Stream of Education, 1970–90

Level of Education	1970	1980	1990
Primary	46.8	48.6	48.6
Secondary	40.6	47.6	50.5
Postsecondary	42.6	45.5	59.3
University	29.1	35.5	44.3
College			
Polytechnics	13.2	21.5	25.2
Teacher Training Institutions	41.9	48.3	56.1
MARA Institute of Technology	32.4	42.9	45.8
Tunku Abdul Rahman College	23.5	33.9	37.2
Stream			
Arts	46.4	61.0	64.8
Science	24.5	36.3	44.7
Vocational	24.2	30.4	22.0
Technical	4.3	27.1	35.9

Source: Federation of Malaysia, *Sixth Malaysia Plan, 1991–1995*, (Kuala Lumpur: National Printing Department, 1991), p. 421.

At the primary and secondary levels the gender gap in enrollment has narrowed. The enrollment rate for all primary-school-aged children was about 87% in 1980 and about 98% in 1989.[19] While the statistics indicate little difference in enrollment between boys and girls, some disparity exists between the urban and rural groups. Among the limiting factors were poverty, health conditions, and the demand on both boys' and girl' time and energy to help the family with household chores.[20] Attitudinal factors no longer play a predominent role.

The relatively high enrollment rates drop after the lower secondary school examination. The percentage of urban boys and girls who enrolled in upper secondary school in 1980 were 65% and 64% respectively. For rural girls it was less than 50% of the age-cohort.[21] This implies that a number of students were eliminated from schools after age 15. Only those students who performed well in the lower secondary school examination were selected for promotion to government schools. While some students repeat lower levels in private schools, others seek employment or join nonformal skill training or craft-making courses or receive on-the-job training. However, the chances for students to enroll in these courses are limited. Thus there is a need to provide some useful training for youths so that they will not become a source of social problems.

A bigger problem emerges if we consider the situation of school leavers after form 5, which is the highest level of secondary schooling, equivalent to the General Certificate of Education Ordinary Level (GCE "O" level). All students in Malaysia aged 16 to 17 and over and at the end of form 5 are required to sit for the Malaysian Certificate of Education, or Sijil Pelajaran Malaysia (SPM). This is equivalent to the GCE "O" level examination and determines whether students can continue with their further studies, including "A" level, Malaysian Higher Certificate of Education, or matriculation for further degrees either locally or abroad. As places in government institutions are limited, only students who obtain good scores in the SPM are accepted to the above programs. In 1990 they represented about 19% of the 17–18 age group.[22] Those who do not make it will have to seek employment or, if they are girls, settle down to family life. The percentage of girls seeking employment is high, perhaps as high as that of boys.

All these facts imply that while a larger number of girls receive education up to the secondary level, there are only limited promotion routes or occupational training prospects. To a certain degree the government has taken measures to reduce this problem. It has established government vocational schools and at the same time encouraged various agencies to offer skills and craft training for youths. An analysis of the provision of vocational education is therefore necessary to enable us to understand the preparation of young women for employment.

Vocational and Technical Education

The Malaysian government has long recognized the importance of vocational and technical education. As early as 1956 the Razak Education Report mentioned that vocational and technical education should be conducted in Bahasa Malay and should meet local economic needs.[23]

The emphasis was reiterated in the Cabinet Committee Report on Education in 1979. Vocational schools provide students with career skills in such areas as engineering, home science, agriculture, and commerce. Technical schools place greater emphasis on technical and scientific subjects. After two years in vocational schools students sit for the Sijil Pelajaran Vokasional Malaysia (SPVM), or Malaysian Vocational Certificate of Education. The technical-stream students qualify to sit for the SPM with a bias in the technical subject areas.

The Sixth Malaysia Plan (1991–1995), which emphasizes human resource development, states that this period will see the strengthening of vocational education through restructuring of the curriculum and the existing training system and a call for greater private sector participation. The main aim is to make vocational education more attractive to students and to produce more competent graduates.[24] Vocational and technical education are important to women because although they comprise about half the population, they are only one third of the labor force in Malaysia. They should therefore be given more opportunity to become professionals or workers. In 1990 about 29% of female employees had had a primary education, 19% lower secondary education, 26% upper secondary education, and 16% had not had any formal education. Of the total, only about 6% had college/university degrees and 4% had "A" level qualifications.[25] The generally low educational attainment of women and girls necessitates that they be provided with training to increase their employability.

However, the participation of girls in vocational and technical education is still low. In 1987 girls made up only 24% and 35% of the total enrollment in vocational and technical schools run by the Ministry of Education. In comparison, girls formed about 54% of the enrollment in the arts stream and 47% in the science stream.[26]

Vocational education for girls is provided by the Ministry of Education, by various government agencies and statutory bodies, and by private agencies. In 1990 there were only 57 government vocational and nine technical schools throughout the country, with a total enrollment of 24,548 and 2,548 students respectively, which was about 8% of the total upper secondary school enrollment.[27] Girls made up about a quarter while boys about made up three quarters of the vocational and technical enrollment.[28] There is an inclination for girls to enroll in traditionally "feminine" courses such as home economics and commerce, which includes clerical and secretarial skills; boys are predominantly in engineering works, metal crafts, and technical skills such as electrical and electronic works, building construction, welding, and metal fabrication. Table 6.5 below shows the distribution.

Table 6.5 Number of Students in Government Vocational Schools by Courses, 1990

Type of courses	Number of Students		
	Male	Female	Total
Engineering Works	15,768 (96%)	595 (4%)	16,363
Commerce	773 (20%)	3,003 (80%)	3,776
Agricultural Science	532 (71%)	219 (29%)	751
Home Science	0 (0%)	1,480 (100%)	1,480
Technical Skills	2,154 (87%)	321 (13%)	2,475
Total	19,227 (77%)	5,618 (23%)	24,845

Source: Ministry of Education, *Educational Statistics 1990*, Table 5, p. 3.

Most of the vocational courses run by other government agencies are short courses in basic trades and skills to enable school leavers and adults to enter specific businesses and trades. For females the courses are mostly in crafts, domestic science, agriculture-related trades, and teaching at the preschool level. In general this type of vocational education reveals an uneven distribution by sex similar to that run by the Ministry of Education.

While technical education has a similar pattern in enrollment, an encouraging phenomenon has emerged. Females made up more than a third of the total enrollment in 1990 and about as much in civil engineering, which is traditionally "male." (See Table 6.6 below)

On the whole, girls' access to formal or nonformal vocational and technical education has the following characteristics. First, opportunities for girls are increasing as the number of schools, agencies, and courses increases. Second, in relative terms, girls comprise a low proportion of the overall enrollment in vocational and technical education, a proportion which has slightly dropped from 24% in 1970 to 22% in 1990.[29] Third, there is a tendency for girls to enroll in traditionally "feminine" courses, mainly tailoring, agriculture-related trades, crafts, and home economics. However, there is also a move away from this tradition. Some girls are enrolled in courses such as electrical works, radio

Table 6.6 Enrollment in Technical Schools, 1990

Type of courses	Number of Students		
	Male	Female	Total
Civil Engineering	1,316 (63%)	765 (37%)	2,081
Mechanical Enigneering	1,606 (92%)	145 (8%)	1,751
Commerce	296 (29%)	722 (71%)	1,018
Agriculture	188 (44%)	239 (56%)	427
Total	3,406 (65%)	1,871 (35%)	5,277

Source: Ministry of Education, *Educational Statistics 1990*, Table 5, p. 3.

and TV mechanics, and furniture making. Although the number is still small, a mild trend is discernible.

Tertiary Education

In Malaysia postsecondary education includes sixth-form matriculation courses, college education provided by teacher training colleges, and degree-granting tertiary-institutions—the universities and polytechnics. Currently there are eight public universities, twenty-eight teacher training colleges, one institute of technology, one college for commerce and banking, and five polytechnics. Colleges do not award degrees. There are also several private colleges that offer nondegree postsecondary education and part-time/external degrees for overseas universities. Tertiary institutions play a very significant role in the preparation of professionals and semi-professionals.

Postsecondary and college-level enrollment represented about 3.7% and about 4.4%, respectively, of the total student population in 1990—approximately 19% of the 17- to 18-year-olds in that year.[30] At the university level the enrollment in 1990 was about 2.8% of the 19–24 age group.[31] Girls form about 43% of total college enrollment and 45% of university enrollment.[32] Thus girls are not left far behind in enrollment. However, they are unevenly distributed in fields of study. For example, at the University of Malaya in 1975, girls formed a majority in dentistry (58%) and education (68%) and almost half (50%) in arts and law. They were a small minority in engineering (2%) and about 22% to 30% in economics, agriculture, medicine, and science.[33] The pattern had changed little by 1990, except for an increase in engineering (Table 6.7). This pattern of uneven distribution also prevails at the diploma- and certificate-level courses and has caused concern among the government and women's leaders, especially when the focus of current development is on industrialization and a wider application of science and technology. This unevenness has been caused by streaming. The streaming of students into arts and science classes at the upper secondary level has resulted in more girls in arts classes. Besides, girls are channeled into home science and secretarial courses at secondary school and boys into areas such as mechanics, industrial arts, and electrical engineering.

Table 6.7 Number and Female Percentage of Local University* First-Degree Graduates, 1990

Discipline	Male	Female	% Female
Medicine	192	170	47
Dentistry	28	32	53
Basic and Applied Sciences	500	442	47
Engineering	561	91	14
Arts and Social Sciences	742	1,068	59
Economics and Public Administration	546	529	49
Business and Accounts	231	291	56
Islamic Studies	185	215	54
Law	55	67	55
Education	215	325	60
Home Science	0	107	100
Agriculture	102	59	37
Town Planning	19	5	21
Architecture	5	1	17
Survey (Land and Quantity)	44	6	12
Total	3,425	3,408	50

* Includes all universities except the Universiti Sains Malaysia, whose statistics were not available at the time of writing. Percentages have been rounded up or down.
Source: Ministry of Education, Higher Education Division, December 1992.

As in other countries, the higher the level of education, the fewer women participating. In Malaysia in 1990 women's representation decreased from 48% at the first degree to 28% at the doctoral level (see Table 6.8).

In areas of study, the student picture was reflected in the faculty. Relatively few women lecturers specialized in science. Of those who did, most were in biological sciences, chemistry, computer, and agriculture rather than inmathematics, physics, or engineering.[34] Thus the role models to be derived from women scientists themselves are still limited. Nevertheless, this situation has greatly improved since the 1970s.

Table 6.8 Enrollment and Male and Female Percentages in Malaysian Universities, 1990

Level of graduates	Enrollment Numbers (percentage)	
	M	F
Ph.D.	388 (72%)	154 (28%)
Master's	1,738 (66%)	905 (34%)
Postgraduate Diploma	674 (40%)	1,032 (60%)
First Degree	24,334 (52%)	22,197 (48%)
Diploma	4,867 (72%)	1,877 (28%)
Certificate	72 (67%)	36 (33%)
Nondegree Program	15 (50%)	15 (50%)
Total	32,088 (55%)	26,198 (45%)

Source: Ministry of Education, *Educational Statistics 1990*, Table 7, p. 5.

Various suggestions have been voiced on how to improve women's involvement in higher education. These include programs to enrich girls' interest in science-based subjects in secondary schools; career guidance to students about supply and demand in the labor market; and encouragement to female students from lecturers in male-dominated disciplines.

WOMEN'S ROLES IN NATIONAL DEVELOPMENT

National development in Malaysia essentially refers to development in the economic, political, and social spheres. Women's contribution to development can be considered in these three spheres.

Throughout the centuries a woman's primary role has been that of wife and homemakers, a role women still play. However, their arena has extended to the workplace. Education is one of the factors that have enabled women to enter the labor market. Research has shown education to have a positive effect on one's paid employment.

Other factors have also encouraged women to move forward. Various national development programs have increased the demand for educated female employees. The government has also been supportive by providing infrastructure such as schools and hostels, and by formulating policies in favor of women's employment. Currently the most comprehensive policy is the National Policy for Women, formulated in December 1989, which aims to bring about greater equality between males and females in access to resources and information, and to integrate more women into all aspects of national development.[35]

Women in Paid Employment

Women's economic role is shown in their labor force participation. Overall, women's labor share increased from 31% in 1970 to 35% in 1990, while men's correspondingly decreased. However, women's representation by industry is uneven, being light in "male" industries, such as mining and quarrying, electricity, gas and water, construction, and transport and communication, and slightly heavy in manufacturing (Table 6.9).

As Malaysia becomes industrialized, there has been a decreasing proportion of both men and women in primary industry over the last two decades and conversely an increase in secondary and tertiary industries (Table 6.10).

Apart from horizontal segregation, women are also vertically segregated. In service industries women cluster in manual jobs at the bottom, which require little education, or in clerical jobs, which require a secondary education. There are few women at the top.[36]

In professional and technical categories, teaching and nursing, now as in the past, are receptive to women. For example, in 1990 51% of all secondary teachers in Malaysia were women;[37] and 82% of female employees in government services were teachers, nurses, clerks, or junior administrators. Increased access to education has facilitated some women's entry into such professions as medicine, dentistry, law, tertiary teaching, accounting,

Table 6.9 Percentage Distribution of Employment by Sector and by Sex, 1970–1990

	1970		1980		1990	
Industry	M %	F %	M %	F %	M %	F %
Agriculture and Forestry	62.0	38.0	61.0	39.0	65.6	34.4
Mining and Quarrying	87.4	12.6	89.7	10.3	87.1	12.9
Manufacturing	71.9	28.1	59.9	40.1	53.6	46.4
Electricity, Gas, and Water	94.7	5.3	92.5	7.5	93.1	6.9
Construction	93.3	6.7	92.9	7.1	95.7	4.3
Wholesale and Retail Trade Hotels and Restaurants	81.1	18.2	70.7	29.3	61.4	38.6
Transport, Storage, and Communications	95.7	4.3	93.7	6.3	88.9	11.1
Finance, Insurance, Real Estate and Business Services	*	*	70.5	29.5	65.8	34.2
Community, Social, and Personal Services	71.1	28.9	70.6	29.4	62.1	37.9
Average	69.0	31.0	67.3	32.7	65.0	35.0

* Data not available.
Source: Federation of Malaysia, *Sixth Malaysia Plan 1991–1995*, p. 415.

and architecture. For example, by 1990 in the eight universities there were over 2,100 women faculty members, constituting about 40% of the faculty. Despite their increase in number, however, few women are in decision-making positions in education. The Universiti Kebangsaan Malaysia had 59 male professors and 185 male associate professors in 1993, but only five female professors and 53 female associate professors.[38] Similarly, while 51% of all secondary school teachers were female in 1990, only 15% of principals of teachers colleges at point G, the lowest point of the senior salary scale, were female.[39]

Women in Social Development

Education is also important for social and political development. Its main contribution to the social development of women is by helping them achieve literacy, and become aware of themselves as individuals, parents, and agents for social change. Statistics show that about 47% of women were literate in 1970, a figure which subsequently rose to 64% in 1980 and is projected to be higher in the future.[40] Education accelerates women's self-development as well as

Table 6.10 Percentages of Total Number of Male and Female Workers Employed in Primary, Secondary, and Tertiary Industries, 1970–1990

Industry	1970 M %	1970 F %	1980 M %	1980 F %	1990 M %	1990 F %
Agriculture and Forestry	49.6	67.9	37.5	49.3	28.9	28.2
Mining and Quarrying	2.3	0.7	1.4	0.3	0.7	0.2
Manufacturing	9.3	8.1	11.8	16.3	15.2	24.3
Electricity, Gas, and Water	1.0	0.1	0.2	0.1	0.9	0.1
Construction	3.1	0.5	6.4	1.0	8.7	0.7
Wholesale and Retail Trade, Hotels, and Restaurants	11.6	5.8	13.1	11.2	16.9	19.7
Transport, Storage, and Communications	5.0	0.5	5.0	0.7	5.9	1.5
Finance, Insurance, Real Estate, and Business Services	—	—	1.9	1.6	4.0	3.9
Community, Social, and Personal Services	18.1	16.4	22.7	19.5	18.8	21.4
Total	100.0	100.0	100.0	100.0	100.0	100.0

* Data not available.
Source: Federation of Malaysia, *Sixth Malaysia Plan 1991–1995*, p. 417.

the development of their families. Both formal and nonformal education programs attempt to imbue women with skills and concepts that enable them to cope with change. Education also fosters a positive self-concept in women and helps them plan and manage their own growth.

Apart from government-sponsored programs for women's enhancement, there exist numerous nongovernment organizations. The National Council for Women Organizations is an umbrella group comprising well over 60 constituent associations. It was formed in 1963 and has been working to remove gender inequalities.

Women's Participation in Politics

Education has pushed women to the forefront of Malaysian politics. Today women hold positions as leaders, planners, and party workers. Education gives them the ability and confidence to perform alongside men. Almost all of the women in Malaysian politics today are highly qualified and worked as professionals before taking up political positions. Today there are two full women ministers, three deputy ministers, and a number of members of parliament. The women ministers are Dato' Napsiah Omar, who heads the Ministry of National Unity and Community Development, and Dato' Seri Rafidah Aziz, of the Ministry of International Trade and Industry. The deputy ministers are in the Ministry of Public Enterprises, the Ministry of Transport, and the Ministry of Youth and Sports. Most have had a graduate education or have been trained in law, business, or accountancy.

As leaders, these women struggle to become the spokespersons for their sisters and to fight for equal pay, equal opportunities, and the implementation of policies aimed at enhancing the situation of women.

At a lower level, education has raised both men's and women's awareness of their rights to participate in different levels of public life and to assess the performance of government.

Problems and Issues

The new roles of women have revealed the dilemma they are caught in. Working women find themselves juggling the traditional role as homemakers and their workplace demands. For professional women, the new demands include geographical mobility and absence from home while on business trips, issuing orders to male subordinates, and socializing with male bosses. For working-class women, the balance between household work, long hours of labor on the assembly line or on plantations, and meager pay remains a great challenge.

The ways women cope with the dilemma vary. Professional women obtain domestic help from maids, who were once locally recruited. But as manufacturing recruits more and more women workers, the maids are now drawn from neighboring Indonesia and the Philippines. Among young couples without maids, there is a tendency for men to share some of the household chores. However, for low-paid women the double burden of home and work is extremely heavy. Organized childcare has released women's burden to some extent. In cities, nurseries and crèches are mostly fee-charging. Some companies have set up similar services, but the number is small, and low-income groups have little access to them. In rural areas there are no such services. Some women enlist the help of their neighbors at a small fee, and a few call on their in-laws.

Industrialization has caused a movement of rural women to urban areas. Such migration has brought social problems such as lack of accommodations and facilities, social adjustment, and, in the case of married women, childcare. The issue is to encourage women to continue working while ensuring that they face minimal social and personal problems. Furthermore, as most of the women are at the lower rung of the employment ladder, training and retraining for better prospects become necessary.

The emergence of women leaders and professionals in managerial and executive roles has brought much pride and raised hopes among women. However, the number of women in this category needs to be increased. At the same time they need to move strategically from marginal positions to the center of organizations. Only then can women define and clarify their goals, understand their specific leadership and organizational capabilities, alleviate barriers that they face from within and without, and work out strategies from their own perspective.

Education and training activities promise to provide answers to some of the above problems. The issues that most need to be addressed concern the workplace, conflict between women's traditional and modern roles, and leadership.

Conclusion

In Malaysia women have made many inroads into society. Education in particular plays a significant role in providing knowledge as well as in shaping attitudes to meet the needs of society.

But, as always, there is room for improvement. The country will be better served if more women are educated, especially in nontraditional areas like applied sciences and technology. Society should also give full recognition to the spectrum of women's efforts and regard them as equal partners of men in development. Only then can women continue to complement men's efforts in economic and political development as well as continuously better themselves and their families.

Notes

1. Department of Statistics Malaysia, cited in *Berita Harian* (a Malay daily), Kuala Lumpur, 24 December, 1992.

2. Federation of Malaysia, *Sixth Malaysia Plan 1991–1995* (Kuala Lumpur: National Printing Department, 1991):414.

3. See, e.g., unpublished reports of numerous reseach projects carried out by lecturers and students of Universiti Kebangsaan Malaysia (UKM) that specifically discuss the relationship between education and national development.

4. W. Makepeace, G. E. Brooke. and R. J. Braddel, *One Hundred Years of Singapore*, Vol. I (London: John Murray, 1921). Cited in Loo Lai May, *Women in Higher Education Institutions: A Survey of Female Students and Their Disciplines of Study at UKM* (Assignment for Bachelor of Arts degree, Faculty of Social Sciences and Humanities, UKM, Bangi, 1987):24 (in Bahasa Malay).

5. L. Wanita Manderson, *Politik dan Perubahan: Pergerakan Kaum Ibu UMNO, Malaysia, 1945–1973* (Women, Politics and Change: The Malaysian Women UMNO Movement, 1945–1973) (Kuala Lumpur: Fajar Bakti, 1981):29.

6. Ministry of Education, *Education in Malaysia* (Kuala Lumpur: Dewan Bahasa dan Pustaka, 1968):10–11.

7. A. G. Smith, *Report of the Committee on Malay Education* (Kuala Lumpur: Government Press, 1951):3.

8. Manderson, *Politik dan Perubahan,* p. 263, and Musa Daia, *Sejarah Perkembangan dan Persekolahan* (The History of Development and Schooling) (Kota Bahru: Pustaka Aman Press, 1976):202–203.

9. Federation of Malaya, *Education Act, 1961* (Kuala Lumpur: MDC Sdn. Bhd., 1988):20.

10. Ministry of Education, *Educational Statistics of Malaysia 1970.*

11. Ainon Muhammad, "Pengaruh Pendidikan Tinggi terhadap Nilai dan Kebebasan Wanita" (The Influence of Higher Education on Values and Women's Freedom) in: *Dewan Masyarakat,* August 1975 (Kuala Lumpur: Dewan Bahasa dan Pustaka):43–44.

12. Federation of Malaysia, *Second Malaysia Plan, 1971–1975* (Kuala Lumpur: Government Press, 1971):2–3.

13. Federation of Malaysia, *Rangka Rancangan Jangka Panjang Kedua 1991–2000* (The Second Outline Perspective Plan, 1991–2000) (Kuala Lumpur: National Printing Department, 1991):8–9.

14. Federation of Malaysia, *Sixth Malaysia Plan, 1991–1995,* op. cit., p. 11.

15. Ibid.

16. Ibid, p. 414.

17. Federation of Malaysia, National Policy for Women (Kuala Lumpur: National Printing Department, 1992):2.

18. Federation of Malaysia, *Sixth Malaysia Plan, 1991–1995,* op. cit., p. 170.

19. Federation of Malaysia, Department of Statistics, *General Report of the Population Census,* Vol. 1 (Kuala Lumpur,1983):91; and Ministry of Education, Educational Planning and Research Division, *Educational Statistics 1990* (Kuala Lumpur: Dewan Bahasa dan Pustaka, 1992):3, Table 4.

20. Ministry of Education, *Kajian Keciciran* (Dropout Study) (Kuala Lumpur: Government Printer, 1973):2–3.

21. Federation of Malaysia, Department of Statistics, General Report of the Population Census, Vol. 1 (Kuala Lumpur, 1983):91.

22. Ministry of Education, Educational Planning and Research Division, *Educational Statistics 1990,* op. cit., p. 4, Table 6.

23. Federation of Malaysia, *Report on Education for 1956* (Kuala Lumpur: Khee Meng Press, 1956):17.

24. Federation of Malaysia, *Sixth Malaysia Plan, 1991–1995,* op. cit., pp. 158, 169.

25. Federation of Malaysia, Department of Statistics, *Penyiasatan Tenaga Buruh Malaysia 1989–1990* (Report on Labour Force in Malaysia 1989–1990) (Kuala Lumpur, 1991):60.

26. Asiah Abu Samah, "Wanita dalam Pendidikan: Beberapa Isu dan Cabaran" (Women in Education: Issues and Challenges). A working paper for Malaysian Women Graduates Association, 1992:4.

27. Ministry of Education, *Educational Statistics, 1990,* op. cit., p. 3, Table 5; p. 5, Table 7.

28. Ibid.

29. Asiah Abu Samah, "Wanita dalam Pendidikan," op. cit.

30. Ministry of Education, *Educational Statistics 1990,* op. cit., Tables 2 and 6.

31. Ibid.

32. Ibid., p. 6, Table 10; p. 7, Table 11.

33. Fatimah Hamid Don, "Opportunities for Women in Education." Paper presented at the Seminar Peranan Wanita dalam Bidang-bidang Pelajaran Tinggi dan Implikasinya, at Universiti Malaya, Nov. 14–15, 1975; pp. 27–28.

34. Azizan Baharuddin, "Malay Women's Involvement in Science in the Universities in Malaysia." Paper presented at the conference on ASEAN Professional Women 1992, Universiti Teknologi Malaysia, Johor (Sept. 1992):18.

35. Federation of Malaysia, *Sixth Malaysia Plan 1991–1995*, op. cit., p. 413.

36. Federation of Malaysia, *Sixth Malaysia Plan*, op. cit., p. 418.

37. Ministry of Education, *Educational Statistics 1990*, op. cit., p. 8, Table 13.

38. Calculated from the calendars of all local universities and the Institute of Technology MARA, 1990, and Statistics from the Registrar's Office, Universiti Kebangsaan Malaysia, 1993.

39. Asiah Abu Samah, "Wanita dalam Pendidikan: Beberapa Isu dan Cabaran," op. cit., p. 21.

40. Department of Statistics, Malaysia, *General Report of the Population Census*, Vol. 1, 1983, pp. 102.

7 SINGAPORE

Guat Tin Low

INTRODUCTION

In her book *A Room of One's Own,* Virginia Woolf[1] questioned a social system that deprived women of an education, a vocation, and a sense of mission. Now, some 65 years after its publication, great strides have been made, not only in Woolf's country, England, but even in Asia, where women were often considered second-class citizens. In Singapore women have made rapid progress in all of Woolf's three respects. Increasingly, more women have availed themselves of tertiary education, and according to data, women in Singapore have made inroads into traditionally male-dominated occupations such as law.

However, what Singapore is today is a far cry from what it was in the 1800s and even in the early 1900s. In the early years Singapore was a man's world. The imbalance of the male-female ratio in its population—mostly male immigrants—was redressed only in the 1960s. In 1834 there were 20,000 males and only 6,000 females in Singapore, and the male-female ratio was 3.3/1. By 1990 the ratio had fallen to 1.024/1.[2]

It was a male-dominated society, in which social pressure and traditional attitudes about sex-roles required that females play a subordinate and submissive role. As males were traditionally economic providers, any educational opportunties were first offered to them. The education of girls was neglected although not nonexistent. In fact, education for females in Singapore was first established in the mid-nineteenth century with the founding of its first girls' school in 1842. The schools were started not merely to educate girls but often to prevent them from going astray. Raffles Girls' School, established in 1844, had as its objective "sheltering the girls from the many temptations to which they appeared to be exposed."[3] Whatever the intentions, education for girls was a potent force not only in raising the economic status of females by giving them the necessary skills but also in getting them to accept and internalize attitudes that were essential for them to survive in the world of work away from their homes.

This chapter starts with a historical sketch of education in Singapore. It will then examine female participation in the education of girls in general and in tertiary education in particular. Finally, it will discuss the impact of education and other possible factors, notably Singapore's development experience, on the pattern of labor force participation of females.

A Historical Sketch

Commercial reasons drew the British to Singapore. In 1819 Stamford Raffles secured Singapore as a British trading post and Singapore remained a Crown Colony until 1959. She became a part of Malaysia in 1963, only to be separated from that country in 1965. Since then Singapore has remained an independent republic. For a nation of three million people with a total area of only 620 square kilometers with no natural resources whatsoever, she has done very well indeed. Today she is considered one of the four Asian dragons, with a per capita income second only to Japan in Asia.

After the arrival of the British, immigrants from China, India, and other countries also came. These immigrants stayed for years, and when they had made their fortunes most returned to their homelands.

Raffles saw a need to educate the populace, for to him "(E)ducation must keep pace with commerce, in order that its benefits may be ensured and its evils avoided."[4] This led to his attempts to encourage the community as well as mission bodies to set up schools. Thus individual Chinese, Indian, and Malay businessmen set up schools to cater to their community's needs. As a result, vernacular schools flourished in the eighteenth and early nineteenth centuries. However, many schools appeared for a while and quietly disappeared with the departure or death of their founders. In a "floating" population, the phenomenon of "floating" schools was not uncommon.[5] A second type of education—i.e., the Western type, where English was the medium of instruction—was set up mainly by missionaries. Thus education was left very largely in the hands of missionaries and various local communities.

The history of education in Singapore has been characterized by the word *compartmentalization*. As T.R. Doraisamy describes it, "The compartmentalization of education—education in Christian mission schools . . ., education through the medium of Chinese, Tamil, English and Malay, education for boys and education for girls—was quite distinct and each educational institution was a separate entity."[6] Besides differences in the medium of instruction, the curricula differed too. Textbooks were imported from the immigrants' home countries.

The educational system in Singapore today is just the opposite of compartmentalization and ethnic community sponsorship. There is centralized control, and all pupils are exposed to a common curriculum. In the 1960s and 1970s, education was used as a device to achieve national cohesion. Numerous policies were introduced, one of the most important being biligualism, which became compulsory for all students in 1966. The rationale was that if all students were proficient in a second language, it would help break down communication and racial barriers. Singapore is a multiracial society. The four main groups are Chinese (77.7%), Malays (14.1%), Indians (7.1%), and all others not accounted for in the above categories (1.1%).[7] Today all schools use English as the medium of instruction and students study their mother tongue as a second language. The policy of bilingualism has become a cornerstone of the educational system.

Control of schools is centralized, though attempts are currently being made to give more autonomy to school principals. Education in Singapore is not compulsory. Children who opt for education, and almost all do, attend six years of primary schooling, followed by four to five years of secondary schooling. (Slower students take five years to complete their secondary education.) All receive at least ten years of basic education and most go on to the polytechnics, junior colleges, or vocational institutes. Everyone who qualifies will be able to continue studying. If education today is marked by a drive toward excellence and equal opportunity for all, what was it like for girls in the early days?

GIRLS' AND WOMENS' EDUCATION
Primary and Secondary Education

In 1860 there were three girls' schools in Singapore. Enrollment in these schools was small and restricted to a few girls from the privileged class or to those who needed financial help. The latter were mostly girls from homes connected to the Christian church. By 1941 there were 31 government and partially government subsidized English schools, and slightly more than a third of the school population was girls. By 1952 almost half of the secondary school population was female,[8] and in 1980 females constituted 51% (see Table 7.1).

Before reaching near parity in education for males and females—especially at primary and secondary levels—by the 1980s, the education of girls lagged behind that of boys. The literacy rates of females and males can be taken as an indication of this. (In Singapore literacy is defined as "the ability to read with understanding a newspaper in a specified language."[9]) In 1957, out of every thousand men 686 were literate, compared

Table 7.1 Female Enrollment in Educational Institutions, 1960–1991

Educational Institutions	1960			1970			1980			1991		
	Total	Females	% of total	Total	Females	% of total	Total	Females	% of total	Total	Females	% of total
Primary	290,576	128,104	44.1	363,518	169,693	46.7	296,608	140,087	47.2	260,286	123,292	47.4
Secondary Schools and Junior Colleges	58,057	22,669	39.0	145,740	70,690	48.5	170,316	87,731	51.5	185,713	92,963	50.05
Technical/Vocational and Economic Dev. Board's Institutes	1,257	516	41.1	3,039	251	8.3	12,543	2,414	19.2	28,871	6,956	24.1
Technical Colleges/Industrial Training Centers	—ª	—	—	1,688	75	4.4	11,105	2,494	22.5	—	—	—
*University of Singapore/NUS	1,444	355	24.6	4,320	1,438	33.3	8,634	3,926	45.5	14,597	7,972	54.6
Nanyang University	1,861	378	20.3	2,310	918	39.7	—	—	—	—	—	—
**Nanyang Technological Institute/N.T.U.	—	—	—	—	—	—	—	—	—	11,138	4,786	43
Singapore Polytechnic	2,342	55	2.3	4,094	217	5.3	8,274	1,712	20.7	16,566	5,404	32.6
***Ngee Ann Technical College/Polytechnic	—	—	—	598	161	26.9	2,831	782	27.6	14,278	5,668	39.7
Teachers Training College/Institute of Education/National Institute of Education	2,327	1,202	51.7	2,001	1,390	69.5	2,328	1,977	84.9	2,012	1,597	79.4
Temasek Polytechnic	—	—	—	—	—	—	—	—	—	1,468	1,003	68.3
Singapore Institute of Management	—	—	—	—	—	—	—	—	—	5,455	2,135	39.1

Sources: *Yearbook of Statistics Singapore*, 1970, 1980, 1991; *1960 Ministry of Education Annual Report*; Singapore Institute of Management–data from Public Relations Office; National University of Singapore–data from Public Relations Office; *Economic and Social Statistics Singapore, 1960–1982*.

* The University of Singapore and Nanyang University were merged in 1980 to form the National University of Singapore.
** Nanyang Technological Institute and the Institute of Education were merged in 1992 to form the Nanyang Technological University and the National Institute of Education. (Teachers Training College, established in 1950, became the Institute of Education in 1973.)
*** Ngee Ann Polytechnic was known as Ngee Ann Technical College prior to 1982.
ª Nonexisting (not begun or closed)

with only 336 in the case of women. The gap has narrowed significantly over the decades, reaching 955 to 844 in 1990 (Table 7.2). These data show that in the early days only sons were sent to schools. With expansion in education, younger generations of women have been catching up. The illiteracy rate among females aged 15–24 decreased from 15.5% in 1970 to 3.8% in 1990.

Table 7.2 Male-Female Literacy Rate (per thousand), 1957–1990

	1957	1970	1980	1990
Male literacy rate	686	800	915	955
Female literacy rate	336	600	762	844

Source: *Census of Population, Singapore 1957, 1970, 1980, 1990.*

This closing of the gap can be attributed to the rapid industrialization of Singapore. With industrial growth came greater occupational opportunities and a shortage of manpower, which in turn led to a realization of the need to maximize the potentials of females. In 1975 the then Prime Minister of Singapore said in a speech to women at the National Trade Union Congress seminar, "Societies which do not educate and use half their potential because they are women are those which will be worse off . . . we cannot not educate and use the energy and ability of our women."[10] From the days of Raffles College to this day, the need to provide education for Singapore's citizens has always been linked to productivity. Education is seen more as a national need than a citizen's right. This point will be discussed in greater detail later in this chapter.

Tertiary Education

Tertiary education started in 1905 with the establishment of King Edward VII College of Medicine. This was followed in 1928 by Raffles College for the study of arts and science. To meet the growing demand for teachers, the Teachers' Training College was established in 1950, and to provide for those educated in the Chinese medium, the Chinese community set up Nanyang University in 1956. The Singapore Polytechnic and the Ngee Ann Technical College, set up in 1954 and 1963 respectively, produced technicians and other diploma holders. The aim was to produce expertise to speed up the industrialization program. The provision of education was once again shown to be closely tied to economic development and productivity.

Table 7.3 Female Students Admitted to Institutions of Higher Learning by Course, 1960–1992

Institution and Fields of Study	1960				1970				1980				1991/2			
	Total Enrolled	Females Enrolled	% of Females to Total Enrollment	% of Females to Total Female Enrollment	Total Enrolled	Females Enrolled	% of Females to Total Enrollment	% of Females to Total Female Enrollment	Total Enrolled	Females Enrolled	% of Females to Total Enrollment	% of Females to Total Female Enrollment	Total Enrolled	Females Enrolled	% of Females to Total Enrollment	% of Females to Total Female Enrollment
Singapore University/NUS	434	136	31.3	100.0	1,300	520	40	100.0	3,074	1,554	50.1	100.0	4,437	2,395	53.9	100.0
Arts and Social Science	116	65	56.0	47.8	216	182	84.3	35.0	674	485	71.9	31.2	1,388	961	69.2	40.1
Science (including pharmacy)	100	29	29.0	21.3	165	93	56.4	17.9	609	392	64.4	25.2	940	599	63.7	25.0
Medicine	84	8	9.5	5.9	118	37	31.4	7.1	170	65	38.2	4.2	152	53	34.9	2.2
Dentistry	38	11	28.9	8.1	39	8	20.5	1.5	38	18	47.4	1.2	35	7	20.0	0.3
Law	96	23	23.9	16.9	89	42	47.2	8.1	120	61	50.8	3.9	203	103	50.7	4.3
Accountancy and Business Administration	*	—	—	—	262	133	50.8	25.6	656	424	64.6	27.3	559	275	49.2	11.5
Architecture and Building	—	—	—	—	74	15	20.3	2.9	205	63	30.7	4.1	273	153	56.0	6.4
Engineering	—	—	—	—	337	10	2.9	1.9	602	46	7.6	2.9	436	66	15.1	2.8
Computer Science	—	—	—	—	—	—	—	—	—	—	—	—	451	178	39.5	7.4
Nanyang University	651	137	21.04	100.0	645	335	51.9	100.0	—	—	—	—	—	—	—	—
Nanyang Technological Institute/NTU													3,028	1,197	39.5	100.0
Engineering													1,254	142	11.3	11.9
Accountancy													704	391	55.5	32.7
Business													613	471	76.8	39.3
Computer Technology													289	73	25.3	6.1
Materials Engineering													49	14	28.6	1.2
Arts with Diploma in Education													89	82	92.1	6.9
Science with Diploma in Education													30	24	80.0	2.0
Teachers Training College/Institute of Education/MIE	890	433	48.3	100.0	1,480	1,003	67.8	100.0	875	748	85.5	100.0	1,077	888	82.5	100.0

Table 7.3 (continued) Female Students Admitted to Institutions of Higher Learning by Course, 1960–1992

Institution and Fields of Study	1960			1970				1980				1991/2			
	Total Enrolled	Females Enrolled	% of Females to Total Enrollment	Total Enrolled	Females Enrolled	% of Females to Total Enrollment	% of Females to Total Female Enrollment	Total Enrolled	Females Enrolled	% of Females to Total Enrollment	% of Females to Total Female Enrollment	Total Enrolled	Females Enrolled	% of Females to Total Enrollment	% of Females to Total Female Enrollment
Singapore Polytechnic**	874	51	5.8	1,679	121	7.2	100.0	3,479	736	21.1	100.0	6,142	2,180	35.5	100.0
Engineering				1,392	109	7.8	90.0	2,847	531	18.7	72.1	4,496	1,199	26.6	55.0
Architecture and Building				185	12	6.5	9.9	537	205	38.1	27.9	365	210	57.5	9.6
Nautical Engineering				102	0	0	0	95	0	0	0.0	173	20	11.6	0.9
Business Studies												810	580	71.6	26.6
Computer												298	171	57.4	7.8
Ngee Ann Technical College/Ngee Ann Polytechnic**				481	116	24.1	100.0	1,112	379	34.1	100.0	5,075	2,157	42.5	100.0
Engineering								782	163	20.8	43.0	3,398	816	24.0	37.8
Business Studies and Accountancy								330	216	65.5	56.9	1,268	1,021	80.5	47.3
Computer Studies												304	232	76.3	10.8
Mass Communication												105	88	83.8	4.1
Temasek Polytechnic												1,512	1,037	68.6	100.0
Business												849	648	76.3	62.5
Design												362	245	67.7	23.6
Science and Technology												301	144	47.8	13.9
Singapore Institute of Management												3,646	1,506	41.3	100.0

* — = nonexisting (not begun or closed).
** Includes part-time students.

Sources:
Economic and Social Statistics Singapore 1960–1982.
National University of Singapore -- data from Public Relations Office.
Yearbook of Statistics 1980, 1991.
Singapore Institute of Management -- data from Public Relations Office.

In the main, female enrollment in tertiary institutions, in particular at the National University of Singapore (NUS), has been on the increase; by 1991 there were more female (54.6%) than male students in NUS. In the mid-1970s about 9% of a primary I cohort went to a tertiary institution and by the mid-1980s the percentage trebled to 27%.[11] Females appear to have benefited more from the general expansion than males. Table 7.1 shows a very encouraging trend. In every decade the enrollment of females in every tertiary institution has been on the increase. This is due to both expansion in educational provision and a successful family-planning policy in the 1970s that asked couples to stop at two children. As family size shrinks, opportunities for daughters to be sent to tertiary institutions increase. When family size was larger, daughters were not sent to tertiary institutions until the education of sons was well taken care of. The message to Singaporeans in the 1970s was "boy or girl, two is enough." Underlying this is the message that girls are just as good as boys.

While enrollment of females in tertiary institutions has increased over the years, an examination into their fields of study reflects biases in their choice of courses. Table 7.3 shows that in the academic year 1991/2 females constituted 35.5% of the students admitted to the Singapore Polytechnic and 82.5% of those in the National Institute of Education. Thus a large majority of females were being trained to be teachers. And in the National University of Singapore a high proportion of females concentrate in "feminine" disciplines like arts and social sciences.

It is noteworthy that, in 1960, 28.9% and 23.9% respectively of the students in dentistry and law were females. Even as far back as 30 years ago females were making inroads into these two male-dominated professions. However, the university had only five faculties then (Table 7.3), and so there was really no other choice for females who wanted a profession, not just a degree, in the 1960s. In law there has been an even greater female increase through the years, and at present female lawyers represent 39% of the legal profession. However, female lawyers are mainly in conveyancing. Only among the younger women lawyers today are many doing litigation work.

An interesting aspect is the number of females who were admitted to accountancy and business studies in the various institutions of learning. These two courses are dominated by females in every tertiary institution. Here again it could be because of limited choice and the less gender-biased nature of accountancy.

Although there is an increase in the number of females admitted to engineering in every institution, most female students still avoid it. There is little published knowledge on how social factors such as peer/parental pressure discourage women from becoming engineers.

While females tend to shy away from engineering and other technical courses offered by the Polytechnics and the Nanyang Technological University, signs of changing trends have emerged. Today female enrollment in these tertiary institutions, in particular the Singapore Polytechnic, has increased by leaps and bounds. In 1960 only 2.3% of the enrollment in that institution was female and in 1970 only 5.3%. By 1991 the figure had increased to 32.6%. While females tend to concentrate in more feminine courses such as business administration and computer studies, a significant percentage (23.3%) graduated in the early 1990s with engineering diplomas from the polytechnics.[12]

The increase in female enrollment at the Singapore Polytechnic was in part a response to the encouragement given by the Ministry of Education to girls to enroll in technical courses. In 1973 the Ministry of Education circulated a Technical Education Guidance Pamphlet, which encouraged girls to enroll in technical education. It states:

> Many people believe that technical education is not suitable for girls. This is only true if ... career ... calls for ... strenous physical effort. In the engineering field, the most important areas of activities are research, design and development, for which imagination, intelligence and creativity are required, not physical strength ... many industries ... provide girls with worthwhile careers.[13]

Through such encouragement, plus careers exhibitions and job guidance, which took place both nationwide and in schools, the interest of female students in male-dominated fields increased. Similar change can be observed in other tertiary institutions (Table 7.3).

On the other hand, the feminization of teaching meant that the enrollment of females in the Institute of Education and today The National Institute of Education increased from 51.7% in 1960 to 84.9% and 79.4% in 1980 and 1991 respectively (Table 7.1). The slight drop of 5.5% in the 1990s may be attributed to the advertising campaign of the Ministry of Education to encourage more males to join the teaching profession. Approximately 45% of secondary schools and junior colleges and 48% of primary schools in Singapore are headed by women. These figures are very encouraging for women compared with those from the United States and other Western countries. Next to Israel,[14] Singapore has one of the highest proportions of female educational administrators.

Adult and Nonformal Education

Besides the established institutions Singapore has numerous private schools/ colleges and foreign universities offering distance learning and other part-time diploma/degree courses. Working adults can register to study law, accountancy, business administration, computer science, and a host of other subjects leading to diplomas or degrees.

The Singapore Institute of Management (SIM), a privately run college, has become a well-established management-development institute offering certificates, diplomas, and undergraduate and postgraduate courses with degrees conferred by foreign universities. In 1992 the Singapore government commissioned SIM to run an Open University program aimed at giving working adults another chance to study for a degree. The government's goal of encouraging those who missed out earlier is evident. For example, in *The Next Lap* it is written that "continuing education through part-time study or training will remain a feature of our education system . . . we will also use the media to offer a wide range of options for self-access learning."[15] The vision of the present government is to maximize the potential of everyone, and to that end they have promised to provide opportunities for lifelong learning.

In this spirit numerous government policies were implemented in the 1980s, all of which aimed at upgrading the work force. Numerous adult education programs were introduced. Some were initiated to address the specific problems of married workers, including videotapes that enabled busy females to study at home.

A recent survey conducted by the National Productivity Board noted that the training participation rate among female workers in Singapore is slightly higher than that of males. In 1991, 44% percent of female workers attended on-the-job training compared to 40% of males. Off-the-job training saw 32% of female and 30% of male workers going on for further training.[16]

The government does not make special allowances for females to undergo training but does offer opportunities for training to all, and motivated females in the last decade have benefited from the numerous training programs. In fact Low[17] found that among educational administrators significantly more female than male administrators attended in-service courses to upgrade and update themselves. Females seem to take every available opportunity to become better equipped for the job.

What drives the government to provide such educational opportunities for all its citizens? Why was there a need to help maximize the potential of each citizen? The reason is that Singapore has no natural resources, and she depends on the one resource she has—people. To the government, the way to utilize and maximize that resource is through education. Back in 1966 the then Minister of Education said, "Singapore's national wealth lies in our human resources, and our human potentials must therefore be developed to the fullest possible extent. An educated and enlightened population is our guarantee for a prosperous future."[18] In 1986 the Minister of State for Trade and Industry and Defense, a son of former Prime Minister Lee Kuan Yew, reconfirmed the government's faith in education when he said, "Akin to infrastructure, in being a prerequisite for growth and doing business, is an educated population... The basic policy of the Singapore government to each individual must be to educate him to his full potentials. This is the way to make the most of our only resource-people... capitalize on a limited talent pool... by making sure that our people are valuable individuals, able to do skilled and rewarding jobs...."[19]

Because of this belief Singapore has a history of relatively generous spending on eduction, skills training, and research and development. In 1993, 19.9% of the Republic's budget was spent on education. This is second only to the budget allocated to defense.[20] The long-term plan is to nurture Singapore as a hub city servicing neighboring countries. As such it must offer top products and services with the best infrastructure. The goal is to become a business hub of the Asia Pacific.[21] With such visions and the capacity to plan long term, it is no wonder that the education of Singapore's people is given top priority.

Thus the government plays a major part in education whether it is for the school-aged or for workers who need to be retrained or upgraded. Singapore sees that her future lies in the training and retraining of her work force to meet changing needs. Singapore has moved from labor-intensive industries to skill- and knowledge-intensive industries and services, and females in Singapore, like males, are seen as human capital. Having received the same basic educationas males, females are encouraged to contribute actively to the labor force.

LABOR FORCE PARTICIPATION OF WOMEN

Back in the early 1970s the then Prime Minister said, "... in case we reach the 'cut off' point for work permits (for foreigners particularly Malaysians, to come to work in Singapore), may I suggest we start planning now how we can employ our young women workers? They are under-utilized."[22] Since then the number of females participating in the labor force has increased about fourfold, from 153,612 to 606,521, between 1970 and 1991. In 1970 females constituted 24% of those employed, and by 1991, the rate was 40% (Table 7.4).

In the main this is because of a few factors, one of which could be increased educational opportunities, but others of more importance are the measures taken by the government. The highly successful family-planning program had far-reaching consequences for females. Not only were married women freed from the extended period of child bearing, but also daughters became more valuable. Further, crèches were built in all housing estates; subsidies were given for childcare; companies were encouraged to provide childcare facilites; factories were built near housing estates; and in recent years good tax relief was given for working professional mothers. The number of childcare centers increased from 25 in 1981 to 290 in 1992, and the number of places available increased from 1,407 in 1981 to 19,711 in 1992.[23] Yet another factor is the presence of foreign maids. Currently, there are 65,000 foreign maids working in Singapore homes. The legal availability of foreign maids has relieved many professional females of childcare and other household chores and enabled them to carry on with their professions. However, these government measures would not have been necessary if not for the economic development needs of Singapore. Labor-intensive industries set up in the 1960s and 1970s and the full-employment situation of male labor meant that the only pool available was female labor, hence the deliberate and intensive effort by the government to induce females to take on the new role of paid worker. Thus, according to Lim, "social structural changes in the economy and technological development have eliminated the biological-cultural factors which earlier limited women's role in direct production."[24]

The labor force participation rate of females correlates positively with the amount of schooling. For instance, in 1990, 91% of females with tertiary education participated in the labor force, compared to 77% of those with primary education, 64% of those who did not complete primary education, and 43% of those with no formal education.[25] Higher education especially facilitates women's entry into the job market. With a higher education, females command better pay and are able to employ maids to take care of the home.

While the 1970s saw multinational corporations setting up labor-intensive industries in Singapore, the 1990s see the shift away from this to skill- and knowledge-intensive industries. Females employed in the 1990s concentrated in four sectors, namely, financing, insurance, real estate, and business services; community, social, and personal services; manufacturing; and commerce. In absolute numbers most females concentrated in the manufacturing sector. The rapid industrializaton in the 1960s saw an influx of females into the manufacturing sector, from 12,298 in 1957 to 48,121 in 1970, and by 1991 the figure stood at 189,366. This accounts for 44.1% of all workers in this sector. All together, 31.2% of all females in the labor force are

Table 7.4 Employed Women Aged 15 Years and Over By Industry, 1957–1991

Industry	1957				1970				1980				1991			
	Total	Females	% of Females to Total	% of Females to Total Female	Total	Females	% of Females to Total	% of Females to Total Female	Total	Females	% of Females to Total	% of Females to Total Female	Total	Females	% of Females to Total	% of Females to Total Female
Total: All Industry	471,918	84,210	17.8	100.0	650,892	153,612	23.6	100.0	1,068,932	373,913	34.9	100.0	1,524,315	606,521	39.8	100.0
Manufacturing	66,754	12,298	18.4	14.6	143,100	48,121	33.6	31.3	312,641	143,860	46.0	38.5	429,612	189,366	44.1	31.2
Construction	24,628	1,761	7.2	2.1	43,126	2,817	6.5	1.8	58,141	5,252	9.0	1.4	98,981	8,626	8.7	1.4
Commerce	121,533	12,102	10.0	14.4	152,910	28,986	18.9	18.9	244,696	86,131	35.2	23.0	345,339	137,404	39.8	22.7
Transport, Storage and Communication	50,347	1,112	2.2	1.3	79,041	3,943	5.0	2.6	122,420	20,760	16.9	5.6	152,931	34,768	22.7	5.7
Financing, Insurance, Real Estate, and Business Services	—	—	—	—	23,071	5,305	22.9	3.5	79,067	37,134	46.7	9.9	163,341	80,208	49.1	13.2
Community, Social, and Personal Services	161,280	42,805	26.5	50.8	177,022	58,843	33.2	38.3	222,783	75,689	33.9	20.2	322,033	154,247	47.9	25.4
Agriculture and Fishing	40,151	13,867	34.5	16.5	22,458	4,796	21.4	3.1	14,108	3,522	24.9	0.9	—	—	—	—
Mining and Quarrying	1,601	165	10.3	0.2	2,168	205	9.5	0.1	1,606	309	19.2	0.1	—	—	—	—
Electricity, Gas and Water	5,624	100	1.8	0.1	7,615	533	7.0	0.4	9,639	1,071	11.1	0.3	—	—	—	—
Others	—	—	—	—	381	63	16.5	0.04	3,831	185	4.8	0.04	12,077	1,901	15.7	0.3

Sources:
Census of Population 1957, 1970.
Singapore Yearbook of Labour Statistics, 1980, 1991.

employed in this sector (Table 7.4). However, females accounted for 49.1% of all workers in the financial insurance and business services sector. Females are very underrepresented, at 15.7%, in administrative and managerial positions.

The number of females in clerical and related areas has increased by substantial numbers, from 4,991 in 1957 to 168,049 in 1991 (Table 7.5). What remains consistent over the decades is the large number of females who are involved in production as operators or laborers. In 1957 the number was 21,093, which doubled in 1970 and nearly trebled in 1980. Jobs in this category are mainly those on the factory floor and the pay is low. Females involved in this work are mostly those who have had only a primary education.

Although the number of females in the professions, technical and related workers had increased from 8,287 in 1957 to 105,999 in 1991 and females constituted 40.3% of all workers in this group, a closer examination reveals that females were the majority in teaching and nursing, followed by accountancy, journalism, and social work. The education they received enabled them to take on these professions. Of the five categories of work listed, only nursing and teaching in primary schools do not require a university degree; the others require three to four years of tertiary education. The higher degree of skill acquisition and educational attainment allowed females successful entry into the professions. However, while females dominate teaching in numbers, they do not in power.

There are encouraging indications of females venturing into new areas such as engineering, and this could be for a number of reasons. First, the technological advancements and innovation reduced the requirement of physical effort to perform the tasks. Second, changes have taken place in work methods. Finally there is, as stated previously, a great demand for labor, and females have made good use of the educational/training opportunities available to qualify them for skilled work.

Besides the drift of females into traditionally male occupations, within the groups of occupations there has also been diversification. For instance, Census Report 1980 shows that within the category of professional, technical, and related workers, women used to fill mainly nursing and teaching categories; today an increasing proportion of women are doctors, lawyers, and accountants.[26] The availability of part-time training, easier access, and greater availability of educational and training facilities have given females greater occupational mobility.

While these movements are extremely encouraging, females are still concentrated in the lower rungs of the professions. They also earn less than

Table 7.5 Employed Females Aged 15 Years and Over By Occupation, 1957-1991

Occupation	1957				1970				1980				1991			
	Total	Females	% of Females to Total	% of Females to Total Female	Total	Females	% of Females to Total	% of Females to Total Female	Total	Females	% of Females to Total	% of Females to Total Female	Total	Females	% of Females to Total	% of Females to Total Female
	471,918	84,210	18.0	100.0	650,892	153,612	23.6	100.0	1,068,932	373,913	34.9	100.0	1,524,315	606,521	39.8	100.0
Professional, Technical and related workers	22,689	8,287	36.5	9.6	55,899	21,818	39.0	14.2	93,380	36,372	38.9	9.7	262,908	105,999	40.3	17.5
Administrative and Executive managerial workers	8,891	340	3.8	0.4	11,344	645	5.7	0.4	51,633	7,311	14.2	1.9	137,434	21,580	15.7	3.6
Clerical and related workers	49,181	4,991	10.1	5.8	84,218	26,029	30.9	16.9	158,236	99,188	62.7	26.5	225,479	168,049	74.5	27.7
Sales workers	86,320	8,630	10.0	10.2	105,558	16,433	15.6	10.7	155,517	45,228	29.1	12.1	215,654	87,958	40.8	14.5
Service workers	80,912	30,206	37.3	35.9	88,812	35,884	40.4	23.7	114,965	50,212	43.7	13.4	(Sales and Service workers combined)			
Agricultural, animal husbandry, and Forestry workers. Fisherman and hunters	37,113	10,057	27.1	11.9	26,943	4,950	1.8	3.2	18,721	4,284	22.9	1.1	2,807	292	10.4	0.1
Production and related workers, Transport Equipment operators and laborers	147,758	21,093	14.3	25.0	254,987	47,412	18.6	30.9	415,125	130,350	31.4	34.9	616,434	221,941	36.0	36.6
Workers not classifiable by occupation	—	—	—	—	23,131	441	1.9	0.3	61,354	968	1.6	0.3	63,600	702	1.1	0.1
Mining and Quarrying	66	3	4.5	0.003												
Transport and communication	38,988	603	1.5	0.7												

Source:
Census of Population 1957, 1970.
Singapore Yearbook of Labour Statistics, 1980, 1991.

men in the same occupations. For example females in professional and technical occupations earn 63% of what their male counterparts earn, while the comparable figure for those in administration and managerial positions is 55%.[27] In 1991 female managers and professionals working on the same job as males received 75% to 80% of men's wages; technical workers received 90%, and clerical, sales, and unskilled workers about 85%.[28]

The conducive factors mentioned above have had a positive impact on the pattern of female age-specific labor force participation. Table 7.6 reveals that whereas in 1957 females tended to drop out of the labor force in the 25–34 age group, presumably to start and care for their families, in 1991 a majority of that group (75.6%) remained active in the labor force. The 1991 figures show that increasingly more females were active in the labor force in every age group except those 65 and above. In part this could be linked to the many schemes and program introduced by the ruling party to increase female participation in the labor force. Females in the civil service were given very favorable terms of employment, including 56 days paid maternity leave for the first two children, after which they could apply for four years no-pay leave to look after their children (i.e., the job is kept for them). They are also allowed five days of paid leave to take care of their child each time their child becomes sick.

Conclusion

The impressive movement of females from their homes to the workplace is an index of the change that has taken place in Singapore. The obstacle to equal participation—that of marriage and childrearing—is slowly giving way as crèches, childcare centers and kindergartens are being established at a phenomenal rate. The close links between years of formal education, on-the-job training, and upgrading of workers' skills and participation rate could have encouraged present policies such as the Skills Development Fund, which requires employers to pay 1% of the salary of all workers earning less than S$750 per month into the fund. Employees can then apply for funding to enroll in courses to upgrade their skills or level of education.

With parity of education achieved at all levels, Eng Soo Peck has written: "with increasing consciousness of the importance of women's contribution to the economy, with deliberate government encouragement and intervention to increase women's participation in all spheres of life, women's role, whether it be in the economy, social or political arenas, will assume greater significance vis-a-vis man's roles in these spheres."[29] The changes that have taken place thus far will proceed with greater momentum and transform further social relationships, attitudes and norms.

Table 7.6 Age-Sex-Specific Labor Force Participation Rates, 1957, 1970, 1980, 1991

Age Group (in years)	1957			1970			1980			1991*		
	Total	Males	Females	Total	Males	Females	Total	Males	Females	Total	Males	Females
Persons 15 yrs and over	57.0	87.6	21.6	56.5	82.3	29.5	63.2	81.5	44.3	64.8	79.8	50.5
15-19	42.0	59.4	23.4	49.5	55.7	43.0	49.1	47.5	50.7	30.4	31.1	29.8
20-24	58.6	92.3	22.9	73.5	92.9	53.6	86.1	93.4	78.4	82.9	83.1	82.6
25-29	60.1	98.0	16.5	64.5	98.0	30.8	78.3	97.2	58.7	86.0	97.0	75.6
30-34	62.6	98.6	17.5	60.6	98.3	22.7	71.5	97.9	44.2	79.8	98.7	61.9
35-39	64.5	98.5	20.8	60.2	98.4	19.3	68.0	98.0	37.1	77.5	99.1	56.0
40-44	66.8	98.0	26.3	60.8	98.1	17.8	65.8	97.6	33.2	75.9	98.4	54.2
45-49	67.9	97.0	30.1	60.0	96.2	17.5	61.8	95.7	26.5	70.3	96.5	46.2
50-54	65.4	93.5	28.8	55.0	88.1	17.5	56.3	89.6	20.4	63.2	92.5	34.1
55-59	57.9	85.1	24.7	46.2	73.9	16.2	43.6	70.7	14.5	46.3	71.0	21.2
60-64	41.8	66.9	17.1	35.0	55.6	13.4	31.9	52.5	11.3	29.7	46.9	12.3
65-69	27.7	49.7	25.3	25.3	41.2	9.8	23.5	38.6	9.5	11.0	19.8	4.1
70-74	14.9	30.9	4.7	14.5	25.8	5.7	15.0	25.1	6.2	—	—	—
75 and over	6.9	17.4	2.1	6.3	14.4	2.1	6.6	13.3	2.5	—	—	—

1. Age-sex-specific labor force participation rate: Percentage of economically active persons to the total population in the same age group and sex.
* 65 and over

Sources:
Census of Population 1957, 1970, 1980.
Singapore Yearbook of Labour Statistics, 1991.

But this trend may not continue. There is already a reversion among employers toward hiring males. There seems to be a concern in some quarters that certain professions may end up having too many females. A positive discrimination toward hiring and even admitting more male members into certain professional courses in the university may be taking place. Government policies may have changed again. While the emphasis in the past was on getting females into the work force, the emphasis in the 1980s and 1990s seems to be on getting females "matched" and then encouraging them to have children. In a 1994 address to a business conference held in Sydney, Australia, Lee Kuan Yew, former Prime Minister of Singapore, said that he regrets giving Singapore females equal opportunities in education and employment rights. He noted that this has in fact made it very difficult for women to find husbands. He said: "The Asian male does not like to have a wife who is seen to be his equal at work, who may be earning as much if not more than he does. . . . That is an enormous loss of face." He said that when his government took office they were "young, ignorant and idealistic." Today he says he favors the Japanese system, in which many "attractive and intelligent young ladies went on to finishing colleges where they learned modern languages and all the social graces which would make them marvellous helpers of their husband's career."[30] Will females in Singapore be discriminated against where university courses are concerned? Will there be a mushrooming of finishing colleges all trying to encourage parents to send their daughters there? If so, with what results? It is too soon to see what implications all these developments will have.

NOTES

1. Virginia Woolf, *A Room of One's Own* (New York: Harcourt, Brace, 1929).

2. S. C. Chua, *Report on the Census of Population 1950* (Singapore: Government Printers, 1964); P. Arumanainathan, *Report on the Census of Population 1970* (Singapore: Department of Statistics, 1973); Chian Kim Khoo, *Report on the Census of Population 1980. Singapore Release No 4. Economic Characteristics* (Singapore: Department of Statistics, 1983); Kak En Lau, *Singapore Census of Population 1990, Statistical Release No. 1, Demographic Characteristics* (Singapore: Department of Statistics, 1993).

3. T. R. Doraisamy, ed., *150 Years of Education in Singapore.* (Singapore: Teachers' Training College, 1969):22.

4. Ibid., p. 4.

5. Ibid., p. 39.

6. Ibid., p. 23.

7. Lau, p. 5.

8. *Annual Report of the Department of Education for the Year 1952* (Singapore: Government Printing Office):4.

9. Arumanainathan, p. 100.

10. Kuan Yew Lee, *The Prime Minister's Speech at the National Trade Union Congress Seminar for Women.* Mimeographed, 1975.

11. *Singapore: The Next Lap* (Singapore: Times Editions, 1991):45.

12. *Singapore Yearbook of Statistics* (Singapore: Department of Statistics, 1992):302–303.

13. Yee Shoon Yu, "The Singapore Women," in: Devan C.V Nair., ed., *Socialism That Works: The Singapore Way* (Singapore: Federal Publications, 1976):114.

14. Ellen Goldring and Michael Chen, "The Feminization of School Administration: How do Women Use their Academic Studies to Legitimate their Authority?" (Paper presented at American Educational Research Association Conference, Washington DC, 1987).

15. *Singapore: The Next Lap*, p. 50.

16. "National Productivity Board Survey on Work Attitudes" (Singapore: National Productivity Board, 1991).

17. Guat Tin Low, *A Comparative Study of Educational Administrators in Singapore: Emphasis on Successful Women* (Ph.D. Thesis. Ann Arbor, MI, University of Michigan Press, 1988):81.

18. Pang Boon Ong, "Education for Industrial Development and Multi-Racial Living" (People's Action Party 15th Anniversary Celebration Souvenir Publication, 1966).

19. Hsien Loong Lee, "Singapore's Economic Policy: Vision for the 1990s." *Speeches*, Vol. 10 (1). (Speech given at Commonwealth Institute in London, 1986):56–75.

20. Republic of Singapore: *Budget for the Financial Year 1993/94*. (Budget Division, Ministry of Finance, 1993):8.

21. *Singapore: The Next Lap*, pp. 57–75.

22. Ilsa Sharp, *Womanpower in Singapore*. (Singapore Trade and Industry, 1972).

23. Figures supplied by Singapore's Ministry of Community Development, Public Relations Dept., 1993.

24. L. Lim, "Women in the Singapore Economy." Occasional Paper, University of Singapore, Economic Research Centre, 1982.

25. Lau, p. 6.

26. Khoo, pp. 230–238.

27. *Report on the Labour Force Survey of Singapore 1980* (Singapore: Research and Statistics Division, Ministry of Labour, 1981):66–67.

28. Aline K. Wong and Wai Kum Leong, ed., *Singapore Women. Three Decades of Change* (Singapore: Times Academic Press, 1993):9.

29. Soo Peck Eng, *Women's Education, Occupational Attainment and Income in Singapore* (Singapore: Institute of Education, unpublished Paper, 1982).

30. Lee Kuan Yew, *Jobs or Husbands?* (Singapore: The New Paper, April 19, 1994):15.

PART III
SOUTH ASIA

8 INDIA

Ratna Ghosh and Abdulaziz Talbani

INTRODUCTION

Women have always played an extremely important role in the economic, social, and cultural development of India. The position of women in India is complex because of regional, cultural, and religious differences and sharp socioeconomic disparities. A very small number of women are educated and visible in positions of power and prestige, while the vast majority, whose basic concern is survival, are illiterate, powerless, and vulnerable.

The status of Indian women is generally believed to have shifted dramatically through the ages. In the Vedic age (which spans a period of 17 or 18 centuries) they are said to have had some freedom in the early phase. But by the eighth century B.C. their condition had deteriorated. The decline in women's status can be traced to the socioeconomic changes brought about by the shift from a pastoral to an agricultural mode of life, which corresponded with Aryan expansion. Prevented from an active role in productive labor (their labor was reproductive and not productive in economic terms), women were removed from accumulation and inheritance of wealth, and thus their status was reduced to a subservient position.[1] Women's access to education was progressively withdrawn during the Vedic age; by the end of that period women were forbidden to read the scriptures. Their barriers and disabilities had worsened during successive invasions over the centuries (when women needed "protection") and with the increasing oppression of the developing complex caste system.

During the greater part of British rule women continued to be subjected to many disadvantages. Social reformers in the nineteenth and twentieth centuries, mostly men but also women, achieved success in questioning and eradicating some social customs that debilitated women. Education of women was given great prominence as the most significant instrument for changing their subjugated position. A dramatic change in women's status occurred when Mahatma Gandhi underscored the importance of their participation in the civil disobedience movement. Women from various social levels in urban and rural areas responded to the call for independence. Nehru wholeheartedly supported women's involvement in the freedom movement and believed that "in a national war, there is no question of either sex or community."[2] The impetus for women's education was greatly emphasized in the wake of equality legislation and the social and economic reconstruction initiated after independence in 1947.

Since then female participation in the economy and in education has increased significantly. Given the sociocultural and political disabilities of women on the eve of independence, women's progress in literacy, educational enrollment, employment, and status has been remarkable. However, despite the progress, a vast majority of women are still illiterate, impoverished, and marginalized. There has been a *de jure* reduction in inequalities and discrimination. But there continues to be an absence of a dynamic orientation in social policy that could break the cycle of subjugation and enable women to participate fully in social, political, cultural, and economic spheres and thus contribute to national development.

This chapter examines Indian women's achievements in education and national development in the last four and a half decades since independence. It discusses the barriers that hinder their equal participation in society and the lack of recognition of their contribution to national development.

A HISTORICAL BACKGROUND TO WOMEN'S EDUCATION

Although it is about one hundred years since the first Indian woman obtained a university degree, there was very little improvement in women's educational status before independence. The root of the problems of education in post-independence India can be traced back to the colonial period when the formal education of women started.[3] The impact of the British Government in the evolution of formal education in India was profound. The colonial administration initially cast the education system in a male mold[4] and favored the education of boys for government service jobs. Added to the prevailing social norm of female seclusion, the Victorian concept of females that excluded women from the public sphere during the late nineteenth and early twentieth centuries further relegated Indian women to the private or domestic sphere. In general, the British policy was cautious with regard to women's education. Even Indian social reformers who emphasized the importance of educating women during that period did so to raise their status within the family or to make them more capable in their traditional roles as wives and mothers[5] in the private sphere, rather than for participation in the wider public sphere.

The goal of women's education was linked to the concept of marriage as the only career for women. A differentiated curriculum supported by the Education Commission of 1882 was based on the view that certain subjects were more suited for the desirable roles girls were expected to perform in society. Hygiene, domestic science, needlework, and music are examples of subjects that emerged as "feminine," while physics, chemistry, and mathematics became "masculine" subjects.[6] Private girls' schools, both missionary and those run by social reformers, emphasized feminine subjects and did not generally have female staff trained in science. During the colonial period social class, religion, culture, and region prevented women from access to education. At this time several private organizations took initiatives to promote women's education. However, most of these organizations were active in urban areas while rural areas were almost entirely neglected. Social handicaps such as sati,[7] child marriage, the ban on widow remarriage, and *purdah* (or seclusion) denied women access to education. In 1959, the Report of the National Committee on Women's Education summarized the problem thus:

> Illustrious women who, in spite of such adverse social conditions made their mark as statesmen, rulers, soldiers or saints, appeared in all parts of the country from time to time and were honoured by men and women alike. But even such exceptions do not reduce the gloom of the general picture of the subjection of women who were denied opportunities for education.[8]

Although practices such as *sati* and child marriage are now illegal, the effects of *purdah* and the related concepts of female chastity and honor continue to this day to have their impact in terms of early withdrawal from school and fear of coeducational institutions.

Independence became a "watershed in the history of women's education in India."[9] At the time of independence female literacy was only 7.9% as compared to male literacy of 25%.[10] The wide disparity in the education of men and women at the end of the colonial period, the impact of colonial policies and practices, and a long history of poor education for women were great handicaps that the new government faced in its attempts to promote gender equality in society.

After independence there was a fundamental shift in the Indian government's policies toward women. The new social agenda accepted the principle of equal female participation in national life in general and in the economy and education in particular. The issue of gender equality became a major policy concern for the Indian government and was guaranteed in the Constitution. The prevalent duality in the curriculum was removed, and the purpose of female education was recognized as being the same as that of male education. It was seen as a means of providing equal opportunity as well as responding to the need for human resource development in the process of national development.

However, the acceptance of the principle of equality was not sufficient to achieve de facto equality. The 1975 Report of the Committee on the Status of Women[11] points out the ambivalence between the old and new views regarding the content and purpose of women's education both among individuals and in official documents. The impact of this ambivalence on educational planning, allocation of resources, and development of societal values was vital. Policy was aimed at reforming the situation of women, not at changing social traditions and social conditioning that kept them subservient. Neither the education system nor constitutional guarantees strike at the structures of patriarchal subordination in which class, caste, religion, and sociocultural norms continue to exploit women. Until the perception of social relations and the roles of men and women change drastically, the idea of women's education and career training will continue to be viewed as being at the cost of their traditional social roles of wife and mother (whereas men's education and career development have never been questioned in terms of their social roles as husbands and fathers).

Constitutional Rights for Women

In modern India the demand for independence and the adoption of Fundamental Rights in the Indian Constitution of 1950 were based on the principle that democracy cannot be established unless certain rights are assured to all citizens, and that guaranteeing these rights would be meaningless unless inequalities were banished and each individual assured of equality of status and opportunity. The Preamble of the Indian Constitution mentions essential individual rights, reflecting the spirit of Article I of the United Nations Declaration: "All human beings are born free and equal in dignity and rights."[12]

The classification of Fundamental Rights in the Constitution of India begins with the right to equality. A number of provisions related to the rights and status of women are enshrined in the Constitution. According to it, discrimination on the basis of sex is illegal (Article 15:2); equality of opportunity in employment is guaranteed (Article 16); and, equality before the law is guaranteed (Article 14). The provision of education for all up to the age of 14 is a Constitutional responsibility (Article 45). An important goal is "to guarantee equality of opportunity for all in education to improve their quality of life and to participate in the tasks of promoting the general well-being of society."[13]

The equality provisions in the constitution have had tremendous impact on social policy in India. Immense changes have taken place in the status of women, and some gains have been made in economic and educational fields. Nevertheless, inequalities in all fields are pervasive and deep-rooted. Social and cultural values and norms obstruct the achievement of national goals set by the constitution and policy agenda.

FEMALE PARTICIPATION IN EDUCATION

The modern system of education was introduced by the British during the colonial period. The colonial education primarily served the interest of the imperialist power. After independence in 1947, the colonial legacy remained intact, paralleled with the struggle to redefine educational goals and reorganize the structure of education. The Indian education system is an amalgamation of heterogenous subsystems run by central and state governments and private agencies.

In 1968 the First National Policy on Education was announced. The Commission, known as Kothari Commission, proposed an organizational pattern of 10, 2, and 3, meaning ten years of primary and secondary education, two years of higher secondary education, and three years of college education for the Baccalaureate degree. In 1986 another major policy initiative was taken, and the National Policy of Education of 1986 proposed major organizational changes. It recommended that a 5, 3, 2 structure should be adopted by 1995. This structural change suggests five years of elementary, three years of middle (lower secondary), and two years of higher secondary schooling.

The essential shift in educational policy that took place after independence was its reorientation from an elitist model to popular education. The state's commitment to make free and compulsory elementary education accessible to all resulted in the investment of resources for the expansion of the education system. The result was that literacy quadrupled in a forty-year span. A threefold increase in educational institutions occurred between 1950 and 1983; 73% of all institutions were primary schools.[14] Accessibility of education through adult literacy programs has made little impact on the overall literacy of the nation. Endemic disparities between the genders and rural and urban areas remain significantly high. Female literacy is in the 1990s 24.8% as compared to male literacy at 46.9%. In rural areas female literacy is merely 18% while male literacy is over 40%.[15]

Participation at Primary and Lower Secondary Levels

The government acknowledges that social and economic disabilities are major obstacles to female participation in education. Efforts to redress the situation have produced some results. Social class and gender appear to be the two most significant factors in determining the level of education one achieves. Women from lower castes or social classes suffer from a double disadvantage; hence their participation and retention rates are the lowest while their dropout rate is the highest in the nation.

According to statistics, the primary level had a gross male and female enrollment of 93.4% in 1986, but because of the high dropout rate among school-aged girls only 30.6% reached the sixth grade (lower secondary).

Table 8.1 shows the relative growth of females as a percentage of total enrollment. It indicates that at the elementary level female enrollment increased from 28.1% of total enrollment in 1950-51 to 42.4% in 1985-6. Similarly, at the upper primary level female enrollment increased from 16.1% to 35.5%. Though these figures show an encouraging trend of increasing female participation in education, 57% of all school-aged girls still do not have access to schooling.

Table 8.1 Percentage of Male and Female Students to Total Enrollment by Sex and Level of Education, 1950–1986

Year	Primary		Lower Secondary	
	Boys	Girls	Boys	Girls
1950–51	71.9	28.1	83.9	16.1
1960–61	67.9	32.1	76.1	23.9
1970–71	62.7	37.3	70.8	29.2
1980–81	61.4	38.6	67.2	32.8
1985–86	57.6	42.4	64.5	35.5

Source: Government of India (1951); (1986); NCERT, 1992.[16]

The above statistics indicate that in India as a whole the participation of girls in education remains lower than that of boys. Rural residence also reduced girls' educational opportunities. In rural areas male-female disparity in enrollment is staggering (Table 8.2). At the primary level enrollment was about 60.5% boys and 39.5% girls in 1986. At the lower secondary level it was 68.2% boys to only 31.8% girls in the same year. In the period between 1978 and 1986, there was an increase of 11.2% in number of schools in the country, from 474,636 to 528,730. The corresponding increase in rural and urban primary schools has been 10.2% and 22.9% respectively.[17] Data on educational expansion indicate that the government has focused on improving access in urban rather than in rural areas. Thus urban girls fare better than their rural counterparts. At the lower secondary level, female participation has decreased, indicating a high dropout rate and/or early withdrawal from schools. In the middle level, although girls' enrollment has grown fast, only 30.6% of girls in the relevant age group are enrolled as compared to 56.3% of boys.[18]

Table 8.2 Percentage of Male and Female Students to Total Enrollment by Level of Education and Residence, 1986

Region	Primary		Lower Secondary	
	Boys	Girls	Boys	Girls
Rural	60.5	39.5	68.2	31.8
Urban	54.8	45.2	58.2	41.8
Total	57.6	42.4	64.5	35.5

Source: NCERT, 1992

Secondary and Higher Secondary Levels

The secondary and higher secondary schools comprise grades 9 to 10 and 11 to 12. Higher secondary is considered equivalent to pre-university education. In grades 9 and 10, boys' enrollment in rural areas is 72.7% of the total as compared to 62.7% in urban areas. Disparity on the basis of gender persists. Hence, the comparable figure for girls in rural areas in grades 9 and 10 is only 27.2%. In urban areas female participation at the same grade levels is 37.5% as indicated in Table 8.3.

Table 8.3 Percentage of Male and Female Enrollment at the Secondary (Grades 9–10) and Higher Secondary (11–12) Levels, 1986

Region	Boys %		Girls %		Total
	9–10	11–12	9–10	11–12	
Rural	72.7	75.9	27.2	24.1	49.9
Urban	62.7	65.1	37.5	34.9	50.1
Total	67.7	70.5	32.3	29.5	100

Source: NCERT, 1992.

At the higher secondary level, access is drastically reduced for rural students in general and female rural students in particular. At the higher secondary level, female participation grew from 16.7% in 1950/1 to 31.0% in 1985/6. The figures in Table 8.3 illustrate much lower participation of girls at the higher secondary level. Their proportion to total enrollment is merely 24.1% in rural areas and 34.9% in urban areas. According to the 1986 survey, only 4.18% of the rural population had access to higher secondary education in their immediate vicinity.[19] Rural students have to travel long distances to get to school. This lack of educational facilities in close vicinity hinders female participation in higher secondary education.

Dropout Rates of Female Students

Another problem is the high dropout rate at all levels of education, constituting a very expensive educational wastage. The female dropout rate is considerably higher than the male rate. This indicates the severity of circumstances under which girls are seeking education. At the primary level the dropout rate for female students was 55.5% in 1981/2, a 11.2% decrease since 1977/8 (as compared to a 9.8% decrease in the dropout rate for boys in the same period) (Table 8.4). At the secondary level, the female dropout rate has decreased from 81.7% in 1977/8 to 77.7% in 1981/2 (similar figures for boys are 73.9% and 68.5%). This shows that while some advances have been made toward making education accessible, the problems of accessibility and retention have remained unresolved. To redress the situation, policymakers must look beyond the educational system. The government must take into consideration the social and economic disabilities of rural and underprivileged classes in society.

Table 8.4 Dropout Rates by Sex and Levels of Education, 1977-81 (in %)

	1977–78			1981–82		
	Male	Female	Total	Male	Female	Total
Primary	56.9	66.7	62.7	47.1	55.5	50.5
Secondary	73.9	81.7	76.9	68.5	77.7	72.1

Source: Government of India, *Women in India*, 1988.

Participation in Tertiary Education

Evidence suggests that while far-reaching changes in women's position have taken place in the post-independence era and some gains have been made by females, particularly in higher education,[20] inequality in the education of women is pervasive and substantially disparate in terms of access, survival, sex-differentiation by field and content, and socioeconomic outcome.[21] As a matter of fact, the 1975 Committee on the Status of Women Report[22] points out that the acceleration in the process of women's education that took place in the 1960s gave way to a deceleration trend since the late 1960s because of withdrawal of special programs. In India today, as is the case in many countries, women still have a lower status in society than men, fewer women are literate, and stereotypes and prescribed social roles ghettoize educated women in "female" fields of study, thus restricting their economic opportunities.

Table 8.5 Women as a Percentage of Enrollment in Higher Education: 1950–51 to 1988–89 (Undergraduate and Graduate)

Discipline	1950–51	1981–82	1988–89
Arts	16.1	38.2	43.2
Science	7.1	28.6	32.6
Commerce	0.6	16.7	20.5
Education	32.4	48.3	52.4
Engineering/Technology	0.2	4.5	6.2
Medicine	0.2	4.5	31.7
Law	2.1	7.1	8.7
Agriculture/Veterinary Sciences	5.8	18.3	10.2
% of Total Enrollment	10.9	27.7	25.4

Source: *University Grants Commission, Annual Report 1988-9* (New Delhi: University Grants Commission, 1989).

The growth rate of higher education has fluctuated in different periods. As in primary education, the growth rate for higher education has declined from 12.4% in the 1950s, and 13.4% in the 1960s, to 3.8% in the 1970s. In 1986 only 4.8% of the total relevant age group was enrolled in higher education and female students constituted only 27.7% of the total enrollment.[23] Although the gap in male-female enrollment has rapidly narrowed in higher education, women still go into "feminine" fields of study with restricted job opportunities.

Distribution by Field of Study

At the tertiary level, apart from accessibility there is also the issue of female ghettoization in certain subject areas. Women continue to be concentrated in the faculties of education and arts. These two faculties have the highest proportion of female students (43.2% and 52.4% respectively). High female enrollment in education is partly explained by the fact that teaching is considered a profession that fits well with women's schedule as shaped by their traditional roles. It is also a low-status and low-income profession. In other fields the male-female disparities are enormous. A marginal improvement has been noticed in prestigious professions such as medicine, science, and commerce, but in areas that are perceived as careers for men female representation is insignificant. For instance, while female enrollment in engineering has increased by 17 times, women still constitute only a little over 6% of total enrollment. The same applies to law, agriculture, veterinary science, and commerce.[24] However, the gains women have made do not always last. Women entered the medical profession as doctors rather early in India. Their proportion was comparatively large in medicine partly because of the symbiotic role between female doctors and female clients. Indeed, the need for women doctors led to a system of reserved places for them in medical schools.

During the 1960s and 1970s efforts by the University Grants Commission to give preferential treatment to girls' colleges for developing facilities for science education narrowed the gender gap in science.[25] Mathematics and general science are now compulsory for all students up to grade 10. Consequently, 40% of enrollments in science are girls, which makes their proportion in India among the highest in the world.[26] This trend weakens somewhat in higher education (Table 8.5) and deteriorates in graduate programs. The enrollment figures in Table 8.6 indicate that at the Master of Science level in 1979–80 only 27.19% were women. A disproportionate number were in Home Science: 98% in 1978–79 and 100% in 1979–80. Women's enrollment in research programs, not surprisingly, is very low. Women have been discouraged from going into sciences by the fact that there is disproportionally high (50%) unemployment among women qualified in the sciences. The distribution of the Council of Scientific and Industrial Research (CSIR) fellowships in 1981 indicates that 30% were held by women, although their percentage at the junior category (36%) was larger than in the senior category (12.5%). Females show a preference for biochemistry, biology, and medicine and less interest in engineering, earth sciences, and physics.

Table 8.6 Percentage of Total Enrollment According to Fields of Study in Post-Graduate Education, 1978–80

Subject	Enrollment Master of Science		Research Enrollment	
	1978–79	1979–80	1978–79	1979–80
Physics	16.7	18.1	14.7	16.3
Chemistry	23.6	24.9	20.4	21.2
Mathematics	18.7	21.0	25.9	15.7
Statistics	18.7	19.8	16.8	12.9
Biological Sciences	34.9	31.5	21.7	26.1
Bio-medical Sciences	40.1	37.0	27.1	32.7
Botany	38.6	33.5	31.1	28.0
Zoology	40.7	35.4	26.6	26.4
Geology	4.6	32.5	11.9	4.33
Geography	34.8	—	25.4	39.2
Home Sciences	98.0	100.0	96.5	95.5
Microbiology	40.3	43.2	49.9	50.1
Anthropology	45.3	43.3	50.0	50.1
Others	34.0	25.3	21.5	20.3
Total	26.6	27.2	23.2	22.1

Source: Government of India, *Report of the Working Group on Personnel Policies for Bringing Greater Involvement of Women in Science and Technology*, 1981.

Enrollment figures[27] for 1977 in the 356 Industrial Training Institutes in India show that in the 32 engineering trades (such as draftsperson, electrician, mechanic) there were 597 women as compared to 134,313 men. In nonengineering trades (such as the manufacture of utensils, sporting goods, footwear, etc.) there were 5,093 women and 11,346 men. The total figure for women is boosted because of high enrollment in tailoring and stenography. In the apprenticeship training program there were 3,092 women and 101,923 men. Urban/rural disparities remained very high. In addition to attitudinal problems, structural problems such as lack of hostel facilities for women become significant constraints for those wishing to pursue science and technology courses away from home. In 1978–79 there were estimated to be 12,731 women's hostels as compared to 65,364 for men.[28]

Issues in Employment

One of the most significant phenomena of this century is women's entry into paid employment. A large part of women's work is still unpaid and in the private sphere, while in the public sphere it is overwhelmingly in the informal and unorganized economic sector. This makes female contribution to the economy and national development unrecognized. Despite their entry into the labor force, the majority of Indian women continue to cluster at the lowest rungs of the occupational hierarchy in low-status and low-pay jobs. They do not have decision-making powers or control over means of production or property.

Science and technology have largely by-passed women and marginalized them. Modernization and industrialization have increased mechanization, which has displaced female labor. This is because technology demands sophisticated skills that need to be developed through education and training generally available only to males. Hence women are hardest hit by a patriarchal system of technology. Lack of education in technological fields effectively cuts women off from the increasing number of technical jobs in a modernizing nation.

Statistics show a startling picture of female participation in the work force. Only 11.87% of the total female population in the age group of 15-59 years is in the work force as compared to 52.51% of men in the same age group. Census figures show that in 1971, 94% of women in the work force were in the unorganized sector, of which over 80% were in agriculture and the rest in nonagricultural occupations. Being in the unorganized sector means being outside the reach of laws and thus having little job protection and the worst working conditions. Women in this sector are subject to exploitation and, with little or no education, they lack confidence and are unaware of their rights. The organized sector is related to the formal education system. Therefore, while increase in women's formal education has resulted in a rapid increase in the number of women in the organized sector—jump from 241,000 in 1965 to 1,370,000 in 1975—these figures represent but a minority of women in India.

Women in the Civil Service

Women have competed for the prestigious civil service jobs since independence. Table 8.7 indicates that while women's representation in the civil service and administration is increasing, their proportionate participation is very low indeed. The percentage of women in government services is astonishingly low. For instance, female employment in 1987 was merely 9.94% in the Indian Foreign Service, 7.45% in the Indian Administrative Service, and

12.8% in Indian Economic Services. But their representation is even lower in other services, such as 0.86% in the Indian Police Service, 0.57% in Indian Forestry, and 3.37% in the Central Secretariat. Their total representation in government services is only 5.85%.[29]

Table 8.7 Representation of Women in Selected Government Services, 1987

Service	Female %
Indian Administrative Service	7.4
Indian Police	0.8
Foreign Service	9.9
Income Tax	8.0
Custom and Excise	5.3
Audit and Account	10.0
Postal Service	10.3
Indian Economic Service	12.8
Statistical Service	4.7
Indian Forest	0.6
Central Information Service	8.2
Central Secretariat	3.4
Total Female % in Services	5.8

Source: Government of India, 1988.[30]

Female representation is insignificant in the state-owned Indian Railways, one of the largest employers in India. The railways staff is only 3.12% women. Some of the departments, such as engineering and telecommunication, have no women staff.[31] The Delhi office of Doordarshan, the state-owned Indian Television Network, has only 4.70% women. These percentages indicate that female representation is negligible in positions that are politically and economically significant.

Women Academics

More than half of women degree-holders and technical personnel are in the teaching profession, and their percentage of those jobs goes down as the level of education progresses. University Grants Commission figures for 1981-82 indicate that only 12.5% of university faculty are women, and they are concentrated in the lower ranks. A study done in 1983[32] indicates that while there are a few women in senior positions at the university level who are academically very prominent, the majority of women are on the periphery. An analysis of women scientists at the Council of Scientific and Industrial Research in 1980 indicated that representation at the senior levels was very low—4% of women held senior posts although they comprised 14% of all scientists. In the Indian Space Research Organization representation of women in the scientific and technology staff increased from 2.6% of the total in 1976 to 4.5% in 1980.[33]

It appears that women's primary role is that of wife and mother and that for these women teaching is a second income. Their satisfaction is derived from their primary role, and they generally do not feel the need to publish or excell in research. They do not compete for research awards and do not perceive any inequalities vis-à-vis men. A very small minority, who view themselves as being active in the academic milieu, have a strong consciousness of women's issues and perceive many subtle forms of discrimination (such as being overlooked for committee memberships). For the majority, equal rights with men is not an issue, either because their careers have less value in the hierarchy of roles or because they lack awareness of differential treatment. Although their pay scales are the same, women end up in the lower ranks.[34] The majority occupy low-status positions; only 19% of doctors are women (high status) but 95% of nurses are women (lower status), and 25% of all school teachers (mostly primary) are women but only 17% of teachers at colleges and universities are women. Women become principals only in girls' schools. Women lawyers are not usually appointed as judges. A very small number of women who come from the upper-middle class are succeeding in management positions in such areas as advertising, public relations, and market research. Nonprofessional women with some education concentrate in clerical services.[35]

Women in Politics

Indian women's presence in politics appears to have declined. In 1957, 1,474 males and 45 females contested Lok Sabha (the lower house in parliament) seats, and 467 males and 27 females were elected, representing 94.5% and 5.5% respectively. In 1977, 2,369 males and 70 females contested, while 523 males (96.5%) and 19 females (3.5%) were elected. Although more females contested, their number and proportion in parliament dropped. This is even more obvious in the State Legislative Assemblies where, in 1957, 193 females were elected as compared to only 28 in 1974–77.[36] While economic necessity, especially in the urban middle-class, has changed social attitudes toward female employment, there continues to be discrimination in recruitment and further advancement and subtle obstacles in the utilization of women's education. The demand for unskilled women's labor is shrinking but the range of jobs open to educated women has widened in public and private spheres.

SOCIAL OUTCOMES

Inequality in the status of men and women is a universal occurrence. Sexual stratification is a complex phenomenon, and while some women of some sections in India are better off than men of other sections, the salient feature is that in each section of society women are underprivileged in social, economic, and political spheres.[37] The impact of inequality is magnified among women from lower socioeconomic groups. In India the situation is more complex because of urban-rural disparities as well as regional, religious, and cultural differences. To the extent that women in India suffer from disadvantages or repressions because of gender and class, they are victims of what can be called the multiple negative, and therefore face both vertical (class) and horizontal (gender) oppression. The economic aspect must preclude equality of distribution because equal opportunity is meaningless if it means equal deprivation. Notwithstanding this, it must be pointed out that although females form roughly half the population, they are nevertheless the most vulnerable among the powerless groups in all societies. What is more serious is that there has been a decline in India's female population[38] so that the sex ratio has dropped from 972 women per 1000 men in 1901 to 933 women per 1000 men in 1981.[39]

The small group of women who have university degrees form about 3% of the female population. They are part of the urban middle class and are the elite for whom education and modernization are generating new life options. Their lives are in no way similar to the masses of illiterate women whose basic concern is survival. When women are excluded from participating in any sphere of activity on the basis of their gender, that phenomenon is sexism. Sometimes discrimination is overt, but in the face of equality legislation it tends to acquire covert barriers, such as, for example, by denying opportunities through social restrictions. Some classes of elite women may not see themselves as being unfairly treated because they enjoy social and economic privileges that are denied to average Indian women.[40] Many are not aware of their rights (even among educated women) and do not perceive discrimination because their socialization teaches them to accept differential treatment without question. For the majority, economic needs are so overriding that the issue of discrimination may not seem important.

Better education of women generally results in increased life options such as marriage choices, increased sharing of authority within the family, lower fertility patterns, greater participation in social and political activities, and increased economic power.[41] Economic power is usually accepted as a most influential factor in determining power and privilege. The overall impact of inequalities in education is due to differences in economic potential that eventually render a difference in the status of men and women.

Equal access to the education system, regardless of social circumstance and retention, depends both on availability of facilities and the disposition to take advantage of these facilities. In India these in turn are affected by a constellation of variables such as socioreligious norms and values relating to women that are critical in defining women's roles and thus affect all dimensions of their education and decision making.

While there are regional, religious, and class differences, it is the lack of special facilities that makes access and retention for girls less likely. Girls' schools are few and tend to be run by private organizations. Norms that disapprove of coeducation lead to the withdrawal of girls, especially in rural areas. Lack of female teachers in secondary schools, the absence of suitable transportation and boarding schools for girls, and early marriages are additional reasons why only about a quarter of all girls enrolled in grade 1 complete primary school.

The benefits of female education are maximized when the traditional value system is conducive to the expansion of women's roles.[42] Not only are there urban/rural disparities regarding women's roles, but there is an overlap between regional and religious factors, since different religious communities respond according to the variations in their sociocultural traditions.[43] Traditional patterns of female seclusion designed to preserve female virtues view the education of girls as perilous. Communities that have historically practiced *purdah* (or seclusion) and sex-segregation have low education rates among their female populations.

The 1959 Report of the National Committee for Women's Education identified regional imbalance as a major drawback in women's education, and *Towards Equality,* the report of the Committee on the Status of Women (1975), stressed the need for equal distribution of educational privileges not only among males and females but also among women from different regions, castes, and religious groups. Scheduled Caste[44] women in rural areas are the most disadvantaged in the country in spite of the government's discrimination policy for Scheduled Castes and Tribes. Several tribal groups of the North-Eastern States (some of whom practice matriarchy) are distinct from other tribal groups in the position they accord to women, and the rapid advances made in the education of their women, not surprisingly, have been significant. But the impact of modernization has eroded women's power, and there is a reversal of this trend. Cities and regions with a high proportion of Muslims or Scheduled Castes and Tribes show low literacy rates while those with relatively high percentages of Christians have high literacy rates, possibly as a result of missionary activity in education. In general, the Southern States have maintained higher literacy rates.[45] A survey conducted by the Status of Women Committee in 1974 indicates that lack of formal education among Muslim women continues at a very high rate even in those states that have made considerable progress in women's education.[46] The wide gap in urban/rural education is universal in India, but interestingly the rural literacy rate in Kerala (in the south) is higher than for the country's urban population as a whole.[47] There are several reasons for this: purdah is not practiced even among the Muslims of Kerala; the Nairs traditionally follow a matriarchal system; and Kerala has a fair-sized Christian population. The gap between the education of boys and girls at the primary level is largest in the northern provinces of Bihar, Gujerat, Rajasthan, and Uttar Pradesh and least in Kerala (south), Meghalaya and Manipur (east), and Punjab (north).[48]

Cultural bias is an important determinant of opposition to female education. The perception of women as dependent—first as daughter, then as wife, and finally as mother—is not an incentive for investment in their education. Fathers, in general, continue to be unwilling to invest in the education of their daughters and would rather divert funds for their dowry, a practice still prevalent in many areas, social classes, and religious groups. Their greater claims to boys' incomes in the absence of social security in old age incline parents to give preferential treatment to boys. Girls are "lost" to the family after marriage, and in any case they do not need to go to school to learn to be wives and mothers. In fact education is often viewed as making them defiant and unsuitable for their traditional role. Not surprisingly, dropout rates for girls are higher than for boys, and two-thirds of this wastage occurs in class 1.[49] University education is more or less confined to urban centers and middle and upper-middle classes where educated men have a preference for educated brides. In addition, economic need in the middle class is encouraging double-income families, and women must have some education for the service-oriented jobs which they generally enter, although a small percentage get into professional fields.

In addition to other disadvantages in lower socioeconomic groups, inequities in income, high social stratification, and social differentiation result in less prosperity for the majority of women.[50] In India it is sometimes difficult to distinguish between cultural and economic forces as major determinants in the lack of access and high wastage levels. With the majority population below the poverty line, extreme poverty coupled with cultural disparities reduces aspirations, and the costs of educating girls (who are most useful at home) enforce a legacy of limited opportunities and displace girls in the education system.

Conclusion

Disparities in the proportion of men and women at different levels of responsibility are important indicators of the unequal employment status and opportunity for men and women, which are the direct result of a combination of factors, namely, the educational system, training, job orientation, and cultural conditioning.[51]

While there are no visible constraints to educational access and little direct evidence of inequality in employment, the foregoing discussion indicates the following picture of contemporary India. First, the gap in the educational enrollment of boys and girls at all levels is very wide, leading to a phenomenal disparity in male and female literacy rates. Second, women concentrate in "female" fields of study and still have very low enrollment in technical and engineering schools and professions. Third, women consequently are in sex-segregated employment ghettos. This occupational balkanization means that women are concentrated in lower status, lower paying jobs, and this is a glaring manifestation of sexism in education and society. Moreover, in a transitional society like India's, where modernization is causing rapid changes, the impact of the application of technology on women's employment is severe. The urgency for development requires flexibility and adaptability in all workers, but low levels of education and literacy make this less feasible for women.

Studies examining women's entry into the labor force indicate problems of role conflict and discrimination (overt or covert) in employment.[52] Those who utilize their education in the work force share the common burden of double work. Even reproductive technologies, which affect the lives and bodies of women most dramatically, are proving to be not so liberating because of women's lack of decision-making power. But familial roles are seen as giving intrinsic rewards and satisfaction, and the higher priority given to them obviates the need for competitive rewards at work, thus minimizing role conflict. Education in science and technology must lead toward reducing the drudgery in what is now women's work. The utilization of scientific and technological knowledge should make it possible for all workers to enjoy more leisure. The majority of India's women do not have a group consciousness of denial of opportunities and societal rewards. Socialization, through education and society, limits their aspirations, and they are either not aware of being discriminated against or they accept the differential treatment. Nanda points out that Indian women have paid terribly for society's insensitivity, "but they also extracted a heavy toll from a society which has not yet learnt to live with all aspects of womanhood . . . (they) participate in a structurally violent system because of the unawareness of one's power to intervene in the real world and because of the indirect psycho-social benefits of being a victim."[53] The nature of society's attitude, both men's and women's, regarding women's roles and behaviors contributes significantly toward preventing women from action and innovation. What is most important is the way women view themselves and their capabilities. Nehru reminded women ". . . that no people, no group, no community, no country, has ever got rid of its disabilities by the generosity of the oppressor . . . the women of India will not attain their full rights by the mere generosity of the men of India. They will have to fight for themselves . . ."[54]

Education is known to bring greater confidence to people. But to the vast majority of women who do not exercise this right, and to those who are subjected to unequal opportunity in the educational process, fighting for rights is as remote as is equality in their status. The minority who have higher levels of education use it to improve their social position in the present structure without changing the hierarchical structure itself. Therefore, women continue to play traditional roles as they take on an additional occupational role. It thus follows that they go into the teaching profession in such large numbers because teaching, particularly at the lower levels, is an extension of their traditional roles. Crossing the frontier by taking up paid employment did not violate these women's traditional image; rather it was a happy combination of the domestic and occupational spheres.

In India political revolution and social revolution did not go hand in hand. The failure to implement a national educational policy at independence resulted in political development that was not accompanied by the essential social changes. The existing education system did not emphasize the ideological foundations of the new India. Traditional Indian values are hierarchial, not egalitarian. A deliberate and focused attempt must be made not only to promote the new values of human rights and equality for women and other oppressed groups but to avoid perpetuating elements in the Indian tradition that justify inequality. A general level of education is imperative for democratic socialism with the attendant social justice. This is so because education is not only the means to political awareness but also to a consciousness of civic and fundamental rights. Values cannot be legislated, and progressive legislation is not much use to the majority of women who are not aware of their rights and who, because of differential socialization of males and females, do not perceive discrimination and inequality. Education is viewed in National Development Plans as a force capable of generating new life options by socializing men and women for a modern society. Paradoxically, education often contributes to the maintenance of existing situations.

The real beneficiaries of education and equality legislation have been urban middle-class women, who constitute a small minority. The majority of women do not, or cannot, exercise their rights in education and society because social and structural changes produced by modernization and the egalitarian ideology since independence have not been accompanied by parallel changes in values and attitudes toward women. Fortunately, there are signs of an emergence of new women's movements, which show trends toward crossing class boundaries, as well as the development of poor working women's organizations for self-help. Nehru remarked, "Political revolution is important and economic revolution is still more important, but the most important of all is the social revolution in the people . . . Women play the most important part in the social revolution."[55]

There are many inequalities to be dealt with and there are no magic solutions. The function of Indian education in the next few years will be as crucial for national development as is the achievement of equity for women. The role of education is not to provide schooling for its own sake but to enable both women and men to participate fully in societal change and national development.

NOTES

1. S. Bhattacharya, "The Position of Women in Vedic Society," *India International Quarterly* 19 (1992):40–52.

2. S. Gopal, ed., *Selected works of Jawaharlal Nehru* (New Delhi: Orient Longman, 1972).

3. Ratna Ghosh, "Women's Education in the Land of the Goddess Saraswati," *Canadian and International Education* 15 (September 1986):25–44.

4. Audrey Chapman Smock, *Women's Education in Developing Countries: Opportunities and Outcomes* (New York: Praeger, 1981).

5. Government of India, *Report of the Secondary Education Commission* (New Delhi: Government of India, 1953).

6. Karuna Ahmad, "Equity and Women's Higher Education," *Journal of Higher Education* 5 (no. 1, 1979) (New Delhi, Monsoon):33–49.

7. *Sati* is the practice of cremating the widow in the funeral pyre of her husband. This inhuman act was made illegal during British colonial rule through the efforts of male social reformers such as Raja Ram Mohan Roy.

8. Government of India, *Report of the National Committee on Women's Education* (New Delhi: Government of India, Ministry of Education, 1959):13.

9. Karuna Ahmad, "The Social Context of Women's Education in India, 1921–81; Tentative Formulations." Occasional papers on history and society, 6. (New Delhi: Nehru Memorial Museum and Library, 1982).

10. Government of India, 1959, op. cit.

11. Committee on the Status of Women in India, *Towards Equality* (New Delhi: Government of India, Ministry of Education and Social Welfare, 1975).

12. Ratna Ghosh, "Human Rights and Sexism in Indian Education," in: U. Baxe, et al., eds., *The Right To Be Human* (New Delhi: Lancer International, 1986):57–76.

13. Government of India, *Education in India, 1970–71* (New Delhi: Government Of India, Ministry of Education and Social Welfare, 1981):43.

14. Government of India, *Report of the Education Commission, 1948–49. Vol.I* (Delhi: Manager of Publications, 1950):393–5; *National Council of Educational Research and Training (NCERT), Fifth All-India Educational Survey. Vols. I and II* (New Delhi: National Council of Educational Research and Training, 1992).

15. NCERT (1992), op cit.

16. Government of India, *First Five Year Plan* (New Delhi: Government of India, 1951); Government of India, *National Policy on Education* (New Delhi: Ministry of Education, 1986); NCERT (1992), op. cit.

17. NCERT, 1992, op. cit.

18. Ratna Ghosh and Abdulaziz Talbani, *A Critical Analysis of the New Educational Policy of India—1986* (Monograph) (Montreal: McGill University Press, 1989).

19. NCERT, 1992, op. cit.

20. Ahmad, 1979, op. cit.

21. Ghosh, 1986, *Women's Education in the Land of the Goddess Saraswati,* op. cit.

22. Committee on the Status of Women in India, *Towards Equality* (New Delhi: Government of India, Ministry of Education and Social Welfare, 1975).

23. Ghosh and Talbani, op. cit.

24. Prabhash P. Singh, *Women in India: A Statistical Panorama.* (New Delhi: Inter-India Publications, 1991).

25. University Grants Commission, *Annual Report 1988–1989,* New Delhi: University Grants Commission, 1989.

26. University Grants Commission, *About Higher Education in India: Some Statistics Relating to Women's Education* (New Delhi: University Grants Commission, 1981).

27. S. Chitnis, "Dimensions of Discrimination in the Employment of Women—Legal Protection and Education for Equity." Paper presented at the Seminar on Sex Discrimination in Gainful Employment, Pune, India, 1981.

28. Government of India, 1981, op. cit.

29. Government of India, *National Perspective Plan for Women 1988–2000. A Perspective From Women's Movement.* (Report of a debate, August 1988) (New Delhi: Government of India, 1988).

30. Government of India, *Women in India—A Statistical Profile* (Department of Women and Child Development, Government of India, 1988).

31. Ibid.

32. Ratna Ghosh, "General Job Satisfaction and Perceptions of Academic Roles: A Study of Male and Female Academics in India." *Report to the Shastri Indo-Canadian Institute, Calgary,* 1981.

33. Government of India, *Report of the Working Group on Personnel Policies for Bringing Greater Involvement of Women in Science and Technology* (New Delhi: Government of India, Ministry of Social Welfare, 1981).

34. Maithreyi Krishna Raj. "Women, Work and Science in India," in: Gail P. Kelly, and Carolyn M. Elliott, eds., *Women's Education in the Third World: Comparative Perspectives* (Albany: State University of New York Press, 1982):249–263.

35. Ghosh, 1986, *Women's Education in the Land of the Goddess Sarawati,* op. cit.

36. Government of India, *Women in India: A Statistical Profile.* (New Delhi: Government of India, Department of Women and Child Development, 1978).

37. Ghosh, "Introduction," in: G. Kurian, and R. Ghosh, *Women in the Family*

and the Economy: An International Comparative Survey (Westport, CT: Greenwood Press, 1981).

38. The decline in female population in India is related to the social stigma attached to having a female child. The preference for a male child leads parents to abort female children.

39. Government of India, *India: A Reference Manual, 1987* (New Delhi: Publications Division, 1987).

40. Vina Mazumdar. "Education and Women's Equality," (New Delhi: Center for Women's Development Studies, 1985).

41. Ghosh, 1981, op. cit.

42. Smock, 1981, op. cit.

43. Ahmad, 1982, op. cit.

44. Scheduled Castes were identified by the British as "untouchable" Hindu castes and put on a schedule for certain safeguards. At independence the Indian Government retained the term for similar use.

45. K. Gopal and S. Madhav, "Patterns of City Literacy," *Economic and Political Weekly* (18 May 1974):20.

46. Government of India, 1975, op. cit.

47. Gopal and Madhav, 1974, op. cit.

48. Government of India, 1981, op. cit.

49. India, 1959, op. cit.

50. Smock, 1981, op. cit.

51. Committee on the Status of Women, 1975, op. cit.

52. B. Chiplin and P. J. Sloane, *Sex Discrimination in Labour Market* (London: Macmillan, 1976); A. Myrdal, and V. Klien, *Women's Two Roles, Home and Work* (London: Routledge and Kegan Paul, 1956); R. J.Schonberger, "Inflexible Working Conditions Keep Women Unliberated," *Personnel Journal* 50 (1971):834–837.

53. B. R. Nanda, *Indian Women from Purdah to Modernity* (New Delhi: Vikas Publishing, 1976):160.

54. Gopal, 1972, op. cit.

55. Gopal, 1972, op. cit.

9 PAKISTAN

Kowsar P. Chowdhury

Pakistan, a country with a predominantly Muslim population (97%), inherited its education system from the British in 1947 when it became independent.¹ Some had hoped that the liberation from colonial control would change the lot of the country, including the status of women. The constitution guarantees women two fundamental rights: equality for all citizens under the law, and equality between the sexes.² Have these rights been realized in education, employment, and other aspects of women's lives? If not, what has gone wrong? What action is required to change the situation of women?

This chapter focuses on women's education in Pakistan and how educational opportunities, or lack of them, have affected women's lives in the work force, politics, and the family. It analyzes efforts that have been made to increase women's access to education in Pakistan, and it questions whether or not such efforts have contributed to reducing the gender gap in education, paid work, and politics. The analysis rests on the belief that women's education profoundly affects their social status and welfare.³

HISTORICAL BACKGROUND

Pakistani women's access to knowledge varied with the times in which they lived. In ancient India, around the second millennium B.C., knowledge was highly exclusive and access to it was differentiated by caste. The Hindu caste system categorically excluded the untouchables and some of the other lower castes from obtaining knowledge. Knowledge was considered sacred and therefore inaccessible to those with a low ritual status.⁴ Religious reform movements, which created new egalitarian religions like Jainism and Buddhism, could not eliminate inequality based on caste. Nor could Muslim rule, despite its ideology of equality for all.⁵

It is, however, claimed that in the early Vedic period (2000–1500 B.C.) Hindu women from higher castes had the same access to learning as men. Women had a voice in the selection of their partners and could remarry without any social censure. There was no segregation between the sexes, and women enjoyed considerable freedom of movement and action.[6] Over the centuries, however, women gradually lost their status, and knowledge became men's prerogative. *The Code of Manu,* formulated around 200 B.C., states that like the shudras, the lowest stratum in the caste structure, women are unfit for knowledge and learning.[7] Rather than setting new rules, *Manu's Code* simply reinforced the gradual deterioration of women's status as shown by the practices of *sati,*[8] child marriage, and female infanticide.[9]

Women's fortunes rose again during the Mughal rule (A.D. 1200 to 1800). Respect for knowledge and learning was evident. There were many female scholars, poets, philosophers, and mystics during this period. Education was quite common. Its provision varied by social class. There was a well-established education system for both Hindus and Muslims.[10] The masses also had access to rudimentary education. For example, there were 1,000 indigenous schools in Delhi during the reign of Mohammad Tughlaq (A.D. 1346). Such schools existed in every town and village. There were classes for imparting basic education to girls in private houses where elderly women taught the Koran, Persian literature, and ethics.[11] Education for both girls and boys was supported by native rulers, the local elites, as well as by the community.[12]

The support for mass education was lost as the British displaced the native rulers and local elites in the eighteenth century. The goal of British colonial education was control, not change. The main purpose of British colonialism was trade—extracting Indian raw materials for industrial needs in Britain and opening markets for British manufactured goods. Therefore education policies were mainly designed to control the subcontinent politically and to keep its people economically dependent on Britain.[13] To attain these goals British education policies were changed from time to time.[14] In the mid-nineteenth century the education policy focused on imbuing the Indian elites with British norms and values and teaching them the English language. A small group of English-speaking, Europeanized local elites were needed to serve as mediators between the British high administration and "important elements" of Indian society. A cadre of English-trained Indians were also required to serve as junior bureaucrats in the colonial service. This demanded the expansion of higher levels of education. The Wood's Despatch of 1854 confirmed the government decision to concentrate on higher education for the upper classes. In contrast, primary education among the masses was completely neglected.[15] The emphasis on elite education rested on the filtration theory, which assumed that the benefits of education for the upper classes would trickle down to the masses. The support for mass schooling, especially for females and the poor classes, was lost. By 1902, the last village school was gone.

Christian missionaries had been providing schooling for girls from the families of converts since the beginning of the nineteenth century. They also tried to extend education to non-Christians in the hope of propagating Christianity. English education for Indian women of the elite class began around 1830 with the establishment of Zenana schools. These schools aimed at inculcating Western values in elite women who could then mingle with Europeans. Muslim girls were not encouraged to attend school, which was held in suspicion because of its Western and colonial biases. By the turn of the century the situation had changed considerably. With the emergence of a growing nationalist sentiment and the efforts of several educated reform movement leaders, more women from aristocratic families were sent to schools in the latter part of the nineteenth century.[16]

In 1919 legislation was enacted for the first time for the introduction of free primary education in the municipalities, and in 1921 this was extended to the rural unions.[17] The period between the World Wars saw further expansion of the education system.

Development Effort in Pakistan

Similar to many postcolonial countries, Pakistan has placed great emphasis on economic and social development since independence. Education was viewed as a means to achieve it. The ultimate goal of economic development is to improve the well-being of society and to ensure that the benefits of economic progress are distributed fairly among the entire population. It is believed that the alleviation of poverty, containment of excessively high incomes, provision of greater economic opportunities, and a more equitable distribution of income and wealth will bring about economic justice.[18] Despite high rates of economic growth during the past decade and an increase in average per capita income in real terms, the gap between rich and poor in Pakistan has widened. Of all households in Pakistan, 40% fell into the lowest and another 40% into the middle-income brackets and 20% into the highest income bracket. However, the share of the lowest group in total income fell from 20.5% in 1970–71 to 17.9% in 1984–85, while that of the highest bracket increased from 41.4% to 46.7%. The share of the middle group also declined slightly. Thus the highest income households reaped the most benefit from economic growth between 1971 and 1985.

Notwithstanding a lower share of income, the poor have experienced an improvement in standard of living. According to the Seventh Five Year Plan, absolute poverty, in terms of minimum calorie intake, is almost eradicated. Relative poverty, in terms of basic needs (food, shelter, clothing, etc.), has declined considerably. The percentage of households below the poverty line (700 rupees per household in 1979 prices)[19] decreased from 65% in 1969–70 to 40% in 1984–85. The average income of the remaining poor had also increased by 20%. The phenomenon of declining poverty along with increased income inequality is explained partly by the extraordinarily large remittances from workers abroad and partly by higher domestic wage levels brought about by large-scale emigration. Although the incomes of the lower groups increased in real terms, the incomes of higher income groups increased at a faster rate.

While income distribution is one way of quantifying the development of a country, it is not an adequate indicator. To understand the development or welfare of the population, one needs also to understand how public services[20] are distributed among different segments of the population according to residence (rural and urban), sex, and social class. In general these services are much less accessible to rural dwellers and do not in any way compensate for lower rural incomes. They are also differentially allocated between males and females. This will be discussed in the section on women's status in Pakistan. There is no information available on the subject by social class.

WOMEN'S STATUS IN PAKISTAN

Women's status cannot be defined by a single indicator, since many forces determine the overall status of women in a society.[21] Nonetheless, the welfare and productivity of women in Pakistan rank almost the lowest in the world. On average they fare worse, on virtually every socioeconomic indicator, than their South Asian counterparts (including women in Bangladesh—whose per capita income is significantly lower), as well as worse than women in most other low-income countries.[22]

Broadly, the indicators of women's welfare and productivity, which reflect women's status as a whole, fall into four categories. The first is mortality rate and life expectancy, which indicate how well women are able to survive. The second is human resources development, e.g., in education and health, of women themselves and of their children. The third is women's role in bringing down the population growth rate, which is high in most poor countries and which is an impediment to women's development. The last category is women's participation in the economy and their contribution to household income.[23]

Pakistan has the lowest women-to-men ratio in the world, and the situation has deteriorated over the last 20 years. In 1985 there were only 91 Pakistani women for every 100 men, down from 93 in 1965, and compared with 97:100 in developing countries and 104:100 in industrial countries. Women in Pakistan also suffer from poor health, partly because of their excessive reproductive burden. During their peak childbearing years they are almost constantly in pregnancy and lactation. On average they each give 6.8 births and they die of childbirth-related complications at a rate of 600 per 100,000 live births, which is among the highest maternal mortality rates in the world, the same as that of Bangladesh but higher than those of other developing countries. Further, the poor health of mothers is passed on to their babies. Only three countries in the world had a higher percentage of low-birth-weight babies than Pakistan's 28% in 1984.[24] Despite a decrease in infant mortality rates (IMR) from 142 per 1,000 live births in 1970 to 97 in 1991,[25] the problem remains serious. Pakistan had a population of 116 million in 1991 and an annual population growth rate of 3.1% between 1980 and 1991.[26] Its population has doubled in just over 20 years, and is likely to double again in another 20 years unless strong measures are taken. This high growth rate since 1951 is largely due to a drop in overall mortality without a corresponding drop in fertility rates.[27]

The status of women in education is also strikingly lower than men in Pakistan, which will be discussed later in the chapter. Before that we need to understand the linkages between women's status and development. In the past development was often equated with economic growth, but in recent years this definition has undergone tremendous change. It is argued that the fundamental goal of development is not only economic growth but also improvement in human welfare, which is often equated with human or social development.[28] Human development is possible only by improving women's socioeconomic status, especially their educational status. There is evidence that the economic and social rates of return from schooling are quite high and on the whole higher for women than for men.[29] It is argued that female education increases women's productivity and contributes to higher economic returns. Further, women's education accrues long-term intergenerational benefits. Educating women reduces fertility, maternal mortality, and infant mortality rates. Educated mothers also produce better educated children. In other words, women's education plays a very crucial role in the development of a country. Yet in Pakistan girls do not receive the same quality and level of education as do boys. The situation in rural areas is worse than in the cities.

Planning for the welfare of women in Pakistan has evolved gradually.

In the initial years of the planning process, efforts were directed toward a development strategy that neglected women. However, in recent years the government recognized that in spite of the religious, constitutional, and legal rights of women, their status remained inferior because of ineffective enforcement of these provisions. In 1979 the Women's Division was created at the federal level to articulate policies, prepare projects, and act as a catalyst for women's development. As provinces were the implementing authorities, Women's Project Cells were created at the provincial level to monitor implementation.[30] These are positive measures aimed at raising women's status. With the above as context, I will discuss women's participation in education and its role in development.

WOMEN AND EDUCATION IN PAKISTAN
Structure of the Education System

The formal education structure has three distinct levels. The first is the primary level (grades 1–5), which lasts five years and enrolls 5–9-year-old children. The next is secondary schooling, which has three stages: a three-year middle stage (grades 6–8), a two-year secondary stage (grades 9–10), and a further two-year higher secondary stage (grades 11–12). The higher secondary stage is also called the intermediate stage and is considered a part of college education. Vocational education is a part of secondary education. It is offered to students who have completed the middle stage (grade 8) or the secondary stage (grade 10). To obtain a degree, four years of higher education after successfully completing the matric examination (held at the end of 10 years of schooling) are required. Students who pass their first-degree stage are awarded a baccalaureate degree in arts or science, typically at the age of 19. In order to complete an honors course, an additional year of study is required.[31]

With an upper secondary education, one can go on to university or non-university tertiary education in liberal arts and sciences or professional studies. The duration of postsecondary education varies. A bachelor's degree in medicine (MBBS) requires five years of study after higher secondary school; the same degree in engineering or veterinary medicine requires four years. An additional two years after the bachelor's degree is required to complete a master's degree. A doctoral degree may require a further two to three years of study. Schooling in Pakistan is sex-segregated at all levels to conform with Islamic ideology. However, in rural areas, where girls' schools do not exist, parents often send their daughters unofficially to boys' schools. Universities are coeducational.

Besides the Western education system, there is the traditional religious education system, which provides education in Islam based on the Koran, the Hadish (the sayings of Prophet Muhammad), Islamic jurisprudence, logic, and so on. Elementary education, which comprises regular basic knowledge, memorization of the Koran, and religious instruction, is provided at *makhtab* schools attached to mosques. *Madrassahs* (or *darul-uloom*) impart advanced Islamic education. In recent years attempts have been made to introduce secular subjects into the *madrassah* system in order to integrate religious education with Western education. In addition, nonformal education is provided by nongovernment organizations and local communities.

Government Policy and Women's Education

The expansion of women's education was subsumed in the education agenda. The importance of education was highlighted by the national leaders of Pakistan as early as 1947. The Pakistan Education Conference in that year first resolved that five-year free and compulsory education be introduced. Since then universal primary education (UPE) has been a major goal of the nation.

The Planning Board was set up in 1953, and systematic effort toward educational development started with the First Five Year Plan (1955–60). The subsequent national plans also underscored the importance of human resources development for the overall development of the country. The First Five Year Plan asserted that implementation of UPE was imperative.[32] Increasing girls' enrollment was considered a key to achieving UPE. The plan recommended that primary schooling be opened to girls wherever possible and that new schools be set up for them. It hoped that a better distribution of primary schools would reduce inequalities in primary education.[33] It also recommended the setting up of quality teacher-training institutions for women and recruitment of female teachers to primary schools. The report of the National Commission on Education in 1959, the education policies of 1970 and of 1972–75, and other subsequent five year plans contained recommendations for universalizing primary education and increasing girls' enrollment at the secondary level. For the higher level, the report of the National Commission on Education of 1959 recommended that female students have access to programs such as nursing, adult education, and civil defense.[34] The national education policy in 1979 recommended that *mohallah* (community) schools for girls be established and girls' participation rates be increased.

Nevertheless, not until the Sixth Plan (1983–88) did the government actually undertake any major action to enhance the condition of women's education. The Sixth Plan officially endorses integration of women into national development. To raise women's status, it recommended an increase in health facilities, more positions in the government, and additional educational and vocational training to increase employment opportunities for women. Specifically, the plan suggested that polytechnics and technical training and skill development centers be built, that existing vocational institutes be expanded, and that a new paramedical staff be trained.

The Sixth Plan set a target of increasing female participation in the primary schools from 32% to 60% and the female literacy rate from 13.7% to 47%. These targets were to be achieved by establishing 4,198 primary schools and 40,000 mosque schools for girls. However, these targets fell short as only 4,300 mosque schools were established. Neither were the literacy programs for 15 million adults called for in the plan implemented.[35]

The Seventh Five Year Plan (1988–93) again reiterated the importance of uplifting women's position and of integrating women into national development processes. The plan recognizes the gender gap in education and outlines strategies to remove it, such as: develop a network of educational institutions and undertake planned programs and activities for their proper development; provide women with the opportunities for studies in various fields, including the physical and social sciences, as well as a wide range of vocational, technical, and professional subjects, similar to the courses available to men. Further, girls' enrollment in primary schools was targeted to increase from 3.1 million in 1987–88 to 5.9 million in 1992–93 (from 45% to 70%). The enrollment of girls in grades 6 to 8 would be increased from 0.7 million to 1.4 million and that of girls in grades 9 and 10 from 0.2 million to 0.4 million. The plan also proposed to recruit mainly female teachers for all primary schools for both boys and girls. The literacy rate was planned to rise to 40% by 1992–93 and to 80% by the end of the century.[36] No results are yet available for these targeted goals.

Despite the repeated proclamation of the importance of education in human resources development, very little has been done to improve it. Public expenditure on education has been nominal, reflecting its low priority on the national agenda. During the first six plans, the shares of government expenditures on education as a proportion of the GNP were only 0.88%, 1.55%, 1.38%, 2.06%,[37] 1.70%, and 2.04%, respectively.[38] The Sixth Plan asserts that, except for the Second Plan, the performance of the education sector in the planned and the nonplanned period (ending 1977–78) remained deficient. The problem was attributed to inadequate allocation of funds and to the absence of a suitable machinery for planning, implementation, and supervision of schools.[39] The analysis of all the Plans show that the actual expenditure was far less than planned allocations.[40] No wonder women's education remained a neglected area within this low priority, since females are accommodated only after males are.

Literacy Rate

The most common indicator of women's educational status is literacy rate.[41] In Pakistan the literacy rate of the population aged 15 and above was only about 26% in 1981; it was 16% for females and 35% for males. By 1990 the rates rose to 20% and 47% for females and males respectively.[42]

The literacy rate was lower for the rural population. In 1981 it was about 17%, compared with 47% for the urban population. There was a wide discrepancy between rural and urban women, at 7% and 36% respectively.[43]

Enrollment Trends

The low literacy rates are a result of limited female access to education. Even so, there has been a marked expansion of female enrollment at all levels of education (Table 9.1). The rate of expansion was much higher for females than for males. In 1955, the enrollment ratio for girls at the primary level was 6%; by 1987, it had risen to 28%. The increases at the secondary and tertiary levels were also remarkable. Such an expansion, however, has not eliminated gender disparities in education. The proclamation of universalization of primary education entitled girls to equal access to education. However, the goal is far from realization, as indicated in Table 9.2.[44]

Table 9.1 Age-Specific School Enrollment Rates by Selected Level of Education and by Sex, 1951–1987

Year	Primary (age 6–10)			Secondary (age 11–15)			Higher (age 16–19)*	(age 20–24)	
	Total	Male	Female	Total	Male	Female	Total	Male	Female
1951	32.0	—	—	14.0	—	—	—	—	—
1955	37.0	—	—	14.0	—	3.0	—	—	—
	(age 5–9)			(age 10–16)			(age 17–19)*	(age 20–24)	
1960	30.0	—	13.0	10.0	—	3.0	1.0	—	0.4
1965	40.0	—	20.0	12.0	—	5.0	1.8	—	0.7
1970	44.0	57.0	22.0	13.0	20.0	5.0	2.5	3.5	1.0
1975	41.0	56.0	25.0	15.0	22.0	7.0	1.9	2.7	0.9
1980	39.0	51.0	27.0	14.0	20.0	8.0	—	—	—
1985	48.0	61.0	34.0	18.0	24.0	10.0	5.1	6.9	3.2
1987	40.0	51.0	28.0	19.0	26.0	11.0	5.0	6.7	3.1

* Data not available. Dashes also represent unavailable data.
Source: UNESCO, *Unesco Statistical Yearbook*, 1963, 1970, 1980, 1985, and 1991.

Table 9.2 Female Participation in Primary Education, 1948–91

Year	Number of Schools			Enrollment (in Thousands)		
	Total	Schools for Females	Female % of Total	Total	Female Enrollment	Female % of Total
1947–48	8,413	1,549	18	770	110	14
1960–61	20,909	4,057	19	2,060	430	21
1970–71	43,710	12,097	28	3,960	1,040	26
1980–81	59,168	18,595	31	5,474	1,782	33
1985–86	77,207	22,441	29	7,049	2,365	34
1990–91*	127,575	28,535	22	8,856	3,047	34

Note: * = estimated
Source: Government of Pakistan, Ministry of Education, *Review of Educational Policies and Corresponding Five Year Plans (1947–1986)*; Government of Pakistan, Ministry of Education, *Pakistan Education Statistics, Summary Tables, 1980–81 to 1990–91*. (Islamabad: Government of Pakistan, 1991); Government of Pakistan, Women's Division, *World Conference of the United Nations*, Annexure IV.

Educational Wastage at the Primary Level

The enrollment figures, however, do not provide any clue to the high attrition that occurs. The gross enrollment rates, which are usually reported for all primary education or all secondary classes, tend to mask some very important aspects of educational processes—retention, attainment, repetition, and dropout. It has been estimated that more than 50% of students drop out before completing the primary stage. Female dropout rate is much higher.[45] A study of rural Pakistan illustrates that 54% of the boys and 73% of the girls drop out before reaching grade 2. Only 10% of school-aged girls reached grade 5.[46] Wastage at the primary level makes the enrollment rate insignificant, since it does not contribute to long-lasting literacy.

Secondary Education

Secondary education starts with grade 6. In 1947–48 there were 153 middle schools and 64 high schools for females, which comprised 6% and 16% of the total number of schools at the relevant levels. By 1990–91 the figures had risen to 2,333 (32%) and 1,864 (30%) respectively. Females constituted only 10% of middle and 12% of high school enrollment in 1947–48. By 1990–91 they were 28% and 29% respectively (Table 9.3). Again, despite the improvement, gender disparities remain. On average, urban boys are in an advantageous position over urban girls and rural children. Rural girls are the most disadvantaged.

Table 9.3 Female Participation in Secondary Education, 1947–91

	Number of Schools			Enrollment (in Thousands)		
	Total	Schools for Females	Female % of Total	Total	Female Enrollment	Female % of Total
Middle Schools (Grades 6–8)						
1947–48	2,443	153	6	221	21	10
1960–61	1,974	281	14	422	63	15
1970–71	3,560	860	24	899	175	19
1980–81	5,295	1,412	27	1,412	359	25
1990–91*	7,389	2,333	32	2,530	705	28
High Schools (Grades 9–10)						
1947–48	408	64	16	58	7	12
1960–61	1,069	203	19	149	23	15
1970–71	1,995	520	26	337	62	18
1980–81	3,479	917	26	509	130	26
1990–91*	6,215	1,864	30	866	247	29
Secondary Vocational Education						
1947–48	46	18	39	4	2	50
1960–61	109	47	43	15	6	40
1970–71	206	97	47	35	10	29
1980–81	231	88	38	40	7	18
1990–91*	574	299	52	142	42	30

* = estimated
Source: Same as Table 9.2.

To increase women's participation in mainstream economic activities, vocational education is an important avenue. Government Vocational Institutes for Girls provide such education. These institutes generally provide one- to two-year diploma programs in traditional activities such as sewing, knitting, dressmaking, leather goods production, and handicrafts. Vocational and technical education for males embodies different contents, such as accountancy, secretarial practices, bookkeeping, supervision, carpentry, masonry, welding, and so on.

In 1947–48 only 39% of the vocational institutions were for females; yet females comprised 50% of the vocational student body (Table 9.3). By 1990–91 there were 574 secondary vocational institutions, of which 299 (52%) were for females. Females comprised only about 30% of the total vocational enrollment. In recent years a number of women's polytechnics have been established to train middle-level female professionals. Although the number of female students has been increasing, the proportion of females has declined over time. A plausible explanation for this decline is that the institutions were not accessible to females or the courses did not meet the needs of prospective students.

Tertiary Education

Education at the tertiary level is provided either in degree-granting colleges or in universities, which are overwhelmingly male institutions. In general there has been an overall trend of increase in female enrollment except at universities, as shown in Table 9.4.

Table 9.4 Female Participation in Higher Education, 1947–91

	Number of Institutions			Enrollment		
	Total	Female Colleges	Female (%)	Total	Female Enrollment	Female (%)
Arts and Science Colleges						
1947–48	40	5	13	14,000	1,000	7
1960–61	131	33	25	71,000	12,000	17
1970–71	514	87	17	199,000	50,000	25
1980–81	434	120	28	270,000	87,000	32
1990–91*	612	218	36	496,000	182,000	37
Professional Colleges						
1947–48	17	2	12	4,368	327	7
1960–61	42	5	12	12,921	1,929	15
1970–71	73	6	8	37,245	4,612	12
1980–81	100	8	8	77,662	14,426	19
1990–91*	99	8	8	85,500	23,700	28
Universities						
1947–48	2	—	—	644	56	9
1960–61	4	—	—	5,084	1,009	20
1970–71	7	—	—	17,057	3,703	22
1980–81	19	—	—	42,678	7,113	17
1990–91*	22	—	—	73,382	10,310	14

Note: Professional colleges include Agriculture, Medicine, Engineering, Education, Home Economics, etc. Source: Same as Table 9.2.

* = estimated

University education is coeducational in Pakistan. In 1947 there were two universities, which together enrolled only 644 students. Of these, only 56 (9%) were females. By 1990–91 the number of universities had increased to 22 and that of students to 73,382, of which 10,310 (14%) were female. Although the number of students has been increasing, the percentage of female students has been decreasing since 1970–71, when it was 22%. The reasons for decline need further exploration.

At the tertiary level, the pervasive problem is gender streaming. Women are concentrated in subjects that are often characterized as soft fields. This problem is recorded in both industrialized and developing countries.[47] Pakistan is no exception. Women are enrolled mostly in arts and humanities rather than in science subjects (see Table 9.5). The limited professional opportunities and segregated labor market also depress women's aspirations for highly technical and scientific fields.

Barriers to Female Education

If women's education is crucial for social and economic development, as mentioned earlier, why does the gender gap persist? Two factors are cited as the major impediment for female education in Pakistan: sociocultural attitudes and poverty. The existence of long-standing traditions of social segregation of women, early marriage, the exclusion of women from the organized labor force, the subordination of women to male members of the family, and women's unequal status in society in general indicate the negative attitudes. In culturally restrictive environments, adolescent girls may be viewed as morally suspect if they continue going to school. The importance of preserving a girl's "purity" up to marriage leads to widespread withdrawal of girls from school at puberty, particularly if they are attending coeducational schools.[48] The observation of cultural norms further increases the costs of educating girls. For example, parental reluctance to send daughters to school without proper attire increases the cost of girls' school attendance. Education is also perceived as corrupting the traditional attitudes of females. Smock reported the results of an attitudinal survey in Pakistan in which education was believed to be changing women into self-centered beings, defiant of parental authority, and uninterested in household chores.[49] Thus, education of girls becomes socially costly.

In Pakistan the most important findings of relevant studies identified the lack of school facilities as the main reason for nonenrollment of girls.[50] Citing various surveys, Summers reports that girls do not enroll in schools because there are no schools for them. If schools are provided for girls, the gender gap at the primary level may close.[51] These findings imply that the

Table 9.5 Distribution of Women in Higher Education by Field of Study, 1986

Field of Study	Level 6		Level 7		All Levels	
	Total of Male and Female (N)	Female (%)	Total (N)	Female (%)	Total (N)	Female (%)
Education	6,371	45.7	1,440	33.6	7,811	43.5
Humanities and Religion	3,053	22	7,302	33.3	10,355	30
Fine and Applied Science	0	0	0	0	0	0
Law	13,101	8.2	80	0	13,181	8.1
Social and Behavioral Science*						
Commercial and Business Administration	14,028	15.3	2,159	12.6	16,187	14.9
Mass Communication & Documentaries	0	0	0	0	0	0
Home Economics	1,477	10	0	0	1,477	10
Service Trades	0	0	0	0	0	0
Natural Science	6,219	21	6,665	24.4	12,884	22.8
Mathematics and Computer Sciences*						

Table 9.5 Distribution of Women in Higher Education by Field of Study, 1986 (continued)

Field of Study	Level 6		Level 7		All Levels	
	Total of Male and Female	Female (%)	Total (N)	Female (%)	Total (N)	Female (%)
Medical and Health-Related	21,625	33.8	112	2.5	21,737	33.7
Engineering	29,645	2.2	129	0	29,774	2.2
Architecture and Town Planning*						
Trade, Craft, and Industrial Programs	0	0	0	0	0	0
Transport and Communications	0	0	0	0	0	0
Agriculture	6,372	1.5	1,385	1.2	7,757	1.4
Others and Not Specified	15,042	15.7	555	35.3	15,597	16.4

* = data are included elsewhere with another category.
Note: Unesco defines level 6 as programs leading to a first university degree or equivalent qualification and level 7 as leading to a postgraduate university degree or equivalent qualification.
Source: *Unesco Statistical Yearbook, 1991*, Table 3.12.

lack of schools rather than cultural inhibitions is the single most important reason for the low rate of female enrollment in Pakistan.

Mothers' attitudes also influence their daughters' education. Smock, citing a village survey in Pakistan, reported that 83% of the village women did not want their daughters to complete even primary schooling and 90% did not support the notion of the equality of opportunity for women.[52] Shah reported the results of a National Impact Survey which indicated that about 27% of urban mothers and 46% of rural mothers believed religious education or about one year of formal education was enough for girls. The findings show that mothers' aspirations for their daughters are dependent on their social class background. Higher parental socioeconomic status has a positive effect on education for both daughters and sons.[53] However, some studies show that fathers' education exterts more influence than mothers' on daughters' education.[54] Parental background also determines the kind of schools females attend and their fields of study. Female students in engineering, medicine, and other professional programs tend to come from richer families.[55]

Poverty was cited as the major reason for female nonenrollment in most studies on Pakistan.[56] Related to it is the demand for child labor. Data suggest that the opportunity costs of schooling in Pakistan were higher for daughters than for sons. Young girls undertake more useful work than their brothers do. Results of a study show that a much higher percentage (61%) of girls dropped out of school because of the demands of domestic tasks, such as housework, care for younger siblings, and collection of fodder, than did boys (28%).[57]

Another explanation for girls' nonenrollment is level of economic development. Some have argued that gender inequality in enrollment is linked to the general economic development of a country.[58] This argument contradicts several studies on other Third World countries that indicate that level of development does not predict the gender gap.[59] They argued that the gender gap in education will not be eliminated with industrialization or increase in per capita GNP and that it persisted because of cultural factors and parental attitudes. If the dominant culture is indifferent or hostile to female education, few women are found among the adult students even if the country is economically relatively well developed.[60] Further, many argue that Islam and its purdah system restrict female education in Pakistan. However, the correlation between the two is not clear.[61]

The mismatch between labor market opportunities and female education also affects women's enrollment, especially at the tertiary level. Often women are channeled into traditional fields of study irrespective of market demand. Lack of marketability of women with postsecondary education discourages other women from seeking higher education.

Nonformal Education

Information on nonformal education (NFE) for females is very inadequate. In general, the nonformal system comprises mosque schools, *mohalla* schools (community schools), women's education centers, village workshops, and community viewing/adult literacy community centers.[62] These programs are supervised by the Village Education Committees of each village. They mainly impart literacy and vocational training, which often includes traditional skills such as knitting and embroidery, which are not likely to generate income. Mosques have traditionally offered religious education. The nonformal schools, established by the government and by NGOs in mosques, offer both religious and the standard school curricula. In general, mosque schools do not go beyond the third grade, and *mohalla* schools may not include girls. In recent years, the Women's Division has sponsored numerous programs of skills training for women. No information on female enrollment is available.

Marker and Gah describe a home school[63] project in Beldia, a large squatter settlement in Pakistan, which began in 1980. The project, by introducing flexible timing for local women to receive high school education, opened home schools for girls within the community. By the time the report was written 64 schools had been opened, with an enrollment of 1,800 students. The curricula of the home schools include teaching of the Koran, basic literacy, and home management.[64] The project demonstrates that girls and women would respond to educational opportunity if it was accessible and if it took into consideration the financial and social restrictions women face in the community and at home. The demand for home schools shows that the quality of teaching and the curricula are acceptable to parents.

EDUCATION AND LABOR FORCE PARTICIPATION
Female Labor Force Participation Rates

In Pakistan, the process of development has created employment conditions that are beyond the ability of education to resolve. Furthermore, dire economic necessity, rather than education alone, has generated female response to the labor market. Women participate mainly in the agricultural and informal sectors of the economy that do not operate on the basis of formal education. As a result, increase in participation of women in the rural and informal labor force cannot be attributed to education alone.

Women's employment is a difficult subject to deal with. There are ambiguities regarding the definition of employment, such as the type of activities (agricultural work at home or family help), which are not included in employment rates, and the reference period upon which to base these rates. This makes the tools for measuring employment and unemployment very inaccurate. If the measurements are not adequate for men, they are even less so for women. In Pakistan there has been no consensus on the percentage of women in the labor force, since different sources render widely different estimates. Women's economic participation is greatly underestimated in official statistics, mainly due to unsuitable methods of data collection, inappropriate definitions of activities and stress on recording only one activity, and the cultural inhibition against reporting that women are working.

According to the 1961 census more than 70% of all working women (age 10 and above) were employed in agricultural activities; of these the majority (76%) were employed as unpaid family helpers. Since then, the situation has not changed substantially. Probable underreporting of unpaid work is considerable. Moreover, the seasonal nature of work may contribute to miscalculation of the number of hours of such work. According to the 1981 census, there were 0.84 million (3.2% of female population aged 10 and above) economically active women, compared with 21.8 million (72.4%) men.[65] Of the total economically active population, only 3.7% women were in the labor force, compared with 96.3% of males. The official data thus totally ignore women's participation in domestic, unorganized, or informal sectors. Most males do not work at home, while most women try to combine productive activity and household chores. Since a large number of households subsist in absolute poverty, the assumption that more than 90% of women perform only nonincome-generating domestic chores is inconceivable. There are a whole range of productive activities in which women work and fully participate with men but their input goes unrecognized. Shah reports that some small-scale surveys in villages show a much larger percentage of women in rural areas are engaged in economic activities than a typical census or labor force survey reveals. It is estimated that the participation rate is certainly much higher than the percentages recorded in census data.[66] The Agricultural Census of 1980, which made serious attempts to document women's participation rate, showed it to be 73% in agriculture. This is highly inconsistent with the Population Census report of about 3% rural female participation rate. If the former is accurate, official statistics have "omitted" 12 million rural female workers.[67]

In the urban economy the problem of measurement again surfaces because of the existence of an informal sector. According to the 1981 census, female labor force participation rate (FLFPR) was 3.5% in urban areas, while the 1985–86 Labor Force Survey showed it to be 4.7%.[68] A

World Bank study arrived at an urban female participation rate of 25% and argued that official statistics "omitted" about 20% (1.91 million) of the urban female working population. A breakdown of the 25% indicated 4.7% in the urban formal sector and 20.3% in the informal sector in 1986.[69] Although women's contribution to the economy is now widely recognized, much of the increase has been taking place outside the formal sector. While most women in the informal sector have little formal schooling, education is required in the formal sector for women to obtain gainful employment. Within the formal sector women are concentrated in a few occupation groups.

Female Employment by Occupation

The labor market in Pakistan is highly segregated. Although women are being increasingly employed, they are concentrated in low-status and low-paid jobs. Very few women are engaged at the supervisory level in either the public or the private sector.[70]

According to the 1981 Census the highest percentage of women are concentrated in agriculture and related occupations (35.4%), followed by production work (24%) and professional work (15.4%) (Table 9.6). Table 9.6 also indicates that in 1985–86 the highest percentage of labor force in the urban formal sector consisted of production workers (39%), followed by professional (26%) and service workers (13%). The three together accounted for 78% of urban female employment. Data from the Labour Force Survey indicated that females comprise a significant and rising portion of the occupational category of professionals and related workers. Between 1984/85 and 1987/88 the female share of this group increased from 15.5% to 18.3% of the total. Although more women were entering nontraditional fields such as engineering, banking, and law, their participation in them remained very limited, and the major increase in this category was confined to teaching and medicine.

In 1991 women constituted 32.9% of the teaching force in primary schools, 30.8% in middle schools, 32.9% in high schools, 33% in arts and science colleges, 31% in vocational institutes, 27.5% in professional colleges, and only 15% in universities.[71] The Commission on the Status of Women reports that although the largest portion of educated working women was in the teaching profession, they were underrepresented at policy-making or top administrative ranks. In fact, women were often superseded by men of lower qualifications and less experience.[72]

The demand for women in teaching and medicine is itself the result of gender segregation in society. The other reasons for segregation of

Table 9.6 Female Participation in the Occupational Structure, 1981 and 1985-86

Occupation	National 1981				Urban 1985-86	
	Total	Women (N)	Women (%)*	Distribution (%)**	Women (%)*	Distribution (%)**
Professional and tech-related workers	843,529	128,185	15.2	15.4	22.2	25.6
Administrative and managerial workers	292,916	5,850	2.0	0.7	3.3	1.1
Clerical and related workers	689,392	21,138	3.1	2.5	2.5	3.4
Sales workers	1,818,671	36,585	2.0	4.4	1.4	5.1
Service workers	922,642	65,007	7.0	7.8	11.8	13.1
Agriculture, animal husbandry and forestry workers, fishermen and hunters	11,276,644	295,384	2.6	35.4	12.6	12.5
Production related workers, transport equipment operators & laborer	5,604,370	200,738	3.6	24.0	5.8	39.2
Others	476,476	19,524	4.1	2.3	—	—
Unemployed	701,808	62,679	8.9	7.5	—	—
Total	22,626,448	835,090	3.69	100.0		100.0

* Women as a percentage of labor force in group.
** Percentage distribution of women by occupation.

Note: See World Bank, *World Development Report, 1993*, Table 31.

Source: Calculated from ILO, *Year Book of Labour Statistics: Retrospect Edition, Population Censuses*. (Geneva: ILO, 1945–89), Table 2B; for figures on urban occupational structure see Labour Force Survey 1985-86 as presented by the World Bank, *Women in Pakistan*, Table 22, Annex 1.

women in a few occupations include prevailing social attitudes regarding women's aptitudes, job discrimination and/or resistance of employers, denial of training opportunities in higher skills for women, and the lack of access to information regarding opportunities open to women. Recent progress in women's education, though limited, has helped women to enter areas previously monopolized by men. In other white-collar jobs, such as management and clerical work, the proportion of women is still very small.

Although education provides women with a chance to participate in the occupational ladder, women's age, marital status, and conjugal roles all influence their participation rates in the labor force. The activity rates are highest among widowed and divorced women who had less than ten years of schooling. For example, a survey in 1973 showed that 22% of all widowed and 38% of all divorced women who had less than ten years of schooling were in paid employment, compared with 2% of all single and 5% of all married women with a similar educational attainment.[74]

A recent study in Rawalpindi City also indicates that widows are the highest percentage (65%) of working women, and the explanation offered is that widows have the lowest household income and therefore high rates of labor force participation.[75] The higher participation rates of widowed, divorced, and single women suggest that these women have greater economic need than married women and that married women's conjugal roles at home prevent them from gainful employment. Findings of a survey indicate that, on average, working women are slightly younger and have smaller numbers of living children than nonworking women.[76] Hamid reported that the household size and household composition were, among others, major factors that influence women's entry into the labor market. She showed that the rearing of younger children inhibits women's access to the labor market.[77] The conflict between women's productive and reproductive roles is a major reason for women to stay at home. Thus, besides education, women's family structure and economic needs, as well as society's attitudes may influence their participation in the labor force.

In general, the employment opportunities for females in Pakistan are limited. The government's affirmative action plan of introducing a quota system[78] for female employment is neither sufficient nor effective. Barriers to formal-sector employment are much greater for women than for men. On the supply side, women's lower education and skill levels limit them. The labor laws in Pakistan make special provisions of maternity leave, crèches, working hours, and so on for women workers who are hired on a permanent basis (for more than six months). These provisions in effect discourage employers from hiring women on a permanent basis and have led to a widespread practice of hiring women on a temporary basis, which deprives them of work-related benefits as well as the opportunity to raise their productivity through on-the-job experience.[79] Although there are supply-side constraints related to proper skills and educational training, household responsibilities, and cultural barriers, Kazi and Raza argued that keeping women out of regular employment and in casual jobs in the informal sector with no security or benefits is the outcome of a deliberate policy of exploiting a cheap source of labor.[80] To increase female participation, government must take appropriate actions to remove both supply- and demand-side barriers.

Impact of Women's Education on Family and Children

The social benefits from female education have been demonstrated in a number of studies.[81] Evidence shows that women's education reduces fertility, lowers maternal and infant mortality rates, and produces better educated children. Educated women desire to have fewer children and are better able to reach their desired fertility. Research is scarce that would allow one to draw any major conclusions about the impact of women's education on the family and children in Pakistan. Findings of one survey showed that educated women had higher expectations for the education of both their sons and daughters.[82] This study also indicated that many women, especially illiterate and/or poor ones, had a very low educational aspiration for girls. One of the reasons for educating girls is that it increases their future prospect for marriage into middle-class families. It should be noted that in Pakistani society a wife is always expected to have less education than her husband, but increasingly, especially in the middle-class families, education becomes the precondition for marriage into higher status families.

Women's education increases their decision-making power in the family, especially regarding fertility control. Sathar's study, based on data from the Pakistan Fertility Survey of 1975, indicated that educated women desired smaller families.[83] Women with no schooling had an average of 5.1 children, while those with less than secondary education had 4.4, those with secondary education 3.9, and those with college education 3.7 children.[84]

There is also evidence that educated mothers prevent the deaths of their infants and children more frequently than do women without any schooling. Interestingly, female children of educated mothers have a lower infant mortality rate than male children.[85]

Women's Education and Political Participation

The political arena in Pakistan is dominated by males. Although the country has recently elected a female prime minister by popular vote, she is a token. The small number of women who are actively involved in politics come from an urban upper class and politically dominant families. This means women's education alone does not necessarily allow women to take part in the political system.

Women played an important role in the independence movement. However, despite their widely recognized contribution, only two women were included in the Constituent Assembly after independence. Various constitutions (1956, 1962, 1973) and the Legal Frame Work Order of 1970 reserved seats for women in the national and the provincial assemblies. The 1973 Constitution accorded a much higher status to women. It gave complete equality to women to contest for all election posts, and 5% additional seats were exclusively reserved for women in National and Provincial Assemblies. In Pakistan, to ensure women's participation, seats are reserved for them; otherwise they might not be elected to the assemblies.

In the 1985 election the number of seats reserved in the National and the Provincial Assembly was doubled, reaching 20 in the National Assembly. The Constitution guarantees the right to vote and reservation of seats for women and has thus raised women's political participation. But this has not increased the power of women in the political system, nor has it secured them political equality. There were only 66 women candidates for 23 Provincial Assembly seats, compared with 3,853 male candidates for the 483 seats in the 1985 election. Sixty-four women candidates contested for the 20 reserved seats of the National Assembly. There were no women in the Senate; not a single woman was appointed as Federal Minister.[86]

Women's participation at the local government level is low but important. The rural councils are divided into two tiers: the union and the district level. Women councilors in local government exert powerful influence and have wide responsibilities. In the early 1980s, they totaled 8,000 and can be the catalysts of change for women's liberation because they operate at the grassroots level.[87] Women councilors are also elected by the male-elected members of their councils. This does not, however, prevent them from contesting for general seats, and quite a few females have been elected directly in the local level elections.

The foregoing discussion shows women's limited participation in the political system. Urban upper- and middle-class women have occasionally joined political movements, though this has not been converted into sustained political activism. Recently a noticeable degree of political activity by educated women to secure legal and political rights has developed in the country. There are many women's organizations that fight for women's rights. However, most rural women who were not exposed to any education had little opportunity for genuine political participation. Most women exercise their voting rights only when asked to or compelled by the male head of the family.[88] If these women were educated, they probably would exercise their voting rights independently.

Conclusion

Women's roles in Pakistan are constructed by sex-gender systems that influence the availability of women's access to schooling and other social services, as well as the types and quality of social services offered to them. Women's access to goods and services, to productive assets, and to markets (including the right to sell their own labor) is conditioned in a way that men's is not. Sociocultural factors dictate that women remain in the private sphere because of their reproductive and nurturing roles, while men deal with the public sphere. Women retain the traditional responsibilities for childrearing and the welfare of the family; they are responsible for processing foodcrops, preparing food, and carrying a heavy workload of domestic tasks, including time-consuming burdens of fetching firewood and water. In general, women tend to control fewer productive resources than men, they are engaged in a wider range of activities in the working day, and they enjoy less mobility.

Although women contribute substantially to Pakistan's economic development, the gender-specific differences in schooling remain. The lack of school provision limits women's chances to enter the formal economy or to empower themselves. A few women who did get a chance to receive education and managed to enter modern sector occupations remained in professions that are socially segregated. Further, the reproductive roles women play at home limit their full participation in the labor force. At the same time, women who participate in the labor force take the double load of work, while men do not. Thus education alone cannot bring about equality in the development efforts. To achieve this, change in the patriarchal structure is required. While education is a precondition for modern sector jobs, without changing the structure of the country equality cannot be ensured.

In addition, access to education and work options vary for women of different socioeconomic strata. Evidence shows that a large number of women have been entering the labor market in recent years. It is not because education opened up more jobs for women or development needs required women's labor force participation, but because poverty forced women to enter the labor market. The majority of women who are working come from the lower strata and have little formal education. Only elite women enter professions. Thus gender cuts across class in terms of work options.

The above discussion does not mean to undermine the importance of education. The argument is that we have to get into the roots of the problem and simultaneously increase women's educational attainment. It is not only because women's education increases social and economic returns, an argument already well established, but also because education is their fundamental right.

NOTES

*I would like to thank Grace Mak and Junko Kanamura for their valuable comments.

1. Initially, Pakistan comprised two constituent parts, East Pakistan and West Pakistan, which were separated from each other by 1,600 kilometers of Indian territory. In December 1971 East Pakistan, after nine months of bloody civil war, declared itself an independent country—Bangladesh. Pakistan now consists of four provinces (the Punjab, Sind, the North-West Frontier Province, and Baluchistan), the federal capital Islamabad, and federally administered areas.

2. Pakistan Commission on the Status of Women, *The Report of the Pakistan Commission on the Status of Women* (Islamabad: Pakistan Commission on the Status of Women, 1984).

3. The terms women's welfare and women's development are used interchangeably in this chapter.

4. Only Brahmins of the highest caste were allowed to study all the Vedas. The education of the other castes was geared to the occupation assigned to them in the caste system. See Suma B. Chitnis, "India," in: Gail P. Kelly, ed., *International Handbook of Women's Education* (Westport, CT: Greenwood Press, 1989), pp. 135–162; *Report on Status of Women*, p. 23.

5. Chitnis, "India," op. cit.

6. A. S. Altekar, *Position of Women in Hindu Civilization* (New Delhi: Manager of Publications, 1962), pp. 410–414, cited in Chitnis, "India."

7. Chitnis, "India," and *Report on Status of Women*, p. 23.

8. Burning of the widow alive along with the dead body of her husband on the pyre.

9. For an elaborate discussion on how various laws in ancient India dictated women's position, see Malladi Subbamma, *Women: Tradition and Culture* (New Delhi: Sterling Publishers, 1985).

10. Indian Statutory Commission, *Interim Report of the Indian Statutory Commission* (Review of Growth of Education in British India by the Auxiliary Committee Appointed by the Commission) (London: His Majesty's Stationery Office, 1929):9–10.

11. *Report on Status of Women*, pp. 24–26.

12. Chitnis, "India."

13. Martin Carnoy, *Education as Cultural Imperialism* (New York: David McKay Co., 1974):80–82.

14. For an elaborate discussion on how education policies changed, see Aparna Basu, "Policy and Conflict in India: The Reality and Perception of Education," in: P. G. Altbach and Gail P. Kelly, eds., *Education and Colonialism* (New York: Longman, 1978); and Carnoy, *Education as Cultural Imperialism*.

15. Indian Statutory Commission, *The Interim Report*, p. 10.
16. Nasram Shah, ed., *Pakistani Women: A Socioeconomic and Demographic Profile* (Islamabad: Pakistan Institute of Development Economics, 1986): 22; Khawar Mumtaz and Farida Shaheed, *Women's Education in Pakistan: Opportunities, Issues and Challenges* (N.p., [1987?], p. 4; and Chitnis, "India."
17. M.S. Huq, *Education and Development Strategy in South and Southeast Asia* (Honolulu: East-West Center Press, 1965):38.
18. Government of Pakistan, Planning Commission, *Seventh Five Year Plan 1988–93 and 1988–2003.* (Islamabad: Pakistan Planning Commission, 1988), Chapter 5.
19. In 1979 $1=9.9 rupees. The World Bank, *World Tables* (Baltimore: The Johns Hopkins University Press/The World Bank, 1993).
20. These services include education, health care, water supply and sewerage, transport and communications, banking, credit and savings, energy, employment and wages, etc.
21. Of the multiple roles of women in Pakistan, the parental and conjugal roles are primary, while the occupational and community roles are secondary. In Pakistan, the family predominates in major decisions regarding a woman's or a man's life. See Shah, *Pakistani Women*, p. 5.
22. The World Bank, *Women in Pakistan: An Economic and Social Strategy* (Washington, DC: The World Bank, 1989).
23. Ibid.
24. Ibid.
25. World Bank, *World Development Report (WDR) 1993: Investing in Health* (Oxford: The World Bank, 1993), Table 28.
26. Ibid., Table 26.
27. The decline in the fertility rate in Pakistan was only about 6% between 1965 and 1985, compared with almost 40% in all low-income countries. Since the mid-1970s, there has not been a further decline in fertility in Pakistan. World Bank, *Women in Pakistan*.
28. Nancy Birdsall, *Social Development is Economic Development*. HRO Working Paper, Human Resources Development and Operation Policy (Washington, DC: The World Bank, 1993).
29. George Psacharopoulos, *Returns to Investment in Education: A Global Update*. Working Paper, WPS 1067 (Washington, DC: The World Bank, 1993); T. P. Schultz, "Returns to Women's Education," in: E. King and A. Hill, eds., *Women's Education in Developing Countries* (Baltimore: The Johns Hopkins University Press, 1993): 51–99; K. Subbarao and L. Raney, *Social Gains from Female Education*. World Bank Discussion Paper No. 194 (Washington, DC: The World Bank, 1993).
30. Government of Pakistan, *Seventh Plan*, p. 279.
31. A. Ghafoor, "Pakistan: System of Education," in: T. Husen and T. N. Postlethwaite, eds., *International Encyclopedia of Education* (New York: Pergamon Press, 1985): 3745–3749.
32. Commensurate with the Universal Declaration of Human Rights by UNESCO in 1948, basic and primary education in Pakistan was also viewed as one of the rights. As Article 26 of the Declaration stated, everyone has the right to education. It stated that "Education shall be free at least in the elementary and fundamental stages. . . ." See Louis François, *The Right to Education: From Proclamation to Achievement 1948–1968* (Paris: UNESCO, 1968):17.
33. Government of Pakistan, *The First Five Year Plan*, pp. 545–548.
34. Government of Pakistan, Ministry of Education, *Review of Educational Policies and Corresponding Five Year Plans (1947–1986)* (Pakistan: Government of Pakistan, Ministry of Education, 1986):24.
35. Government of Pakistan, *Seventh Plan, 1988–93*, p. 280.
36. Ibid, pp. 245–282.

37. *The Fourth Five Year Plan (1970–75)* was not implemented. During the period 1970–78 no plans were followed. Therefore 1970–78 was considered as a nonplan period.

38. Government of Pakistan, *Review of Education Policies,* Annexure VI.

39. Government of Pakistan, *Sixth Five Year Plan,* pp. 383–84.

40. Government of Pakistan, *Review of Education Policies,* Annexure VI.

41. The definition of a literate person has been a constant problem. The 1951, 1961, 1972, and 1981 censuses defined literacy in somewhat different terms. The percentages of literate persons thus differ. The definition has become more restrictive. For example, the 1951 census collected information on whether a person could "read a clear print in any language," the 1961 census asked whether a person could read a simple letter, in any language, with understanding; and the 1972 census and HED Survey treated literate persons as those "who were able to read and write in some language, with understanding." See Nasra M. Sha, "Education: Level, Enrollment, Facilities and Attitudes," in Shah, op. cit. (note 16), pp. 207–263.

42. UNESCO, *Statistical Yearbook,* 1991.

43. Ibid.

44. Tables 2, 3, and 4 show that some enrollment figures dropped by 1980–81. It seems this was mainly because of the difference in counting system of two government institutions, which often provide different figures.

45. Government of Pakistan, Women's Division (Cabinet Secretariat), *World Conference of the United Nations Decade for Women: 1975–85. Equality, Development and Peace, Pakistan Country Paper.* Nairobi, Kenya, July 15–26, 1985, p. 7.

46. Bureau of Educational Planning and Management (BEPM), *Pakistan Education Statistics* (Islamabad: Ministry of Education, 1976) cited in Shah, Education: Level, Enrollment.

47. K. Subbarao et al. *Women in Higher Education: Progress, Constraints and Promising Approaches.* Background Paper, Education and Social Policy Department, WID Team (Washington, DC: The World Bank, 1993).

48. M. B. Anderson, "On Girls' Access to Primary Education in Pakistan." *The Bridges Forum,* January 3–8, 1988, p. 6.

49. A. C. Smock, *Women's Education in Developing Countries: Opportunities and Outcomes* (New York: Praeger, 1981):91.

50. Shah, "Education: Level, Enrollment"; Meher K. Marker and Shirkat Gah, *Women, Education and Development in Pakistan;* The World Bank, *Women in Pakistan,* p. 3.

51. Lawrence H. Summers, "Investing in All the People: Educating Women in Developing Countries." Speech delivered at Development Economics Seminar, 1992 World Bank Annual Meeting (np).

52. Smock, op. cit. p. 91.

53. Shah, "Education: Level, Enrollment."

54. M. Irfan, "Poverty, Class Structure and Household Demographic Behavior in Rural Pakistan." Pakistan Institute of Development Economics, research report (Islamabad: PIDE, 1985); E. King et al., *Change in the Status of Women Across Generations in Asia* (Santa Monica, CA: The RAND Corporation, 1986):52.

55. King et al., ibid., pp. 28–29.

56. For example, see Zubeida Mustafa, *Women's Education in Pakistan* (N.p., [1986?]); Marker and Gah, *Women, Education and Development;* (N.p., [1985?]); also see studies cited by Shah, "Education: Level, Enrollment;" Khan, "South Asia," in: Elizabeth King and A. Hill, eds., *Women's Education in Developing Countries: Barriers, Benefits and Policy,* pp. 211–246.

57. Cited in Smock, *Women's Education in Developing Countries: Opportunities and Outcomes,* p. 93.

58. See Milton Adams and Susan Kruppenbach, "Gender and Access in the African School," *International Review of Education* 33 (1987): 437–453; N. El-

Sanabary, *Determinants of Women's Education in the Middle East and North Africa: Illustration from Seven Countries*, Education and Employment Division, Population and Human Resources Department, Document No. PHREE/89/14 (Washington, DC: The World Bank, 1989); Ines Bustillo, *Female Educational Attainment in Latin America: A Survey*, Education and Employment Division, Population and Human Resources Department, Document No. PHREE/89/16 (Washington, DC: The World Bank, 1989).

59. Barbara Herz, K. Subbarao, Massoma Habib, and Laura Raney, *Letting Girls Learn: Promising Approaches in Primary and Secondary Education*, World Bank Discussion Paper No. 133 (Washington DC: The World Bank, 1991) Gail P. Kelly, "Achieving Equality in Education—Prospects and Realities" in: Gail P. Kelly, ed., *International Handbook of Women's Education*, op. cit., 547–569.

60. E. Boserup, *Women's Role in Economic Development* (New York: St. Martins Press, 1970):121.

61. Mustafa, *Women's Education in Pakistan*; Marker and Gah, *Women, Education, and Development in Pakistan*. Other muslim societies like Morocco, Kuwait, and Malaysia have relatively high female participation rates in education.

62. Canadian International Development Agency (CIDA), *Nation Builders: Women in Pakistan: A Development Strategy* (Ottawa: CIDA, 1986):19.

63. Home schools are actually run by older women at home.

64. Marker and Gah, *Women, Education, and Development*, pp. 7–9.

65. Economically active population figures exclude armed forces. The civilian labor force comprises population age ten years and above who are presently employed or unemployed. See International Labor Office, *Year Book of Labour Statistics: Retrospective Edition on Population Censuses, 1945–89* (Geneva: ILO, 1990), Table 1, p. 72.

66. Nasra M. Shah, "Female Employment," in Shah, op. cit., pp. 265–301.

67. The World Bank, *Women in Pakistan*, pp. 85–86.

68. Ibid., p. 85.

69. Ibid., pp. 86–89.

70. Shahnaz Kazi and Bilquees Raza, "Duality of Female Employment in Pakistan," *The Pakistan Development Review*, 30: 4 Part II(Winter 1991):733–743.

71. Calculated from Ministry of Education, *Pakistan Education Statistics*, pp. 1–7.

72. *Report on Status of Women*, pp. 91–92.

73. Nursing is not a prestigious profession in Pakistan, and women who continue secondary education and who typically come from middle or upper-middle class families may not find this profession attractive.

74. Calculated from HED Survey (1973) by Shah, "Female Employment," Table 7.6.

75. Shahnaz Hamid, "Determinants of the Supply of Women in the Labour Market: A Micro Analysis," *The Pakistan Development Review*, 30: 4 Part II (Winter 1991):755–766.

76. Shah, "Female Employment," Table 7.7.

77. Hamid, "Women in the Labour Market."

78. The Sixth Plan aimed at a target 10–15 % quota for recruitment of women, mainly in government service. See Government of Pakistan, *Decade of Women*, p. 14.

79. The World Bank, *Women in Pakistan*, p. 98.

80. Kazi and Raza, "Female Employment."

81. For example, see K. Subbarao and Laura Raney, *Social Gains From Female Education*; also see the review of studies by Robert Le Vine, "Influences of Women's Schooling on Maternal Behavior in the Third World," in: G. Kelly and C. Elliott, eds., *Women's Education in the Third World*, pp. 283–310.

82. Shah, "Education: Level, Enrollment." It should also be noted that women with more education come from economically better off families.

83. Zeba A. Sathar, "Does Female Education Affect Fertility Behaviour in Pakistan?" *Pakistan Development Review,* 23: 4 (Winter 1984):573–594.
84. The World Bank, *Women in Pakistan,* Annex 1, table 7.
85. Sathar, "Does Female Education Affect Fertility?"
86. *Report on Status of Women,* p. 119.
87. Ibid, p. 121.
88. Ibid, p. 122.

10 Sri Lanka

Swarna Jayaweera

The complexities of the relationship between education and national and individual development are reflected in the different theoretical stances in social science literature. Education was seen to be a powerful agent of modernization or social transformation.[1] Human capital theories underscored the economic returns from investment in education.[2] Education is valued from a broader perspective of human development as a fundamental individual right. However, education is seen to operate in contradictory ways in society. Sociologists have pointed to the role of education as an agent of socioeconomic mobility, particularly in meritocratic societies.[3] In the 1970s sociologists argued that education as an agent of social control, reproduces unequal social structures and relations.[4]

This review of education and development in Sri Lanka from a gender perspective takes into account all these partially explanatory theories by exploring three facets of the education and development interface as it affects women: gender-based distribution of educational opportunity, the relationship between education and female labor force participation, and the impact of education on gender roles and relations within the family.

Historical Background

A brief historical analysis of the education of women in Sri Lanka (formerly Ceylon) is necessary to understand the genesis of many of the issues that affect women in contemporary society.

Traditional Society

Sri Lanka, a small island located south of India, has a recorded history of over 2,500 years. In traditional Sri Lanka society, with its agrarian economy, feudal social order, and strong Buddhist and Hindu religious foundations, formal education was restricted to religious centers of learning and was complemented by household education and apprenticeship or on-the-job training in vocational skills. In this context, only women ordained as *bhikkunis* (female Buddhist priests) received an institution-based education leading to high intellectual attainment. Although history records examples of women who were accomplished in the arts, the majority of women were limited to informal learning in their homes.

Most women, however, were economic producers, working side by side with men in fields and in domestic industries in gender-differentiated tasks, and were active in aesthetic pursuits, acquiring their skills through nonformal modes of learning or on-the-job experience. Traditional family laws in the majority Sinhalese community were relatively liberal, ensuring equal rights to inheritance, to acquisition and disposal of property, and to transaction of business. Yet household work was perceived to be "women's work," and the majority of women were socialized into nurturing and servicing roles in the family and in the community.

The Colonial Experience

Successive phases of colonial rule introduced economic and social changes. The Portuguese (1505–1658) and the Dutch (1658–1796) in turn ruled the coastal areas from the sixteenth through the eighteenth centuries, and both colonial powers established a few educational institutions to teach chiefly Christianity. In the seventeenth century the Dutch introduced for the first time the concept of compulsory elementary schools that taught Christianity and literacy skills. The numbers that were enrolled in these schools, however, were small.[5]

British colonial rule penetrated the whole island by 1815, and the modern education system in Sri Lanka evolved gradually under the aegis of the colonial administrators who translocated several of their educational institutions. The education system was developed to meet colonial political needs. The children of the elite and the new middle class that emerged in the nineteenth century were educated in a small number of English, fee-levying, urban schools imbued with Christian and British social values. The six State Female Superior Girls' Schools of the mid-nineteenth century and the English missionary girls' schools were, therefore, purveyors of the metropolitan colonial culture. In the second half of the nineteenth century girls' schools were modeled on the high schools in England and had as their goal the Cambridge School Examination introduced from England in 1881. These English schools were important agents of upward socioeconomic mobility. About 80% of the school population went to vernacular schools conducted in the local languages, Sinhala and Tamil, and learned little more than the

3Rs and elementary history, geography, drawing, and needlework. These schools were a blind alley as far as mobility was concerned. By the end of direct colonial rule in 1930 a third of the students enrolled in schools were girls. Male and female literacy rates had risen from 24.6% and 2.5% respectively at the first Census in 1881 to 56.3% and 21.2% at the 1921 Census.

At a higher level, the Medical College established in 1870, the Law College in 1876, and the University College affiliated to the University of London for B.A. and B.Sc. degrees in 1921 were prestigious institutions. Women entered these higher educational institutions at a slow pace initially, as ninteenth-century Victorian norms of domesticity from England seeped into schools for the elite. The first woman entered the Medical College in 1892, and in 1929, at the end of direct colonial rule, 6% of the students in the University College were women. The teacher-training institutions also had women students from their inception in the nineteenth century.

The commercialization of the economy under British rule was largely through the export-oriented plantation industry developed by British planters. They hired immigrant Indian labor, half of whom were women wage workers. Meanwhile, more indigenous people became deprived of land, and peasant agriculture and local industries were undeveloped. Consequently the Agriculture School (established in 1881) and the Technical School (established in 1893) had little success as institutions of further education. There were no women enrolled in them. The vernacular schools were limited largely to the 3Rs, and their students eventually worked in agriculture or as low skilled artisans and service workers in urban centers[6] with very little prospect of upward mobility.

The gender ideology that pervaded the colonial schools was transplanted by British elite and middle-class society. Victorian norms of domesticity underscored the perceptions of a male breadwinner and dependent housewife. Where career aspirations surfaced in English schools, girls were directed to occupations associated with their ascribed nurturing and servicing roles.[7] Patriarchal norms entrenched the colonial legal system and increased gender inequalities in the family.[8] With education, women's economic roles expanded, but the gender division of labor within and outside the household remained.

Postcolonial Development

In post-colonial Sri Lanka priority was given to social development. Local policymakers, responsive to mass needs after the introduction of universal franchise in 1931, sought to reduce socioeconomic inequalities through education and health policies. The colonial economy, however, did not undergo any significant structural changes until the late 1980s. It continued to be dependent on the export of primary commodities—tea, rubber, and coconut. Policies of capital-intensive industrialization in the 1950s and 1960s and labor-intensive industries in the 1970s did not succeed in promoting effective industrialization, but the relatively rapid expansion of the administrative system and social infrastructure helped to expand the services sector until the late 1960s.

The fall in prices of primary commodities (tea, rubber, and coconut) in the world market since the late 1950s and the failure to effectively diversify the economy led to deficits and stagnation in economic growth. The gloom was exacerbated by a controlled or "closed" economy in the 1970s. The GDP growth rate declined from over 4% in the 1950s to around 2% in the 1970s. Population growth rates were high—above 2.5% in the 1950s and 1960s and declined to 1.5% in the 1970s and 1980s. The economy could not absorb the expanding labor force. This resulted in a high unemployment rate of over 13% since the late 1960s. The implications were more adverse for women as the female labor force had expanded rapidly as a result of rising educational attainment and economic pressures for increased family income.

The change of government in 1977 led to a sharp swing in economic policy toward liberalization and reliance on market forces and export-oriented growth. This change, however, coincided with the introduction of the IMF-World Bank-imposed structural adjustment package, enforced policies such as devaluation of the currency, decontrol of prices, removal of consumer and producer subsidies, reduction in social sector expenditure, promotion of export-oriented industrialization, and privatization of public sector enterprises. Consequently, export-oriented industries such as the garment and other labor-intensive industries, which use mostly female labor, have been accelerated. Since the establishment of three Export Processing Zones between 1978 and 1990 there have been spurts of economic growth, and Sri Lanka has set its sights on achieving the status of a newly industrialized country in the early twenty-first century. Nevertheless, income disparities have widened, and unemployment and poverty continue to be critical problems, with women and children in low-income families bearing a disproportionate share of the burden of structural adjustment. The ambitious Mahaweli Settlement Program, aimed at improving agriculture and irrigation, has transformed the Dry Zone but has yet to ensure self-sufficiency in food production. Ethnic conflict and social unrest among youth since the mid-1980s have resulted in continuing tension and violence and have hampered national development.

DEVELOPMENTS IN EDUCATION

In the context of the priority given to social development in the early postcolonial years, rapid educational development took place in Sri Lanka from the 1940s to the mid-1960s. Free primary, secondary, and tertiary education was introduced in 1945, accompanied by free health services and subsidized food policy at about the same time. Central schools were established between 1940 and 1947 to extend secondary education to rural areas. The mother tongue (Sinhala or Tamil) became the medium of instruction to relevant groups in primary and secondary schools. The majority of schools were nationalized in 1961, at which time only 2% of all students were enrolled in private schools. There was a rapid expansion in secondary and higher education between the late 1950s and mid-1960s.

Both education and social policies were implemented without gender differentiation, and 89.2% of all schools were coeducational institutions by 1963. Parents perceive education as an agent of upward mobility and have high aspirations for both sons and daughters. Consequently, gender disparities in participation declined rapidly. At the 1963 Census, 76.7% of boys and 72.0% of girls between 5 and 14 years of age were in school. At the upper end, the percentage of women students in the universities increased from 10.2% in 1942 to 44% in 1970, and the social composition of the university was transformed from its elitist urban middle class ethos to a more representative environment. Seventy percent of women and men students had rural origins.[9]

Literacy rates rose from 76.5% for males and 46.2% for females at the 1946 Census to 90.5% and 82.8% respectively at the most recent Census in 1981.

Priorities shifted from the mid-1960s on, and education expanded at a much slower rate. As indicated earlier, economic growth slowed down in the 1960s and 1970s, and unemployment rates rose from 7.3% in 1963 to 13.9% in 1969/70 and to around 20% in the mid-1970s. Female unemployment rates were at least double those of men from the late 1970s. Meanwhile, curriculum reforms in the 1970s aimed at providing a vocational orientation to general education and university education failed in a stagnant economy. The liberalization of the economy in 1977 and improved economic growth rates have not changed the situation radically.

The International Women's Year and the UN Decade for Women raised consciousness regarding the constraints that women face in many areas of activity. Sri Lanka ratified the UN Convention on the Elimination of All Forms of Discrimination against Women in 1981, but many women's issues such as equality in family law and equal access to employment have yet to be addressed.

Provision and Utilization of Education Opportunities

The 1978 Constitution of Sri Lanka has as a principle "the complete eradication of illiteracy and universal access to education at all levels"(Section 27). Sri Lanka has ratified the UN Convention on the Rights of the Child (1989), endorsed the World Declaration on Education for All (Jomtien, Thailand, 1990), and the World Declaration on the Survival, Protection and Development of Children (New York, 1990) and developed a Plan of Action for Children to promote, *inter alia*, the universalization of education.[10]

Compulsory education legislation, however, has not been enforced, although the Education Ordinance of 1939 provided for enabling regulations. Nevertheless, in addition to free tuition, which has been in force for four decades, other incentives such as an increasing number of scholarships at year 5 in primary schools and in the university, the provision of free textbooks for grades 1 to 10, funds for midday meals and free school uniforms, have facilitated the access of girls and boys of all socioeconomic strata to schooling. Free state schools cater to the educational needs of 98% of the school population. Primary schools are available within a kilometer of the residence of 80% of families. An overwhelming majority (96.5%) of the schools are coeducational. Single sex schools are largely a legacy of a nineteenth-century urban middle class.

There has been very little gender differentiation in the responses of parents to these incentives. Studies have indicated that gender preference is minimal and that most parents tend to have equally high aspirations for their sons and daughters.[11] The aspirations of secondary school girls for higher education and professional employment have been documented in studies over the years.[12]

It is apparent that relatively liberal traditional laws (except in the minority Muslim community) and the absence of oppressive social practices such as *purdah* and *sati* and the joint family structure prevalent in much of South Asia, have provided a cultural context that is conducive to the equal participation of the majority of Sri Lanka's women in education. Sociocultural constraints for women and girls in two minority communities—Muslims (7%) and resident plantation families descended from South Indian immigrant labor in the nineteenth and early twentieth centuries (5%)—have also been diminishing rapidly in recent years.[13] Poverty continues to be a major barrier to educational opportunity, and the reduction of public expenditure and the removal of some aspects of the "safety net" for poverty groups by IMF-World Bank-sponsored structural adjustment policies have resulted in deterioration of the quality of education and in spiralling costs that have increased the constraints of low-income families in utilizing educational opportunities in the 1980s and 1990s.

The education system in Sri Lanka offers 13 years of general education: five years of primary education, six years of secondary education leading to the General Certificate of Education (Ordinary Level) examination, and two years of senior secondary education leading to the General Certificate of Education (Advanced Level) examination. A rather weak and diffuse vocational and technical education sector offers vocational training opportunities to some of the school dropouts and leavers. Entry to the eight universities and some courses in the Open Unversity are on the basis of performance at the GCE Advanced Level Examination.

Educational statistics reflect the equal access of girls and boys to general education. Age-specific education participation rates in the most recent Census in 1981 point to overall gender equality in school enrollment in both urban and rural sectors. (The Census scheduled for 1991 was delayed by civil strife in the north and east.) In 1981, 83.7% of boys and 83.6% of girls in the 5–14 age group and 41.2% of boys and 42.7% girls in the 15–19 age group were in school (Table 10.1). Annual School Censuses since the 1970s have reported that more girls than boys are in senior secondary grades. For instance, in 1991 58% of the students enrolled in the highest grades (school years 12 and 13) were girls (Table 10.2).

Table 10.1 Education Participation Rates—Urban and Rural, 1981 (in % of age group population)

Age	Total			Urban			Rural		
	Total	Male	Female	Total	Male	Female	Total	Male	Female
05–09	84.4	84.5	84.2	86.6	86.4	86.9	83.8	84.1	83.6
10–14	82.4	82.9	81.8	85.2	86.4	84.4	81.6	82.1	81.1
05–14	83.7	83.7	83.6	85.9	86.4	85.6	82.7	83.1	82.4
15–19	41.9	41.2	42.7	46.4	44.9	48.0	0.6	40.0	41.3
19–24	8.9	8.9	9.0	9.7	9.4	10.2	8.7	9.1	8.7
05–24	55.8	56.0	55.6	56.2	55.3	57.3	55.7	56.3	55.2

Source: *Census of Ceylon 1981.*

School dropout rates for school years 1 to 9 are slightly higher for boys than for girls, 4.9% and 3.8% respectively in 1991, partly because boys have easier access to employment.[14] In 1986 more women (32.2%) than men (26.3%) had acquired the General Certificate in Education (Ordinary Level) qualification after a 10-year education.[15]

Table 10.2 Enrollment in Schools, 1991

Grades	Total No.	No. of Girls	% Girls
School Years 1–5	2,078,152	1,000,929	48.2
School Years 6–8	1,021,293	506,126	49.6
School Years 9–11	840,957	436,947	51.9
School Years 12–13			
Science	50,701	23,171	45.7
Arts	82,223	57,301	69.7
Commerce	54,885	23,198	51.4
Total	187,809	108,670	57.9
School Years 1–13	4,128,211	2,052,672	49.7

Source: *School Census 1991*, Ministry of Education, Policy Planning and Review Division.

Nevertheless, education participation has to be viewed from both a gender and a social-equity perspective. The denial of opportunity to some children is illustrated by the fact that 5.8% of boys and 7.1% of girls in the 10–14 age group at the 1981 Census and 21.1% of boys and 22% of girls in the 5–9 age group at the Labor Force Survey in 1985/86 had never been to school, and that around half the population between 15 and 19 years of age does not have access to secondary education.

These macro-statistics also conceal the fact that girls and boys living in different locations do not have the same opportunities. Disparities in educational provision that affect both girls and boys are clearly illustrated in Tables 10.3 and 10.4. In the urban sector 23.2% of the schools are type 1/AB schools, which have, apart from arts and commerce, science education facilities to years 12 and 13 and are the avenue to university courses and prestigious jobs, while only 3.5% of the schools in the rural sector belong to this category. On the other hand, 22.9% of the urban schools and 45.9% of the rural schools are type 3 schools, which provide only a primary education. Hence, while the participation rates of rural women and men are almost as high as those of urban women and men, the quality of the education they receive is unequal.

It will be noted also that more remote districts like Moneragala, Polonnaruwa, and Anuradhapura in the Dry Zone and Nuwara Eliya, a plantation district, are underserved with type 1/AB schools, while 25% of these schools are in the Western Province, that is, in the metropolitan district of Colombo and its contiguous districts. Further, in Sri Lanka around 22% of all schools are small schools with less than 100 students and with minimal facilities, and disadvantaged districts have a larger proportion of these schools.

District-wide disparities in education participation also underscore the disadvantaged situation of girls in remote and plantation districts. Nonschooling in Sri Lanka is not as extensive as in other South Asian countries; it is concentrated chiefly in pockets of disadvantage in urban low-income neighborhoods, in remote villages, and in the plantation sector, where education has been subordinate to economic interests for over a century. Child labor, child prostitution, and street children are visible manifestations of inequalities that education has yet to counter.

Low-income countries have offered a second chance through nonformal basic education to children denied access to the formal school system. In Sri Lanka, literacy centers and learning activity centers were established initally in the 1980s, but have received low priority. In 1992, 382 centers met the educational needs of less than 5% of the out-of-school population, and the location of these centers was not congruent with the distribution of out-of-school children in the country. Just over half of the students enrolled in these centers through the decade of the 1980s were girls.[16]

It appears, therefore, that social class rather than gender determines girls' access to education, and that uneven development, poverty of national resources, and lack of adequate planning underlie the unequal distribution of educational opportunities.

In an attempt to reduce inequalities an official policy attempts to enforce a common curriculum for school years 1–11, with diversification into science, commerce, and arts in years 12 and 13; a uniform syllabus in all school subjects; and state-produced textbooks in all schools. The quality of education, however, depends on the distribution of qualified teachers and the adequacy of physical facilities, and school equipment. The relationship between socioeconomic background of students, school facilities, and educational achievement enables educational disadvantage to follow socioeconomic disadvantage.[17]

Most women have tended to make optimal use of educational opportunities. The female literacy rate was just over 80% in the 1980s (Table 10.5), and there are no serious disparities in male and female literacy rates. A recent study of functional literacy of the population under 25 years of age found that girls performed better than boys at all three levels that were tested.[18] Tests of entry competencies at five years of age showed that girls had a slightly higher level of average achievement than boys.[19] Analyses of performance of boys and girls at the General Certificate in Education (Ordinary Level) Examination found that achievement differed according to school features and the socioeconomic background of the child.[20]

Table 10.3 Distribution of Government Schools and Students by Type of Schools and Sector, 1991

Type of School	URBAN				RURAL				TOTAL			
	No. of schools	% Total No. of Schools	No. of Students	% Total No. of Students	No. of schools	% Total No. of Schools	No. of Students	% Total No. of Students	No. of schools	% Total No. of Schools	No. of Students	% Total No. of Students
Type 1/AB	196	23.2	378,171	50.4	317	3.5	458,753	13.6	513	5.1	836,924	20.2
Type 1/C	159	18.8	155,022	20.7	1,351	14.8	1,039,175	30.7	1,510	15.1	1,194,197	28.9
Type /2	297	35.1	159,839	21.3	3,285	35.9	1,222,380	36.1	3,582	35.8	1,382,219	33.4
Type /3	194	22.9	56,998	7.6	4,199	45.9	664,776	19.6	4,393	43.9	721,774	17.04
Total	846	100.0	750,030	100.0	9,152	100.0	3,385,084	100.0	9,998	100.0	4,135,114	100.0

Notes: Type 1/AB -- secondary school up to GCE(AL) arts, commerce, and science classes (year 13).
Type 1/C -- secondary school up to GCE(AL) arts and commerce classes (year 13).
Type 2 -- secondary school up to GCE(OL) classes (year 11).
Type 3 -- schools up to Grade 5/Grade 8 (years 5 and 8).

Source:
School Census 1991, Ministry of Education.

Table 10.4 Government Schools Classified by Type, District, and Province, 1991

District/Province	Type 1AB	%	Type 1C	%	Type 2	%	Type 3	%	Total
Colombo	55	12.2	78	17.4	201	44.8	115	25.6	449
Gampaha	44	7.5	85	14.4	244	41.4	216	36.7	589
Kalutara	29	6.2	69	14.8	212	45.6	155	33.3	465
Western Province	128	8.5	232	15.4	657	43.7	486	32.3	1,503
Kandy	38	5.5	124	18.1	237	34.6	286	41.8	685
Matale	10	3.2	58	18.6	96	30.9	147	47.3	311
Nuwara Eliya	12	2.6	42	9.2	123	26.9	279	61.2	456
Central Province	60	4.1	224	15.4	456	31.4	712	49.0	1,452
Galle	32	6.3	90	17.7	175	34.4	211	41.5	508
Matara	20	5.1	78	19.7	162	41.0	135	34.1	395
Hambantota	14	4.3	57	17.6	137	42.4	115	35.6	323
Southern Province	66	5.4	225	18.4	474	38.7	461	37.6	1,226
Jaffna	41	8.5	39	8.1	141	29.3	260	54.1	481
Kilinochchi	4	4.9	10	12.2	20	24.4	48	58.5	82
Mannar	6	5.8	10	9.7	27	26.2	60	58.3	103
Mullativu	4	4.1	7	7.1	19	19.4	68	69.4	98
Vavuniya	5	2.7	11	5.9	36	19.6	132	71.7	184
Northern Province	60	6.3	77	8.1	243	25.6	568	59.9	948
Batticaloa	13	4.9	21	7.9	45	17.1	184	69.9	263
Ampara	20	5.8	42	12.1	87	25.1	198	57.1	347
Trincomalee	11	5.0	32	14.5	69	31.4	108	49.1	220
Eastern Province	44	5.3	95	11.4	201	24.2	490	59.0	830
Kurunegala	37	3.9	210	22.1	367	38.6	33.7	35.4	951
Puttalam	20	5.9	37	10.9	153	44.9	131	38.4	341
North Western Province	57	4.4	247	19.1	520	40.2	468	36.2	1,292
Anuradhapura	16	2.9	84	15.4	202	36.9	245	44.8	547
Polonnaruwa	6	2.9	35	17.2	82	40.4	80	39.4	203
North Central Province	22	2.9	119	15.9	284	37.9	325	43.3	750

Table 10.4 Government Schools Classified by Type, District, and Province, 1991 *(continued)*

District/Province	Type 1AB	%	Type 1C	%	Type 2	%	Type 3	%	Total
Badulla	24	4.3	86	15.2	197	34.9	257	45.6	564
Moneragala	5	2.2	33	14.3	105	45.4	88	38.1	231
Uva Province	29	3.6	119	14.9	302	37.9	345	43.4	795
Ratnapura	26	4.4	81	13.7	232	39.3	251	42.5	590
Kegalle	21	3.4	91	14.9	212	34.6	288	47.1	612
Sabaragamuwa Province	47	3.9	172	14.3	444	36.9	539	44.8	1,202
Sri Lanka	513	5.1	1,510	15.1	3,581	35.8	4,394	43.9	9,998

Source: *School Census 1991*, Ministry of Education.

Throughout the 1980s around 42% to 44% of university students were women (Table 10.6). Population-based district quotas were introduced in the 1970s to assist students from educationally backward districts to enter universities. Nevertheless, the eight universities were unable to accommodate a significant proportion of secondary school leavers who passed the competitive General Certificate of Education (Advanced Level) Examinations, and until the early 1990s, only 3% of the relevant age group were in higher educational institutions. The establishment in 1990 of ten Affiliated University Colleges, which provide two-year Diploma courses with future prospects of proceeding to a university degree, was intended to extend higher education opportunities to a larger number of qualified applicants.

Throughout the 1980s around 42% to 44% of university students were women (Table 10.6). Population-based district quotas were introduced in the 1970s to assist students from educationally backward districts to enter universities. Nevertheless, the eight universities were unable to accommodate a significant proportion of secondary school leavers who passed the competitive General Certificate of Education (Advanced Level) Examinations, and until the early 1990s, only 3% of the relevant age group were in higher educational institutions. The establishment in 1990 of ten Affiliated University Colleges, which provide two-year Diploma courses with future prospects of proceeding to a university degree, was intended to extend higher education opportunities to a larger number of qualified applicants.

Table 10.5 Literacy Percentage by Sector and Sex, according to Census 1946–1981, CF and SE Surveys, and LF and SE Survey

	Census 1946	Census 1953	Census 1963	Census 1971	CF & *SE Survey 1978/79	CF & *SE Survey 1981/82	Census 1981	LF & 86 Survey 1985/86
All Island								
Total	62.8	69.0	76.8	78.5	86.2	85.4	86.5	84.2
Male	76.5	80.7	85.6	85.6	90.0	89.9	90.5	88.6
Female	46.2	55.5	82.5	70.9	81.9	81.1	82.8	80.0
Urban								
Total	76.2	82.6	87.7	86.2	90.7	89.7	93.3	89.1
Male	84.5	88.5	91.8	90.3	92.9	92.9	95.3	92.4
Female	65.7	74.1	82.5	81.5	88.7	89.8	91.0	86.1
Rural**								
Total	60.1	66.4	70.1	76.2	87.8	86.0	84.5	84.6
Male	74.7	79.0	83.9	84.1	91.6	90.1	89.0	88.5
Female	43.0	52.4	63.6	67.9	83.2	82.1	79.9	80.7

Table 10.5 Literacy Percentage by Sector and Sex, according to Census 1946–1981, CF and SE Surveys, and LF and SE Survey (continued)

	Census 1946	Census 1953	Census 1963	Census 1971	CF & *SE Survey 1978/79	CF & *SE Survey 1981/82	Census 1981	LF & 86 Survey 1985/86
Estate*								
Total					65.6	64.8		59.4
Male					79.3	78.0		74.5
Female					52.1	52.6		45.9

* Population 5+ years.
** Estate Sector is included in the rural sector in Census.
*** The estate or plantation sector (tea and rubber plantations) has labor families of immigrant South Indian origin who are now citizens. This sector historically formed a separate enclave. Some national surveys have separate data for this sector and for the nonplantation sector.
CF & SE survey—Consumer Finance and Socio-economic Survey, Central Bank of Ceylon.
LF & CE survey—Labour Finance and Socio-economic Survey, Department of Census and Statistics.
Source: Department of Census and Statistics, Central Bank of Ceylon

Table 10.6 Student Enrollment in Universities, 1942–1989, by sex and female percentage

Year	Total (N)	Male (N)	Female (N)	Female (%)
1942	904	813	91	10.1
1945	1,065	932	133	12.5
1950	2,036	1,655	381	18.7
1955	2,431	1,781	650	26.7
1960	4,723	3,587	1,136	24.1
1965	14,210	9,631	4,579	32.2
1970	11,813	6,570	5,243	44.4
1975	12,648	7,496	5,152	40.7
1980	17,494	10,544	6,950	39.7
1985	18,913	10,753	8,160	43.1
1989	29,781	17,110	12,671	42.5

Note: The sharp increase in numbers after 1985 was caused partly by unrest in the country and closure of universities, which delayed examinations.
Source: University Council Reports, Reports of the Vidyodaya and Vidyalankara Universities, Reports of the NCHE, University of Sri Lanka, and University Grants Commission.

In Sri Lanka a major barrier to gender equality in education and subsequently in career mobility lies in the distribution of vocational-related knowledge and skills. Gender-based diversification of vocation-oriented subjects into home science for girls and woodwork and metal work for boys from the eighth school year and gender-role stereotypes in educational materials[21] and in school organization affect the perceptions and aspirations of girls and boys and limit the access of girls to technology. There is a culturally determined gender-based demarcation in the selection of courses in physical and biological sciences, and girls are channeled into the latter courses. At the universities, therefore, disparities in enrollment exist chiefly in engineering studies (Table 10.7). The participation of women is relatively high in "feminine" courses, which are associated with the nurturing roles of women, such as medical and related courses.

Alternative opportunities to general education are inadequate to meet all needs or aspirations. They are confined at the tertiary level to such fields as law, accountancy, teacher education, and computer studies. Agricultural education is poorly developed at the secondary level. Seven state agencies have island-wide networks of centers with clearly demarcated "masculine" and "feminine" courses. Technical courses are considered to be male "areas of excellence" and women tend to be channeled into sewing, typing, and handicraft courses. In technical colleges around 70% of women students are enrolled in commerce courses and are underrepresented in technical studies. While large numbers of women are enrolled in the nonformal vocational training programs of the Ministries of Education, Labor, and Small Industries, the National Apprenticeship and Industrial Training Authority, and the National Youth Services' Council, around 80% to 90% follow dressmaking and other courses perceived to be gender appropriate.[22]

Table 10.7 Distribution of University Students by Faculty, 1966–1987, including percentage of women to total

Faculties	1966 Total	% F	1975 Total	% F	1987 Total	% F
Medicine	1,551	28.8	1,239	47.1	2,413	42.4
Dentistry	95	37.9	193	55.9	284	45.4
Veterinary Science	70	14.3	108	49.9	159	37.1
Agriculture	83	13.3	390	25.6	850	34.2
Engineering	571	1.9	1,210	10.4	1,914	13.1
Architecture	25	—	73	28.8	152	40.8
Science	802	24.6	1,797	30.7	3,462	43.7
Management Studies	—	—	889	29.6	3,807	44.7
Law	72	26.4	144	42.4	571	48.5
Social Sciences/Humanities/ Education	10,902	41.7	6,425	49.4	6,354	50.6
Total	14,171	37.3	12,648	40.7	19,966	42.9

Source: University Reports and University Grants Commission.

It is apparent that women themselves are conditioned by their socialization to prefer such courses, while employers are influenced by gender-role assumptions to reject women applicants for technical training and employment. The social construction of gender thus determines the distribution of women's skills, confining them to a narrow range that often adversely affects their employment prospects.

Before formal education, only 20% of children below five years of age have access to pre-schools, play centers, or crèches, which provide largely custodial care or a "head start" for primary education. Adult education in its wider connotation of non-vocational education continues to receive low priority.

The pattern of distributon of educational opportunities therefore works in such a way as to foster upward mobility and to expand the intellectual horizons of some women and, at the same time, to reinforce others in poverty.

The rising levels of education of most women have been a visible outcome of social development in the last four decades and have contributed in turn to enhancing the quality of life of women and their families. A measure of this contribution is that the Physical Quality of Life Index (based on health indicators and literacy) has been estimated to be 79.7% for men and 78.1% for women in the 1970s,[23] a relatively high figure for a low-income country bedeviled by global and national economic pressures. The increase in educational attainment of women has been associated with improved health indicators such as declining infant and maternal mortality rates and fall in the annual population growth rate to 1.5%.

Women, Education, and the Labor Market

An important gender issue that affects the education-development interface is the extent to which the labor force participation of women is determined by (a) their educational attainment and (b) development patterns.

It is often assumed that there is a positive relationship between education and employment, that education increases aspirations and promotes labor force participation and access to a wide range of remunerative jobs. This issue has been debated widely. The positive gender dimension of education-employment linkages has been supported with macro-data,[24] but micro-studies and empirical evidence have pointed to complexities in these relationships. The Sri Lanka experience does not support the thesis of a positive linear relationship between educational attainment and employment. Expanded access to education and high aspirations have raised educational levels among women, but the supply of female labor for development is limited to a narrow range of skills.

Labor force data need to be used cautiously, for definitions and classifications of "gainful employment," which are transferred from industrialized societies, exclude large numbers of women in home-based economic activities and family labor in the informal sector from the officially reported labor force, and these women belong to all educational levels. In this informal sector access to work is not dependent on educational attainment. Indeed, the highest female economic activity rates have been and are among plantation women workers of immigrant South Indian origin, who are the most educationally disadvantaged group, and their participation rates are the same as those among plantation men.

Nevertheless, the reported female labor force has increased at a faster rate than that of the male labor force since the early 1960s. This happened at a time when gender disparities in access to education disappeared. In the 1980s the female labor force increased even more rapidly, at the rate of 6.9% a year, while the male labor force kept pace with population growth at 0.8% a year. The participation rates of the 20–34 age group among women almost doubled during this period. The increase during these years, however, was irrespective of the level of educational attainment, pointing to the intervention of noneducational factors, chiefly family economic pressures on more women to join the labor market.

Table 10.8 depicts the relationship between educational attainment and labor force participation in recent decades. Female labor force participation rates have not correlated positively with increments in educational attainment except at the higher education levels. Indeed, those with no schooling have higher participation rates than those with some schooling. Male and female labor force participation rates are also closest at the higher educational level.[25]

Table 10.8 Labor Force Participation Rate by Education and Sex, 1971, 1980/81, 1985/86 (in %)

	Male			Female		
	1971	1980/81	1985/86	1971	1980/81	1985/86
No Schooling	69.5	64.4	70.7	30.4	28.9	38.3
Grades 1–4	96.8	64.3	64.1	27.5	21.4	29.3
Grades 5–10	51.5	66.7	53.5	17.9	19.4	25.3
Passed GCE (O Level)	62.0	73.8	79.2	54.2	43.0	46.1
Passed GCE (A Level)	75.4	69.9	83.1	78.6	56.6	67.4
Passed Degree	86.2	95.7	91.9	69.2	85.7	86.7
Total	68.4	66.8	61.2	26.0	25.8	32.6

Note: Data on the 1990 working-age population are not available, and so Labour Force and Socio-economic Survey 1985/86 data are used.
Source: Department of Census and Statistics 1976, 1982, and 1990.

Unemployment data also reflect a relatively weak linear relationship between educational attainment and employment. Unemployment rates rose steeply from the end of the 1960s. Gender differences widened sharply, and the unemployment rates of women have risen much higher than those of men during the last two decades—from 7.6% for female unemployment and 8.9%

for male unemployment at the 1963 Census to 23.4% and 9.1% in 1990.[26]

Among both women and men those with no schooling have the lowest unemployment rates and secondary school leavers have the highest unemployment rates. In 1985/86, 14.4% of men at GCE(OL) and 18.7 percent at GCE (AL) and 35.6% and 44.9% of women respectively were unemployed (Table 10.9).

Education, however, has been necessary for women to obtain jobs in the upper levels of the employment hierarchy and to increase their incomes significantly. The majority of school dropouts are agricultural workers, and over 70% of those with ten or more years of schooling are in the services sector. In fact, the percentage of women of those employed in professional and technical-related occupations increased from 38.7% at the 1963 Census to 49.6% at the Labor Force Survey in 1985/86, and those in clerical occupations from 1% to 25.3% over the same period, as women tended to seek employment in the services sector.

Table 10.9 Unemployment Rates by Sex and Level of Education, 1981/82 and 1985/86 (in %)

Level of Education	1981/82			1985/86		
	Male	Female	Total	Male	Female	Total
No Schooling (illiterate)	2.1	2.6	2.4	7.7	4.8	6.1
No Schooling (literate)	2.4	*	1.9	*	*	*
Primary	3.8	7.8	4.8	7.0	9.4	7.7
Secondary (grades 6–8)	9.6	33.5	14.6	9.5	16.5	11.2
(grades 8–10)				15.4	34.0	20.8
GCE (OL)	14.5	42.0	24.5	14.4	35.6	22.3
GCE (AL)	22.0	52.2	34.8	18.7	44.9	32.0
Undergraduates		40.0	41.2	*	*	*
Graduates				3.3	10.2	6.3
Graduates and Postgraduates	8.1	12.1	9.7			
Postgraduates				4.2	3.2	3.9
Total	7.8	21.9	11.7	10.8	20.8	14.1

* Data not available.
Source: Consumer Finances and Socio-economic Survey 1981/82, Central Bank of Ceylon; Labour Force and Socio-economic Survey 1985/86, Department of Census and Statistics.

There has been a negative trend in the 1980s on employment "status" as defined in labor force surveys. In 1981, 80% of women in the labor force were in "paid employment," but the percentage declined to 58.4% (nonpermanent) in 1985/86 and to 55.6% in 1990, and half these women were in "casual employment." At the same time, the percentage of women "unpaid family workers" increased from 6.5% in 1981 to 23% in 1985/86 and 25.1% in 1990, indicating that the increased female labor force in the 1980s has been marginalized into the informal sector and casual employment despite any gains in education (Table 10.10).

Table 10.10 Employment Status of Sri-Lanka Population, 1981–1993 (in %)

Employment Status	1981 M	1981 F	1985/86 M	1985/86 F	1990 M	1990 F	1993[1] M	1993[1] F
Employer	2.4	1.2	3.0	0.9	4.4	1.2	1.9	0.7
Paid Employees	62.3	79.4	58.2[2]	58.4[2]	59.5	55.6	58.1	64.9
Own account workers	32.5	12.9	29.6	17.7	28.4	18.1	31.8	12.4
Unpaid family workers	2.8	6.5	9.2	23.0	7.7	25.1	8.2	22.0
Total	100.0	100.0	100.0	100.0	100.0	100.0	100.0	100.0

1. Excluding Northern Province.
2. Regular employees: M 28.5, F 29.6. Casual employees: M 34.7, F 28.9
Source: Census of Ceylon, 1981; Labour Force and Socio-economic Survey 1985/86, 1990; Labour Force Survey 1993 third quarter, excluding Northern and Eastern Provinces, Department of Census and Statistics.

There is no evidence of a marked shift in the gender division of labor as a result of increased educational participation. Women continued to concentrate in peasant and plantation agriculture, traditional "feminine" industries, assembly-line work in factories, the education and health-related professions, and domestic service (Table 10.11).

It is apparent, therefore, that education per se cannot assure women remunerative employment or change labor market structures in an environment that is determined by a multifaceted development process. Both quantitative and qualitative indicators of education and labor market operations are affected by social and economic structures and by demands generated by the development process that are also mediated by gendered assumptions.

Table 10.11 Employed Female Population by Occupational Groups, 1963–1986

	% Female of Workers in Specified Occupation			Female % of Total Labor in Specified Occupation		
	1963	1981	1985/86	1963	1981	1985/86
Professional and Technical	8.5	14.1	8.7	38.7	44.9	49.6
Administration and Management	0.2	0.4	0.1	3.4	9.5	6.9
Clerical related	1.0	6.0	4.6	1.0	22.5	25.3
Sales Workers	1.5	3.0	5.7	1.9	7.9	20.1
Service Workers	10.0	4.3	5.9	10.0	17.7	37.7
Agriculture, Animal Husbandry, and Fishing	62.8	42.8	53.4	24.9	24.1	33.9
Production and Transport Workers	14.0	16.8	21.6	12.4	13.2	23.6

Source: Census Reports 1963, 1981; Labour Force and Socio-economic Survey 1985/86.

Despite positive education policies, economic constraints and socioeconomic inequalities created partly by development have limited socioeconomic mobility. IMF and World Bank structural adjustment policies, which aimed at reducing balance of payments deficits, increased the burdens of women in low-income families. Local industries collapsed because they were unable to compete in the open market. Jobs were lost in the reduction in public expenditure. Consequently women were displaced and pushed into the informal sector at home and to domestic work in the international market. Education is at a low premium in this struggle for family survival, as reflected in the number of secondary school leavers employed as domestic aides in the Middle East, Singapore, and Hong Kong (around 60,000 a year) and as casual workers in industry and services.

Major development programs of the last decade increased the demand for female labor. However, in consonance with the gender-role assumptions of policy-makers and entrepreneurs, the employment available to women has been low-skill, low-wage jobs. In the Mahaweli Development irrigation-cum-settlement program, in which about 100,000 families were translocated to new settlements to develop small commercial family farms since the mid-1970s, women were perceived as dependent wives of farmers and not as agricultural producers. Hence the demand was for their unpaid domestic labor to improve family incomes and agricultural productivity.[27] This perception of women as housewives, consumers of services, or low-cost labor rather than as economically viable producers was manifest also in several district-based Integrated Rural Development Programs.

Export-oriented industrialization, the focus of development policy since the late 1970s, has been dependent on female labor. With the relocation of labor-intensive industries in low-income countries and the international division of labor, women have been perceived to be secondary earners and therefore as cheap, dispensable, and pliable labor. In the three Export Processing Zones in Sri Lanka, 80% of the labor force are women, mostly single and between 18 and 30 years of age. They are employed as low-cost semiskilled labor in fragmented assembly line production, while men are mostly technicians, supervisors, and managers. Even women with ten years of schooling have no opportunity for skills upgrading or for upward occupational mobility. Further, they are not protected by labor legislation and unionization.[28]

In the subcontracting industries that have proliferated, women are at the bottom of a vertical process, working long hours in their homes or in small units for poor economic returns, outside the ambit of labor legislation, while entrepreneurs and intermediaries claim a disproportionate share of profits.[29] In the informal sector, in which many women have been compelled to seek a livelihood, self-employment is seen by policymakers as an objective of development. Women, however, tend to be seen as supplementary earners and consequently as targets of ad hoc "income generating" projects that lack critical inputs such as technology skills, management skills, credit, or reasonable terms and market information. Hence economic viability is still unattainable for a majority of women in low-income families. On the other hand, a small group of women with family resources and initiative have responded to incentives offered for private enterprise and have become successful entrepreneurs.[30]

This overview of economic development programs explains why women have not been able to achieve the occupational mobility expected from their rising educational levels and have been pushed instead into casual and marginal economic activities. It is a far cry from the 1960s when education opportunities expanded and women sought entry in large numbers to professional and clerical employment. However, women—whether non-schooled, dropouts, or school leavers—make a crucial economic contribution to agriculture and industrial development and to revenue from foreign exchange earnings to reduce balance-of-payment deficits.

Education and Changing Family Roles

It is assumed also that education changes the lives of women within their primary social unit, the family. The extent of change appears to be dependent on external pressures, such as development needs and cultural definitions of womanhood.

In Sri Lanka such change impinges on family perceptions of gender roles and on individual behavior in intrafamilial relationships. Over the last century education as an avenue of socioeconomic mobility, as well as an instrument to preserve social and gender relations, promoted gender equality in some facets of family life and reinforced inequalites in others. Two agendas in education have been noted—expansion of the economic and public roles of women, and socializing them to conform to social norms and stereotypes.[31] Participation in secondary and higher education has equipped women with knowledge and skills and subsequently led to their improved status in the family. Studies have shown that both parents and daughters see the instrumental value of education.[32] While there is no clearcut positive linear relationship between educational attainment and employment, it is clear that education has expanded the economic roles of women in the family context.

Women in the low-income families, irrespective of educational levels, have been compelled to engage in economic activities within and outside the household and have become even primary income earners and therefore decision makers in the family. In middle-class families women's options in employment outside the family have widened, and education has given them access to leadership roles in the professions, greater visibility in public life, and consequently higher status within the family.

While women have heavier economic roles and responsibilities in the family than before, the division of labor in the household has not changed significantly. Household chores and childcare tasks are still perceived to be "women's work." Women have internalized these gender-role stereotypes and many look askance at the possibility of sharing domestic chores with their spouses. Consequently, women's multiple roles in the family demand on average 14 hours a day, while men, in their perceived "breadwinner's" role, work on average around nine hours a day.[33]

Sharing of childcare and household tasks is increasing in dual-earner families, and there is evidence of a role-reversal in some families in which women are the primary income earners, such as overseas domestic workers and women in home-based piece-rate work.[34] Men in some of these families have taken over a significant share of "women's work." Nevertheless, for the majority of women gender inequalities in the division of labor have remained.

It is assumed that women's education and economic participation ensure economic independence and therefore equitable gender relations in the family. There appears to be no simple relationship between education, employment, and economic independence in the family. The experience of women in farming communities whose economic returns are subsumed as family income and that of resident plantation women workers whose wages tend to be collected and used by their spouses[35] underscore the fact that access to an independent income and control of this income are necessary for economic independence and power in the family.

Rural and urban low-income women who sell their labor as wage earners or outworkers and control independent cash incomes have acquired status and a critical decision-making role in the family, irrespective of their level of education.[36] Educated young women, even unemployed ones, appear to enjoy a status and leadership role in rural families.[37] Professional women have been empowered by both education and employment to become joint decision makers and to achieve equality in family relations. Hence education is one factor that has enhanced the role of women as decision makers in the family, but employment, control of income, and personality continue to be more powerful variables in the family context.

Education, in conjunction with employment, has also affected the reproductive role of women by postponing marriage and increasing the average age of marriage to 25 years, making women more receptive to family planning advice. Girls tend to stay on longer in school, since education is free, and to seek employment before they consider marriage.[38] In the current development context the demand for labor in modern assembly line industries is preferably for young, unmarried, secondary-educated women.[39]

Education also has a crucial role as an agent of socialization and social control. Children learn gender roles in their social environment,[40] initially in the home and the school. Studies in Sri Lanka, as in other countries, have shown that the school often reinforces normative behavior patterns in children.[41]

As a consequence women in Sri Lanka tend to play a crucial role in family strategies, and by and large they are not confined to the domestic sphere. Social conditioning, however, has slowed the pace of change in intrafamilial relationships. The role of the male head of household is accepted, although there is evidence of contradictions between normative and actual behavior and the exercise of autonomy, despite social norms. Control of female behavior is reinforced through puberty rituals and virginity tests,[42] and family honor is used as an agent of social control, enforcing double standards on women and men. Domestic violence toward women is observed in families irrespective of educational attainment. Education, and even university education, does not appear to have increased the capacity of the majority of women to challenge such practices. Marriage and dowry bargaining by parents, practices that negate the individual worth of women and their human rights, have also not been affected.

There appears to be a contradiction in that many women aspire to the highest education and employment while conforming to gender-role stereotypes that promote passivity and inequality. It is likely that perceptions of the instrumental value of education in individual and national development have brought rapid change in some facets of women's lives, while cultural lags reinforced by education and other social forces delay changes in other gender roles and relations.

Conclusion

The situation of women in Sri Lanka has been affected by the interaction of education and other development trends. Although education has yet to be universalized, positive education policies and their linkages with other social development policies have improved the quality of life of women, their families, and the wider community. Women have made a crucial contribution to economic development, in peasant and plantation agriculture, in industry, and in service occupations within and outside the country, irrespective of their educational attainments. However, global and national economic pressures, the social construction of gender, the supply of and demand for labor, and the vertical and horizontal segmentation of the labor market have had an adverse impact on women. Programs that focus on factors such as the comparative advantage of low-cost female labor have resulted in the continuing integration of women in development on unequal terms with men.

Access to education has expanded the economic roles of women in the family without, however, adequate support for the performance of their multiple roles. Education has assisted in improving their status in the family but has not empowered them sufficiently to achieve more equitable family relations and autonomy in the control of their lives.

The interface of ethnicity, class, and gender is seen in the more disadvantaged status of women in resident plantation families, the economic constraints that impinge on the lives of women in low-income families as they struggle for family survival, and in the visible manifestations of success among women professionals and entrepreneurs.

A dichotomous perception of social and economic development has eroded some of the benefits of education that should have accrued to women in the labor force and in the family environment. Nevertheless, education has been perceived often in Sri Lanka as a basic human right as well as an instrument of gender equity and social justice.

NOTES

1. Myron Weiner, ed., *Modernization: The Dynamics of Growth*, (Washington, DC: Voice of America, 1966.)

2. Theodore W. Schultz, *The Economic Value of Education* (New York: Columbia University Press, 1963); F. Denison, *Why Growth Rates Differ* (Washington, DC: The Brooking Institution, 1967).

3. A. H. Halsey, A. C. Heath, and J. M. Ridge, *Origins and Destination: Family Class and Education in Modern Britain* (Oxford: Clarendon Press, 1980).

4. S. Bowles and H. Gintis, *Schooling in Capitalist America* (New York: Basic Books, 1976); P. Bourdieu and J. C. Passeron, *Reproduction in Education, Society and Culture* (London: Sage, 1977).

5. J. D. Palm, "The Educational Establishments of the Dutch in Ceylon," *Journal of the Royal Asiatic Society*, 1, No. 2 (1946) 105–137.

6. Swarna Jayaweera, "A Comparative Study of British and American Colonial Education Policy in Ceylon and the Philippines." Unpublished Ph.D. Thesis, University of London, 1966.

7. Swarna Jayaweera, "European Women Educators under the British Colonial Administration in Sri Lanka," *Women's Studies International Forum* 13, no. 4 (1990):323–332.

8. Savitri Goonasekera, "Colonial Legislation and Sri Lankan Family Law: The Legacy of History," in: *Asian Panorama*, K. M. de Silva et al., eds., (New Delhi: Vikas Publishing, 1990):193–209; Carla Risseeuw, *The Fish Don't Talk about Water* (London: E. J. Brill, 1988).

9. Murray Strauss, "Family Characteristics and Occupational Choice of University Entrants," *University of Ceylon Review* ix, no. 2 (1951); G. Uswatte Aratchi, "University Admissions in Ceylon: Their Economic and Social Background and Employment Expectations," *Modern Asian Studies* 8, no. 3, (1984); Swarna Jayaweera, "Access to University Education—The Social Composition of University Entrants," *University of Colombo Review* 1, no. 4 (1984):6–40.

10. National Planning Department, *A Plan of Action for Children in Sri Lanka* (Colombo: Ministry of Policy Planning and Implementation, 1991).

11. Swarna Jayaweera, "Women and Education," in: University of Columbo, *Status of Women: Sri Lanka* (Colombo: University of Colombo, 1979):254–422; Centre for Women's Research (CENWOR), *Women's Work and Family Strategies* (Colombo: Centre for Women's Research, 1987); Swarna Jayaweera, "The Socialization of the Girl Child in Sri Lanka," Ch.7 in: Centre for Women's Research (CENWOR), *The Girl Child in Sri Lanka* (Colombo: CENWOR, 1993).

12. T. L. Green, "Education and Social Needs in Ceylon," in *University of Ceylon Review*, no. 4 (1952):297–316; Swarna Jayaweera, "Vocational Preferences of Secondary School Girls in Sri Lanka," *Modern Ceylon Studies*, nos. 1 and 2 (1976):207–238; S. Rupasinghe, "Gender Differences in the Career Aspirations of Students in GCE(OL) grades in Sri Lanka," in: Swarna Jayaweera, ed., *Gender and Education in Sri Lanka* (Colombo: CENWOR, 1991):97–106.

13. Swarna Jayaweera. "Quality Development in Education: Badulla Integrated Rural Development Programme," (Colombo: Swedish International Development Agency):24–30.

14. *Annual School Census Statistics* (Colombo: Ministry of Education, 1991).

15. Department of Census and Statistics, *Labor Force and Socio-economic Survey, 1985/86* (Colombo: Government Press, 1987).

16. The data were provided by Non-formal Division, Ministry of Education, 1992.

17. S. Rupasinghe, "Social Environment and its Relationship with Factors Associated with Schooling (Sri Lanka)," *University of Colombo Review* 6, Dec. (1986):82–95.

18. Jayaweera, "The Socialization of the Girl Child in Sri Lanka," op. cit.

19. Chitrangani Abhaydeva, "Gender and Competencies of Children at Entry to Primary School," in: S. Jayaweera, ed., *Gender and Education in Sri Lanka* op. cit., pp. 36–44.

20. Swarna Jayaweera, Sterling Perera, and Sirisoma Rupasinghe, "Gender Differences in Performance at Secondary School Examinations in Sri Lanka," in: S. Jayaweera, ed., *Gender and Education in Sri Lanka*, op cit., pp 5–22.

21. Asoka Jayasena, "Sexism in the Post Primary School Curriculum in Sri Lanka," in: S. Jayaweera, ed., *Gender and Education in Sri Lanka*, op. cit., pp 45–55.

22. Swarna Jayaweera, *Women, Skill Development and Employment* (Colombo: Institute of Policy Studies, 1991).

23. H. D. Sumanasekera, "Measuring the Regional Variation of the Quality of Life in Sri Lanka," *Sri Lanka Journal of Agrarian Studies* Vol. 2, no. 1(1981):27–40.

24. Guy Standing and Glen Sheehan, eds., *Labor Force Participation in Low Income Countries* (Geneva: ILO, 1978); Audrey Chapman Smock, *Women's Education in Developing Countries* (New York: Praeger, 1981); Ram Rati, "Sex Differences in the Labor Market Outcomes of Education," in: Gail P. Kelly and Carolyn M. Elliot, eds., *Women's Education in the Third World: Comparative Perspectives* (Albany: State Unversity of New York Press, 1982); Patricia Alailima, *Education-Employment Linkages: The Macro Profile* (World Bank Sri Lanka Study, 1991).

25. Standing and Sheehan, op. cit.; Audrey Chapman Smock, op. cit.

26. Department of Census and Statistics, *Socio-economic Survey, 1969/70*; Department of Census and Statistics, *Labor Force and Socio-economic Survey 1985/86*.

27. Dharshani Rajapakse, "Agricultural Transformation and Changing Labor Relations: Implications for Peasant Women in Sri Lanka," in: Center for Women's Research, *The Hidden Face of Development*, (Colombo: CENWOR, 1989):41–62.

28. Voice of Women, *Women Workers in the Free Trade Zone* (Colombo, Voice of Women, 1983); Hema Gunatilake et al., "Industrialization and Women Workers in Sri Lanka," in: Noeleen Heyzer, ed., *Daughters of Industry* (Kuala Lumpur: Asian and Pacific Development Center, 1988):189–208; Rohini D. Weerasinghe, "Women Workers in the Katunayake Investment Production Zone of Sri Lanka: Some Observations," in: V. Kanesalingam, ed., *Women in Development in South Asia* (New Delhi: Macmillan Ltd., 1989):306–321.

29. Swarna Jayaweera and Malsiri Dias, *Subcontracting in Industry: Impact on Women* (London: Commonwealth Secretariat, 1989).

30. CENWOR, *Human Resources in Sri Lanka's Industrial Development—The Current and Prospective Contribution of Women* (Vienna: United Nations Industrial Development Program, 1989).

31. CENWOR, *Women's Work and Family Strategies* (1987), op. cit.; Asoka Jayasena, *Sexism in the Post Primary Curriculum in Sri Lanka* (1991), op. cit.; Swarna Jayaweera, *The Socialization of the Girl Child*, op. cit.

32. Status of Women, op. cit., Ch. 5; CENWOR, *Women's Work and Family Strategies*, op. cit.; Jayaweera, *The Socialization of the Girl Child*, op. cit.

33. CENWOR, *Women's Work and Family Strategies*, op. cit.

34. CENWOR, *Women's Work and Family Strategies*, op. cit.; *Women and Export Production Villages. Study Series No. 2* (Colombo: CENWOR, 1990).

35. Rachel Kurian, *Women Workers in Sri Lanka Plantation Sector* (Geneva: ILO, 1982).

36. CENWOR, *Women's Work and Family Strategies*, op. cit.; *Women in Ex-*

port Production Villages, op. cit.; Dharshani Rajapakse, *Agricultural Transformation,* op. cit.

37. CENWOR, *Women's Work and Family Strategies,* op. cit.

38. Jayaweera, *The Socialization of the Girl Child,* op. cit.; *The Vocational Preferences of Secondary School Girls in Sri Lanka,* op. cit.

39. Gunatilake et al., *Industrialization and Women Workers in Sri Lanka,* op. cit.

40. L. Kohlberg, "A Cognitive Development Analysis of Children's Sex Role Concepts and Attitude," in: E. Maccoby, ed., *The Development of Sex Differences* (Stanford, CA: Stanford University Press, 1966); W. Mischel, "Sex Typing and Socialization," in P. Mussen, ed., *Carmichael's Manual of Child Psychology,* Vol 2 (New York: Wiley, 1970).

41. Jayasena, *Sexism in the Post Primary Curriculum in Sri Lanka,* op. cit.; Jayaweera, *The Socialization of the Girl Child in Sri Lanka,* op. cit.

42. CENWOR, *Women's Work and Family Strategies,* op. cit.; Sriyani Basayake, "The Virginity Test—a Bridal Nightmare." Paper presented at the First National Convention on Women's Studies, CENWOR, 1989.

BIBLIOGRAPHY

Abdul Malek bin Mohamed. "Perkembangan Pelajaran Teknik dan Vokasional 1957–1974" (The development of Technical Vocational Education 1957–1974), in: Khoo Kay Kim and Mohd Fadzil Othman, eds., *Pendidikan di Malaysia Dahulu dan Sekarang* (Education in Malaysia Then and Now). Malaysian Historical Society: Kuala Lumpur, 1981.

Abeywickrema, Dorothy. "Career Guidance Needs of the Female Adolescent," in: Sri Lanka Federation of University Women, *Half Our Future.* Colombo: Sri Lanka Federation of University Women, 1991, pp. 67–94.

Abhadeva, Chitrangani. "Gender and Competencies of Children at Entry to Primary School," in: S. Jayaweera, ed., *Gender and Education in Sri Lanka.* Colombo: Centre for Women's Research, 1991, pp. 36–44.

Adams, Milton and Susan Kruppenbach. "Gender and Access in the African School." *International Review of Education* 33 (1987): 437–453.

Aftab, Tahera. *Women and Education in Pakistan.* N.p., [1986?].

Adelman, Irma and C. T. Morris. *Economic Growth and Social Equity in Developing Countries.* Stanford, CA: Stanford University Press, 1977.

Ahmad, Karuna. "Equity and Women's Higher Education." *Journal of Higher Education* 5 (no. 1, 1979): 3–49. New Delhi: Monsoon, 1979.

———. "The Social Context of Women's Education in India, 1921–81; Tentative Formulations." Occasional papers on history and society, 6. New Delhi: Nehru Memorial Museum and Library, 1982.

Alailima, Patricia J. *Education-Employment Linkages: The Macro Profile.* N.p.: World Bank Sri Lanka Study, 1991.

Alavi, Hamza. "Pakistan: Women in a Changing Society." *Economic and Political Weekly (India)* 23 (June 25, 1988): 1328–30.

All-China Women's Federation. *Zhongguo funu falu shiyong quanshu* (Practical Guide to Law toward Women in China). Beijing: Falu chubanshe, 1993.

Altekar, A. S. *Position of Women in Hindu Civilization.* New Delhi: Manager of Publication, 1962.

Anderson, C. Arnold and M. J. Bowman, eds. *Education and Economic Development.* Chicago: Aldine Publishing, 1963.

Anderson, M. B. "On Girls' Access to Primary Education in Pakistan." *The Bridges Forum* (January 3–8, 1988).

Andors, Phyllis. *The Unfinished Revolution of Chinese Women 1948–1980.* Bloomington: Indiana University Press, 1983.

Andrew, Nancy. "History of Women in Japan." In: *Kodansha Encyclopedia of Japan*, Vol. 8. Tokyo: Kodansha, 1983.

Arumanainathan, P. *Report on the Census of Population 1970*. Singapore: Department of Statistics, 1973.

Arumugam, Pathmasamy. "The Education of Girls in Ceylon 1796–1867." Unpublished M.A. Thesis, University of Peradeniya, Sri Lanka, 1965.

Awakening. *Fu-Nu Hsin-Chih* (Awakening Monthly) 112 (Sept. 1991).

———. *Liang-Hsing P'ing-Teng Chiao-Yu Shou-Tse* (A handbook for equal education for the sexes). Taipei: The Awakening Foundation, 1988.

Azizah Kassim. *Wanita dan Masyarakat* (Women and society). Kuala Lumpur: Utusan Publications, 1985.

Azizan Baharuddin. "Malay Women's Involvement in Science in the Universities in Malaysia." Paper presented at the Conference on ASEAN Professional Women 1992, Universiti Teknologi Malaysia, Johor (Sept., 1992).

Bacchus, M. K. *Education for Development or Underdevelopment?* Ontario: Wilfrid Laurier University Press, 1980.

Bandarage, Asoka. "Women and Capitalist Development in Sri Lanka 1977–87." *Bulletin of Concerned Asian Scholars* 20, no. 2(1988): 57–81.

Bank, Olive. *The Sociology of Education*. London: Batsford, 1976.

Basu, Aparna. "Policy and Conflict in India: The Reality and Perception of Education," in: P. G. Altbach and Gail P. Kelly, eds., *Education and Colonialism*. New York: Longman, 1978.

Beauchamp, Edward R. "Education of Women." In: Edward R. Beauchamp, *Education in Japan: Source Book*. New York: Garland Publishing, 1989.

Becker, Gary S. *Human Capital*. New York: National Bureau of Economic Research, 1964.

Bernstein, Gail Lee. *Haruko's World: A Japanese Farm Woman and Her Community*. Stanford, CA: Stanford University Press, 1981.

———, ed. *Recreating Japanese Women, 1600–1945*. Berkeley: University of California Press, 1990.

Bhattacharya, S. "The Position of Women in Vedic Society." *India International Quarterly* 19, no. 4 (1992): 40–52.

Bian, Y. Y. "Nu-hsing lao-kung tuei ching-chi fa-chan te kung-hsian: tai-wan te shih-cheng yen-chiu (The contribution of female workers to economic development: An empirical analysis of the case of Taiwan)," in: N. Chiang, ed., *Kuo-Chia Fa-Chan Kuo-Ch'eng Chung te Nu-Hsing Chiao-Se* (The role of women in the national development process in Taiwan). Taipei: Population Studies Center, National Taiwan University, 1985.

Bilquees, Faiz and Moazam Mahmood. *Women in the Labour Market in Pakistan*. New Delhi: Asian Regional Team for Employment Promotion, International Labour Organization, 1990.

Bingham, Marjorie W. and Susan H. Gross. *Women in Japan: From Ancient Times to the Present*. St. Louis: Glenhurst Publications, 1987.

Birdsall, Nancy. *Social Development Is Economic Development*. HRO Working Paper, Human Resources Development and Operation Policy. Washington, DC: The World Bank, 1993.

Biro Pusat Statistik. *Indikator Sosial Wanita Indonesia 1991* (Social indicators on Indonesian women 1991). Jakarta. 1992.

———. *Penduduk Indonesia, Hasil Sensus Penduduk 1980* (Population of Indonesia, Results of the 1980 Population Census), Series S2, 1983.

———. *Sensus Penduduk 1971* (1971 Population Census), Series D, 1975. Jakarta.

———. *Sensus Penduduk 1971* (1971 Population Census), Series C, 1972. Jakarta.

———. *Sensus Penduduk 1990* (1980 Population Census), Series S2, 1992. Jakarta.

———. *Statistik Pendidikan di Bawah dan di Luar Lingkungan Departemen P dan K, 1988/1989* (Education statistics in and out of the Department of Education and Culture), 1991.

Boserup, E. *Women's Role in Economic Development.* New York: St. Martin's Press, 1970.

Buckley, Sandra and Vera Mackie. "Women in the New Japanese State," in: Gavan McCormick and Y. Sugimoto, eds., *Democracy in Contemporary Japan.* Armonk, NY: M. E. Sharpe, 1986.

Burton, Margaret E. *Notable Women of China.* New York: Fleming H. Revell, 1912.

Canadian International Development Agency. *Nation Builders: Women in Pakistan: A Development Strategy.* Hull, Quebec: CIDA, 1986.

Carnoy, Martin. *Education as Cultural Imperialism.* New York: David McKay, 1974.

Central Bank of Ceylon. *Consumer Finances and Socio-economic Survey 1973, 1978/79, 1981/82, 1986/87.* Colombo, Sri Lanka.

Centre for Women's Research. *Human Resources in Sri Lanka's Industrial Development—The Current and Prospective Contribution of Women.* Vienna: UNIDO, 1989.

———. *Women's Work and Family Strategies.* Colombo: CENWOR, 1987.

Chan, H. C. "Notes on the mobilization of women into the economy and politics of Singapore." Occasional Paper Series, University of Singapore, Department of Political Science, 1975.

Chang, C. H. and L. C. Chen. "Kuo-hsiao hseuh-sheng hsueh-yeh ch'eng-chi yu chiao-shih hsing-pieh kuang-hsi chih yen-chiu" (The relation between academic performance of elementary school students and the sex of teachers). *Chiao-Yu Hsin-Li Hsueh K'an* (Journal of Educational Psychology) 8 (1977): 21–34.

Chang, Ching-Hsi. "A Review of Female Labor Force Participation," in: *Economic Essays*, Vol. 8. Taipei: The Graduate Institute of Economics, National Taiwan University, 1978, pp. 275–284.

Chang, Wei-an. Ke-chia fu-nu ti-wei: yi min-nan tzu-chun wei tuei-chao te fen-hsi (Status of Hakka women: An analysis using Fukien women as the reference group). Paper presented at the Conference on Hakka Culture, Council on Culture Planning and Development (Miaoli, Taiwan, March 12–13, 1994).

Chapman, Christine. "The Meiji Letters of Tsuda Ume, Pioneer Educator of Women." *Japan Quarterly* (July-Sept. 1987): 263–270.

Chen, Ta. *Population in Modern China.* Chicago: University of Chicago Press, 1946.

Chen, Xuexun, ed. *Zhongguo jindai jiaoyushi jiaoxue cankao ziliao Vol. 3* (Reference materials for the teaching of the history of modern Chinese education). Beijing: Remin jiaoyu chubanshe, 1986.

Chenery, Hollis B. *Redistribution with Growth.* London: Oxford University Press, 1974.

Cheng, L. and P. C. Hsiung. "Fu-nu, ch'u-k'ou tau-hsiang, yu kuo-chia: yi tai-wan wei li" (Women, export-oriented growth, and the state: The case of Taiwan)." *Taiwan She-Hui Yen-Chiu Chi-K'an*, (Taiwan: A Radical Quarterly in Social Sciences) 1993, 14: 39–76.

Chiang, L. H. and Yen-Ling Ku. *Past and Current Status of Women in Taiwan.* Women's Research Program, Population Studies Center, National Taiwan University, 1985.

Chiang, Lan-Hong Nora. "The New Social and Economic Roles of Chinese Women in Taiwan and its Implication for Policy and Development." Paper presented at the 30th Annual Conference, Western Social Science Association, Denver, CO (1988).

China, Center for Research on Educational Development, State Education Commission. *Yiwu jiaoyu xiaoyi yangjiu* (A study of the effectiveness of compulsory education). Beijing: Renmin jiaoyu chubanshe, 1992.

———, Department of Planning and Construction, State Education Commission. *Educational Statistics Yearbook of China 1992.* Beijing: Renmin jiaoyu chubanshe, 1993.

———, Department of Planning, Ministry of Education. *Achievement of Education in China 1949–1983*. Beijing: People's Education Press, 1984.
———, Department of Population Statistics, State Statistical Bureau. *China Population Statistics Yearbook 1992*. Beijing: Zhongguo tongji chubanshe, 1993.
———, Ministry of Education. *Educational Statistics of the Republic of China, 1992*. Taipei: Ministry of Education, 1992.
———, Ministry of Education. *Educational Indicators of the R.O.C.*, 1992.
———, State Statistical Bureau. *Zhongguo tongji nianjian 1989* (Statistical yearbook of China 1989). Beijing: Zhongguo tongji chubanshe, 1990.
———, State Statistical Bureau. *Zhongguo tonji nianjian 1993* (Statistical yearbook of China 1993). Changsha: Hunan chubanshe, 1992.
China Yearbook Publishers. *Zhonghua nianjian 1948* (China yearbook 1948), Vol.2. Nanjing: Zhonghua nianjian she,1948.
Chiplin, B. and P. J. Sloane. *Sex Discrimination in the Labour Market*. London: Macmillan, 1976.
Chitnis, S. "Dimensions of discrimination in the employment of women—legal protection and education for equity." Paper presented at the Seminar on Sex Discrimination in Gainful Employment, Pune, India, 1981.
Chiu, Hai-Yuan. "Education and Social Change in Taiwan," in: H. H. M. Hsiao, W. Y. Cheng, and H. S. Chan, eds., *Taiwan: A Newly Industralizated State*. Taipei: National Taiwan University, Department of Sociology, 1988, pp. 187–206.
Cho, Hyoung. "Labour Force Participation of Women in Korea," in: Seiwha Chung, ed., *Challenges for Women: Woman's Studies in Korea*. Seoul: Ewha Womans University Press, 1986.
Cho, Uno. "Industrialisation and Female Labor Absorption in Korea." *Women's Studies Forum*. Seoul, 1985.
Chou, Bih-er. "Industrialization and Change in Women's Status: A Reevaluation of Some Data from Taiwan," in: H. H. M. Hsiao, W. Y. Cheng, and H. S. Chan, eds., *Taiwan: A Newly Industrialization State*. Taipei: National Taiwan University, Department of Sociology, 1989, pp. 423–61.
Chua, S. C. *Report on the census of population 1957*. Singapore: Government printers, 1964.
Committee on the Status of Women in India. *Towards Equality*. New Delhi: Government of India, Ministry of Education, Department of Social Welfare, 1975.
Condon, Jane. *A Half Step Behind: Japanese Women of the 80's*. New York: Dodd Mead, 1985.
Council for Economic Planning and Development (CEPD). *Taiwan Statistical Data Book, 1992*. Taipei: The Executive Yuan, 1992.
———. *An Analysis of the Utilization of Female Labor Force in Taiwan*. Taipei: The Executive Yuan, 1984.
De Mel, Gayanandeni. "Women Primary Teachers—their Work and Problems," in: *Gender and Education in Sri Lanka*. Colombo: CENWOR, 1991, pp. 73–82.
Denison, Edward F. *The Sources of Economic Growth in the United States and the Alternative Before Us*. New York: Committee for Economic Development, 1962.
———. *Measuring the Contribution of Education to Economic Growth*. Paris: OECD, 1964.
Diamond, N. "Women and Industry in Taiwan." *Modern China* 5, no. 3 (1979): 317–40.
Dias-Abeygunawardene, Hema. "Participation of Girls and Women in Formal and Non-formal Educational Programmes in the Nuwara Eliya Educational Region." Unpublished M.Ed. thesis, University of Colombo, 1980.
———. "Non-formal Education for Working Mothers with Pre-school Children." Unpublished M.Phil. thesis, University of Colombo, 1982.
Dodd, C. H. *Political Development*. New York: Macmillan, 1972.

Doraisamy, T. R., ed. *150 Years of Education in Singapore*. Singapore: Teachers' Training College, 1969.
Dore, Ronald. *Education in Tokugawa Japan*. Berkeley: University of California Press, 1966.
El-Sanabary, N. *Determinants of Women's Education in the Middle East and North Africa: Illusration from Seven Countries*. Education and Empolyment Division, Population and Human Resources Department, Document No. PHREE/89/14. Washington, DC: The World Bank, 1989.
Emerson, John Philip. "Sex, Age and Level of Skill of the Nonagricultural Labor Force of Mainland China." Washington, DC: U. S. Department of Commerce, June 1965.
Eng, S. P. *Women's Education, Occupational Attainment and Income in Singapore*. Singapore: Institute of Education, 1982.
Europa World Year Book 1993, The. Vol. II. London: Europa Publications Limited, 1993.
Fatimah Abdullah. "Wanita yang Bekerja dan Pengurusan Rumahtangga" (Working women and managing the house). *Journal Antropologi dan Sosiologi*, no. 15 (1987): 72–92.
Fatimah Hamid Don. "Opportunities for Women in Education." Paper presented at the Seminar Peranan Wanita dalam Bidang-Bidang Pelajaran Tinggi dan Implikasinya (The role of women in higher education and its implications). Kuala Lumpur, 1975, Federation of Malaysia, *Sixth Malaysia Plan 1991–1995*. Kuala Lumpur: National Printing Department, 1991.
———. "The Manifestation of Science and Technology in the ASEAN Heritage: Women in Eduction and Training." Paper presented at the Conference on ASEAN Professional Women 1992, Universiti Teknologi Malaysia, Johor (Sept. 1992).
Francois, Louis. *The Right to Education: From Proclamation to Achievement 1948–1968*. Paris: UNESCO, 1968.
Fujii, Harue. "Education for Women: The Personal and Social Damage of Anachronistic Policy." *Japan Quarterly* 23, no. 3, pp. 301–310.
Fujimura-Fanselow, Kumiko. "Women and Higher Education in Japan: Tradition and Change." Ph.D. dissertation, Columbia University, 1981.
———. "Women's Participation in Higher Education in Japan." *Comparative Education Review* 29 (Nov. 1985): 471–489.
———. "Women's Education in Japan," in: Gail P. Kelly, ed., *International Handbook of Women's Education*. Westport. CT: Greenwood Press, 1989.
Fujimura-Fanselow, Kumiko and Anne E. Imamura, "The Education of Women in Japan," in: Edward Beauchamp, ed., *Windows on Japanese Education*. Westport, CT: Greenwood Press, 1991.
Gates, H. *Chinese Working-Class Lives: Getting By in Taiwan*. Ithaca, NY: Cornell University Press, 1987.
Ghafoor, A. "Pakistan: System of Education," in: T. Husen and T. N. Postlethwaite, eds., *International Encyclopedia of Education*. New York: Pergamon Press, 1985.
Ghosh, R. *General job satisfaction and perceptions of academic roles: A study of male and female academics in India*. Report to the Shastri Indo-Canadian Institute, Calgary, 1983.
———. "Human Rights and Sexism in Indian education," in: U. Baxi et al., eds., *The Right to be Human*. New Delhi: Lancer International, 1986.
———. "Introduction," in: G. Kurian and R. Ghosh, eds., *Women in the Family and the Economy: An International Comparative Survey*. Westport, CT: Greenwood Press, 1981.
———. "Introduction," in: R. Ghosh and M. Zachariah, *Education and the Process of Change*. New Delhi: Sage Publications, 1987.

———. "Women's Education in the Land of Goddess Saraswati." *Canadian and International Education* 15, no. 1 (1986): 25–44.
Ghosh, R. and A. Talbani. *A Critical Analysis of the New Educatinal Policy of India—1986* (monograph). Montreal: McGill University Press, 1989.
Gold, B. Thomas. *State and Society in the Taiwan Miracle*. Armonk, New York: M. E. Sharpe, 1986.
Goldthorpe, J. E. *The Sociology of the Third World: Disparity and Development*. London: Cambridge University Press, 1984.
Gopal, K. and S. Madhav. "Patterns of City Literacy." *Economic and Political Weekly* (May 18, 1974): 20.
Gopal, S., ed. *Selected works of Jawaharlal Nehru*. New Delhi: Orient Longman, 1972.
Green, T. L. "Education and Social Needs in Sri Lanka." *University of Ceylon Review* 10, No. 4 (1952) 297–316.
Greenhalgn, S. "Is Inequality Demographically Induced? The Family Cycle and the Distribution of Income in Taiwan." *American Anthropologist* 87, no. 3 (1985): 571–94.
———. "Sexual Stratification: The Other Side of 'Growth with Equity' in East Asia." *Population Development Review* 11, no. 2 (1985): 264–314.
Gunawardene, Chandra. "A Career Appraisal of Women Teachers in Sri Lanka," in: *Gender and Education in Sri Lanka*. Colombo, CENWOR, 1991, pp. 83–96.
———. "Participation of Women in Higher Education in Sri Lanka." Paper presented at the First National Convention on Women's Studies, CENWOR, Colombo 1989.
———. "The Changing Composition of the University Student Population in Sri Lanka since 1948." Unpublished M.A. thesis, University of Peradeniya, Sri Lanka, 1974.
Hafeez, Sabeeha. *Women in Industry in Pakistan*. Islamabad: Women's Division, Government of Pakistan, 1989.
Hafsah, Nawawi, Ramlah Hamzah, and Hamidah Khalid, "Pendidikan Vokasional Untuk Wanita Malaysia: Satu Tinjauan" (Vocational education for women in Malaysia: A survey). Paper presented at the National Workshop on Technical and Vocational Education for Women in Malaysia. Universiti Pertanian Malaysia, Serdang, March 1992.
Hagen, Everett E. *The Economics of Development*. Homewood, IL: Richard D. Irwin, 1975.
Hall, Ivan P. "Technical/Vocational and Women's Education," in Ivan P. Hall, *Mori Arinori*. Cambridge: Harvard University, 1973.
Hamid, Shahnaz. "Determinants of the Supply of Women in the Labour Market: A Micro Analysis." *The Pakistan Development Review*, no. 30:4 Part II (Winter 1991): 755–64.
Hashimah, Roose, "Changes in the Position of Malay Women," in: B. Ward, ed., *Women in the New Asia*. Paris: UNESCO, 1965.
Herz, Barbara, K. Subbarao, Massoma Habib, and Laura Raney. *Letting Girls Learn: Promising Approaches in Primary and Secondary Education*. World Bank Discussion Paper No. 133. Washington, DC: The World Bank, 1991.
Hewitt, Farida. "Women's Work, Women's Place: The Gendered Life—World of High Mountain Community in Northern Pakistan." *Mountain Research and Development* 9 (November 1989): 335–52.
Hing, Ai Yun, Nik Safiah Karim, and Rokiah Talib. *Malaysian Women*. Kuala Lumpur: Pelanduk Publications, 1984.
Ho, Chi-Min. "Chia Kung Ch'u K'ou Ch'u" (The export process zone), in: Kao Hsi-Chun and Li Cheng, eds., *Tai-wan Ching-yen Ssu-shih Nien* (The Taiwan experience 1949–1989). Taipei: Tien-Hsia, 1991, pp. 380–409.
Ho, Chung-Wen. "Tang-tai t'ai-wan ch'ang-chi wen-ti" (Prostitution in contemporary Taiwan), in: *Tsai-hung Chuan-an Yu-fang Kuo-chi Fu-nu Yun-shu Yen-tao-hui*

Pao-kao-shu (Report on Rainbow Program on the Prevention of International Smuggling of Women). Taipei: 1988.

Honig, Emily. *Sisters and Strangers: Women in the Shanghai Cotton Mills 1919–1949*. Stanford, CA: Stanford University Press, 1946.

Hooper, Beverley. "Gender and Education." In: Irving Epstein, ed., *Chinese Education*. New York: Garland Publishing, 1991.

Hsia, Lin-Ching. "Ts'ung hsueh-hsiao tao kung-ch'ang: kuo-chung pi-yeh nu-sheng kung-ch'ang sheng-huo chin-ju li-ch'eng chih miao-shu yu fen-hsi" (From school to work: A description and analysis of the process of women junior high school graduates entering factory life). *Chung-Hua Hsing-Li Wei-Sheng Hsueh K'an* (Chinese Mental Health) 5, no. 2 (1992): 135–153.

Hsieh, Hsiao-Chin. "Ability Stratification in Urban Taiwanese Secondary Schools." *Chung Yang Yen Chiu Yuan Min Tzu Hsueh Yen Chiu So Chi Kan* (Bulletin of the Institute of Ethnology Academia Sinica) 64 (1987): 205–252.

———. "Chiao-yu chung te hsing-pie-yi-shih" (Gender ideology in school system). *Jen-Pen Chiao-Yu Cha-Chi* (Humanistic Education) 7 (1989): 30–35.

———. "Hsing-pie yu chiao-yu chi-hui: yi pei-shih liang-ssokuo-chung wei li" (Gender difference in educational opportunities in Taiwan: Two Taipei junior high schools). *Kuo-Chia K'e-Hsueh Wei-Yuan-Hui Hui-K'an: Jen-Wen Yu She-Hui K'e-Hsueh* (Proceedings of the National Science Council, Part C: Humanities and Social Sciences, vol. 2 (1992): 179–201.

Hsiung, P. C. "The Social Construction of Paternalism: A Case Study of Taiwan's Satellite System." Occasional paper no. 6, Women's Research Program. National Taiwan University, Population Studies Center, 1991.

Hu, Tai-li. *Daughter-in-law Marries In*. Taipei: China Times, 1982.

———. "The Influence of Industrialization of Taiwan Rural Areas on the Status of Women," in: N. Chiang, ed., *Kuo-Chia Fa-Chan Kuo-Ch'eng Chung te Nu-Hsing Chiao-Sse* (The role of women in the national development process in Taiwan). Taipei: Population Studies Center, National Taiwan University, 1985, pp. 335–356.

Huang, Yu-Hsiu. "1992 Taiwan fu nu jen chuan pao kao" (Women's rights report, Taiwan, 1992). *Fu-Nu Hsin-Chih* (Awakening) 129 (1991): 20–23.

Huntington, S. P. and Nelson, J. M. *No Easy Choice: Political Participation in Developing Countries*. Cambridge: Harvard University Press, 1976.

Huq, M[uhammad] S[hamsul]. *Education and Development Strategy in South and Southeast Asia*. Honolulu: East-West Center Press, 1965.

———. Education, *Manpower and Development in South and Southeast Asia*. New York: Praeger Publishers, 1975.

Imamura, Anne E. Urban Housewives: *At Home and in the Community*. Honolulu: University of Hawaii Press, 1987.

India, Government of. *Education in India, 1970–71*. New Delhi: Government of India, Ministry of Education and Social Welfare, 1981.

———. *First Five Year Plan*. New Delhi: Government of India, 1951.

———. *India: A Reference Manual, 1987*. Delhi: Publications Division, 1987.

———. *National Perspective Plan for Women 1988–2000. A Perspective from the Women's Movement*. Report of a debate 22–23 August 1988. New Delhi, 1988.

———. *National Policy on Education*. New Delhi: Ministry of Education, 1986.

———. *Report of the Secondary Education Commission*. New Delhi: Government of India, 1953.

———. *Report of the Education Commission, 1948–49*. Vol. I. New Delhi: Manager of Publications, 1950.

———. *Report of the National Committee on Women's Education*. New Delhi: Government of India, Ministry of Education, 1959.

———. *Report of the Working Group on Personnel Policies for Bringing Greater In-

volvement of Women in Science and Technology. New Delhi: Government of India, Ministry of Social Welfare, 1981.

——. *Towards Equality: Report of the Committee on the Status of Women*. New Delhi: Ministry of Education and Social Welfare, 1975.

——. *Women in India: A Statistical Profile*. New Delhi: Government of India, Department of Women and Child Development, 1978.

Insan Harapan Sejahtera. *A Study of Women's Issues in Agricultural Transformation*. Study conducted for the World Bank, 1993. Jakarta.

Institute of Ethnology. *1991 Tai-wan Ti-Ch'u She-Hui Pien-ch'ien Chi-Pen Tiao-Ch'a Pao-Kao* (Report on Social Change Survey 1991). Taipei: Institute of Ethnology, Academia Sinica, 1991.

International Labour Office. *Year Book of Labour Statistics: Retrospective Edition on Population Censuses, 1945–89*. Geneva: ILO, 1990.

Irfan, Mohammad. "Poverty, Class Structure and Household Demographic Behavior in Rural Pakistan." Pakistan Institute of Development Economics. Research Report No. 11. Islamabad: PIDE, 1985.

——. *Pakistan Labour Force, its Size and Structure: A Review of Evidence*. Research Report No. 116. Islamabad: Pakistan Institute of Development Economics, 1981.

Ismall, Jezima. "The Status of the Girl Child in the Sri Lankan Muslim Community," in: *Half Our Future*. Colombo: Sri Lanka Federation of University Women, 1991, pp. 95–124.

Jamilah, M. A. "Industrialization, Female Labour Migration, and the Changing Pattern of Malay Women's Labour Force Participation—An Analysis of Interrelationship and Implications." Paper presented at the Seminar on Population and Sectoral Development. Cameron Highlands, Pahang, Malaysia, Jan. 1981.

Japan, Ministry of Education. *The Status of Women in Japan*. Tokyo: Ministry of Education, 1977.

——. *Women and Education in Japan*. Tokyo: Ministry of Education, 1980.

Jayasena, Asoka. "Sexism in the Post-Primary Curriculum in Sri Lanka," in: *Gender and Education in Sri Lanka*. Colombo: CENWOR, 1991, pp. 45–55.

Jayawardene, Kumari and Swarna Jayaweera. "The Integration of Women in Development Planning in Sri Lanka," in: *Missing Women*. Kuala Lumpur: Asian and Pacific Development Centre, 1985, pp. 105–127.

Jayaweera, Swarna. "A Comparative Study of Colonial British and American Education Policy in Ceylon and the Philippines." Unpublished Ph.D. thesis, University of London, 1966.

——. "Access to Education—The Social Composition of University Entrants," in: *University of Colombo Review* no. 4 (1984): 6–40.

——. "Universalization of Elementary Education in Sri Lanka." *Journal of the National Education Society of Sri Lanka* 24 (1985): 50–63.

——. "Colonial Educational Policy and Gender Ideology under the Colonial Administration in Sri Lanka," in: K. M. de Silva, ed., *Asian Panorama*. New Delhi: Vikas Publishing House, 1990, pp. 210–227.

——. "Education and Socio-economic Development," *Sri Lanka Journal of Social Sciences*, 13 nos. 1 and 2 (1990): 47–72.

——. "Education of Girls and Women in the Context of an Economically Developing Society," in: *Women at the Crossroads*. New Delhi: Vikas Publishing House, 1990, pp. 96–118.

——. "Education" and "Aspects of the Role and Position of Women," in: Tissa Fernando and Robert N. Kearney, eds., *Modern Sri Lanka: A Society in Transition*. Syracuse, NY, Syracuse University Press, 1979, pp. 131–154, 165–180.

——. "European Women Educators under the British Colonial Administration in Sri Lanka." *Women's Studies International Forum*, USA 13, no. 4 (1990): 323–332.

———. "Integration of Women in Development Planning," "Women and Education," and "Women and Employment," in: *UN Decade for Women: Progress and Achievements of Women in Sri Lanka*. Colombo: CENWOR, 1985.

———. "The Education of Girls in Sri Lanka—Opportunities and Constraints," in: *Half Our Future*. Colombo: Sri Lanka Federation of University Women, 1991, pp. 45–66.

———. "The Education of the Girls" and "The Socialization of The Girl Child," in: *The Girl Child in Sri Lanka*. Colombo: CENWOR, 1993.

———. "The Education of Women in Sri Lanka," in: *Growth and Development*. Colombo: Sri Lanka Federation of University Women, 1991, pp. 9–17.

———. "Vocational Preferences of Secondary School Girls in Sri Lanka," in: *Modern Ceylon Studies* nos. 1 and 2 (1976): 207–238.

———. "Women and Development: A Re-appraisal of the Sri Lanka Experience," in: *The Hidden Face of Development*. Colombo: CENWOR, 1989, pp. 1–16.

———. "Women and Education" and "Women in the Economy," in: *Status of Women: Sri Lanka*. University of Colombo, 1979, pp. 254–422, 423–550.

———. "Women, Education and the Labour Force," in: *Gender and Education in Sri Lanka*. Colombo: CENWOR, 1991, pp. 107–129.

———. *Women in Sri Lanka in 2015*. Colombo: Organization of Professional Associations, 1988.

———. *Women, Skill Development and Employment*. Colombo: Institute of Policy Studies, 1991.

Jayaweera, Swarna and Thana Sanmugam. *Women Engineers in Sri Lanka*. Colombo: Sri Lanka Federation of University Women, 1992.

Jayaweera, Swarna, Patricia Alailima, Chandra Rodrigo, and R. A. Jayatiss. *Women and Structural Adjustment: the Sri Lanka Experience*. London: Commonwealth Secretariat, 1991.

Jayaweera, Swarna, Sterling Perera, and Sirisoma Rupasinghe. "Gender Differences in Performance at Secondary School Examinations in Sri Lanka," in: *Gender and Education in Sri Lanka*. Colombo: CENWOR, 1991, pp. 5–22.

Jayaweera, Swarna, Thana Sanmugam, Wijaya Jayatilake, and Soma K. Mendis. *Women Graduates in Agriculture*. Colombo: CENWOR, 1992.

Ji, Rong. *Zhongguo funu yundongshi* (History of women's movement in China). Changsha: Hunan chubanshe, 1985.

Jing, Yihong. "The Status and Future Prospect of Rural Women in the Economic Reform," in: Li Xiaojiang and Tan Shen, ed., *Zhongguo funu fenceng yanjiu* (A study of chinese women by social stratum). Zhengzhou: Henan renmin chubanshe, 1991.

Johnson, Kay Ann. *Women, the Family and Peasant Revolution in China*. Chicago: University of Chicago Press, 1983.

Kamiyama, Tamie. "Ideology and Patterns in Women's Education in Japan." Ph.D. dissertation, St. Louis University, 1977.

Kanesalingam, V. *Women in Development in South Asia* (New Delhi: Macmillan, 1989).

Kazi, Shahnaz and Bilquees Raza. "Duality of Female Employment in Pakistan." *The Pakistan Development Review* 30, no. 4, Part II (Winter 1991): 733–743.

Kelabora, Lambert and Kenneth Orr. "Stimulating the Appetite and Coping with the Consequences in Indonesia," in: Kenneth Orr, ed., *Appetite for Education in Contemporary Asia*. Canberra: The Australian National University, Development Studies Centre Monograph No. 10, 1977, pp. 92–107.

Kelly, Gail. *International Handbook of Women's Education*. Westport, CT: Greenwood Press, 1989.

Khan, Shaheen. "Economic Analysis of Personal Earnings in Urban Formal and Informal Sector of Employment." *Pakistan Economic and Social Review* 21 (Summer/Winter 1983): 1–24.

Khawaja, Sarfraz. *Promotion of Girls Education in the Context of Universalization of Primary Education.* Islamabad: Academy of Educational Planning and Management, 1985.

Khoo, C. K. *Census of population 1980, Singapore Administrative Report.* Singapore: Department of Statistics, 1983.

———. *Census of population 1980, Singapore Release No. 4: Economic Characteristics.* Singapore: Department of Statistics, 1983.

Kim, Chayoon. *Study of Social Stratification in Korean Society.* Seoul: Moonjo, 1966.

Kim, Kwangsuk. *Outward-Looking Industrialisation Strategy: The Case of Korea.* Seoul: Korea Development Institute, 1975.

Kim, Kwangsuk and Joonkyung Park. *Estimated Sources of Growth.* Seoul: Korea Development Instiutec, 1985.

Kim, Kwangsuk and Joonkyung Park. *Source of Economic Growth in Korea: 1963–1982.* Seoul: Korea Development Institute, 1985.

Kim, Oksoon. "The Role of Family Background on Educational and Occupational Attainment of Korean Adults." Ph.D. dissertation, University of Southern California, 1988.

Kim, Yoonhwan. *Procedure of Korean Economic Growth.* Seoul: Dolbegae, 1981.

Kim, Yungbong. "Education and Economic Growth," in: Chonkee Park, ed., *Human Resources and Social Development in Korea.* Seoul: Korea Development Institute, 1980.

King, Elizabeth and Hill, A., eds., *Women's Education in Developing Countries: Barriers, Benefits and Policy.* Education and Employment Division, Population and Human Resources Department, PHREE, Background Paper Series, Document No. PHREE/91/40. Washington, DC: The World Bank, 1991.

King, Elizabeth, et al. *Change in the Status of Women Across Generations in Asia.* Santa Monica, CA: The RAND Corporation, 1986.

Kiribanda, B. M. "Education, Female Labour Force Participation Status and Fertility Interrelationships." Unpublished Ph.D. thesis, University of Pennsylvania, 1981.

Kiyooka, Eiichi, translator and ed. *Fukuzawa Yukichi on Japanese Women.* Tokyo: University of Tokyo Press, 1988.

Korea, Bank of Korea. *National Income in Korea.* Seoul, 1982.

———, Economic Planning Board. *Annual Report on the Economically Active Population Survey.* Seoul: 1980.

———, Women's Development Institute. *Women Report.* Seoul, 1985.

Koyama, Takashi. *The Changing Social Position of Women in Japan.* Paris: UNESCO, 1961.

Ku, Yen-ling. "Fu-nu yun-tung yu kung-kung cheng-tse te hu-tung kuan-hsi: tuo-tai he-fa-hua yu p'ing-teng kung-tzuo-chuan te tse-lueh fen-hsi" (The dynamic between women's movement and public policy: An analysis of strategies for the legalization of abortion and equal right for work). Paper presented at the Conference on State and Society in Taiwan's Democratization, March 7 and 8, 1992. Taipei: Chinese Society of Sociology, 1992.

Kung, L. *Factory Women in Taiwan.* Ann Arbor, MI: UMI Research Press, 1978.

Labor Committee, *Liang-Hsing Lao-Tung Ch'ing-Shih T'ung-Chi* (Male and female labor statistics, Taiwan Area, R.O.C.). Taipei: Labor Committee, 1990.

Lang, Olga. *Chinese Family and Society.* New Haven, CT: Yale University Press, 1946.

Lau, K. E. *Singapore Census of Population 1990 Demographic Characteristics Release 1.* Singapore: Department of Statistics, 1992.

Lebra, Joyce, et al. *Women in Changing Japan.* Boulder, CO: Westview Press, 1976.

Lebra, Takie Sugiyama. *Japanese Women: Constraints and Fulfillment.* Honolulu: University of Hawaii Press, 1984.

Lee, K. Y. The Prime Minister's Speech at the National Trade Union Congress Seminar for Women. Singapore. Mimeographed, 1975.

Leys, Collin. *Politics and Change in Developing Countries*. Cambridge, UK: Cambridge University Press, 1969.

Li, Debiao. *Zhonghua renmin gongheguo jingjishi jianbian 1949–1985* (A short economic history of China 1949–1985). Changsha: Hunan remin chubanshe, 1987.

Li, K. T. "Fu-nu tzai tai-wan ching-chi fa-chan kuo-ch'eng chung te kung-hsien" (The contribution of female labor force in Taiwan's economic development process), in: N. Chiang, ed., *Kuo-Chia Fa-Chan Kuo-Ch'eng Chung te Nu-Hsing Chiao-Ssu* (The role of women in the national development process in Taiwan). Taipei: Population Studies Center, National Taiwan University, 1985, pp. 1–7.

———. *Chia-Hu Lao-Tung, Chia-T'ing yu Hsiao-Ch'i-Yeh: Yi Chia Tai Pei Ch'eng-Yi-Ch'ang te Ke-An Yen-Chiu* (Household labor, family and small-scale community). M.A. thesis, Graduate Institute of Sociology and Anthropology, National Tsing-hua University, 1993.

———. *The Evolution of Policy Behind Taiwan's Development Success*. New Haven, CT: Yale University Press, 1988.

Liao, Cheng-hung. "Urbanization in Taiwan." In: H. H. M. Hsiao et al., eds., *Taiwan: A Newly Industralized State*. Taipei: National Taiwan University, 1989, pp. 345–378.

Liao, Long-Li and Wei-Yuan Cheng. "The Contribution of Female Labor Force to Economic Growth in Taiwan." Keynote speech delivered at the Conference on the Roles of Women in the National Development Process in Taiwan, March 14–16, 1985. Taipei: National Taiwan University, Population Studies Center, 1985.

Lim, Heepseup. *Social Equality and Progress*. Seoul: Jungeumsa, 1983.

Lim, L. "Women in the Singapore Economy." Occasional Paper, University of Singapore, Economic Research Centre, 1982.

Lin, Chung-Cheng. "Sex Difference in Wage among First-job Holders." *Economic Essays* (Graduate Institute of Economics, National Taiwan University) 16, no. 3 (1988): 305–322.

Lo, A. and V. Shieh. "A Study from an Educational Perspective to Investigate Sex Equity in the Classroom between Teacher and Student at Elementary School Level in Kaohsiung." Department of Psychology, Kaohsiung Medical College, 1992.

Logsdon, Martha G. "Women Civil Servants in Indonesia: Some Preliminary Observations," *PRISMA* 37 (September 1985): 77–87.

Loo Lai May, *Wanita di Institusi Pengajian Tinggi* (Women in higher education). Academic Exercise for Bachelor of Arts Degree, Universiti Kebangsaan Malaysia, Bangi, 1987.

Low, G. T. *A comparative study of educational administrators in Singapore: Emphasis on successful women*. Unpublished doctoral dissertation, University of Michigan, 1988.

Lu, Yu-Hsia. "Urban-rural Economic Development and Employment of Married Women: An Exploration of the Theory of Female Marginalization." *Population Studies*, 1992.

———. "Women's Informal Employment in Taiwan." Paper presented at the Conference on Gender and Society, National Tsing-Hua University, June 25–26, 1991.

Malayisa, Department of Statistics. *The Labour Force Survey Report 1989–1991*. Kuala Lumpur, 1991.

———, Federation of. *Malaysia Federal Constitution*. Kuala Lumpur: Federal Printers, 1978.

———, Federation of. *National Policy for Women*, Kuala Lumpur: National Printing Department, 1992.

———, Federation of. *Second Malaysia Plan, 1971–1975*. Kuala Lumpur: Government Press, 1971.

———, Federation of. *Third Malaysia Plan, 1976–1980*. Kuala Lumpur: Government Press, 1976.

———, Ministry of Education. *Peranan Wanita dalam Bidang-bidang Pelajaran Tinggi dan Implikasinya* (The Role of Women in Higher Education and Implications). Report of the Seminar (University of Malaya, November, 1975). Kuala Lumpur: Government Press.

———, Ministry of Education. Educational Planning and Research Division, *Education in Malaysia*. Dewan Bahasa dan Pustaka, Kuala Lumpur, 1980.

———, Ministry of Information. *Malaysian 90/91 Official Year Book*, Vol. 22. Kuala Lumpur: Utusan Print Corp Sdn. Bhd., 1991.

Manderson, L. *Wanita, Politik dan Perubahan: Pergerakan Kaum Ibu UMNO, Malaysia 1945–1972* (Women, politics and change: The UMNO women's movement in Malaysia 1945–1972). Fajar Bakti: Kuala Lumpur, 1981.

Marga Institute. *University Education and Graduate Employment in Sri Lanka.* Colombo, 1983.

Marker, Mether K. and Shirkat Gah. *Women, Education and Development in Pakistan.* [S.l.: s.n. 1985?].

Maskiell, Michelle. *The Impact of Islamization Policies on Pakistani Women's Lives.* Working Paper No. 69. East Lansing, MI: Women in International Development, Michigan State University, 1984.

Matsui, Machiko. "A Case Study of Female Students from Japan and the PRC at an American university." Ph.D. dissertation, State University of New York at Buffalo, 1991.

Matsuoka, Yoko. *Daughter of the Pacific.* New York: Harper, 1952.

Mazumdar, Vina. *Education and Women's Equality* (mimeograph). New Delhi: Center for Women's Development Studies, 1985.

Mishima Sumie. *My Narrow Isle: The Story of a Modern Woman in Japan.* New York: John Day, 1941.

Moon, B. G. *Study of Occupational and Social Movement through the Educational Achievement.* Seoul: Seoul National University Press, 1984.

Mumtaz, Khawar and Shaheed, Farida. *Women' Education in Pakistan: Opportunities, Issues and Challenges.* N.p., [1987?].

Mustafa, Zubeida. *Women's Education in Pakistan.* N.p. [1986?].

Myrdal, A. and V. Klien. *Women's Two Roles, Home and Work.* London: Routledge and Kegan Paul, 1956.

Nagy, Margit. "How Should We Live?: Social Change, the Family Institution and Feminism in Prewar Japan." Ph.D. dissertation, University of Washington, 1981.

Nanayakkara, N. C. *The Impact of Employment, Education and Age at Marriage of Females on Fertility in Sri Lanka 1971–81.* Demographic Training and Research Unit, University of Colombo, 1987.

Nanda, B. R. *Indian Women from Purdah to Modernity.* New Delhi: Vikas Publishing, 1976.

Narumiya, Chie. "Opportunity for Girls and Women in Japanese Education." *Comparative Education* 22, no. 1 (1986): 47–52.

National Council of Educational Research and Training (NCERT). *Fifth All-India Educational Survey.* Vols. I and II. New Delhi: National Council of Educational Research and Training, 1992.

Nik Safiah Karim. *Dekad Wanita: 1975–85 Satu Pengenalan Ringkas* (Decade of women: 1975–85, An overview). Kuala Lumpur: NACIWID, 1985.

———. *Wanita Malaysia: Kumpulan Esei dan Ceramah* (Malaysian women: Collection of essays and lectures). Pustaka Ilmu Raya Sdn. Bhd., Kuala Lumpur, 1982.

National Productivity Board, Singapore. *National Productivity Board Survey on Work Attitudes.* Singapore, 1991.

Oey-Gardiner, Mayling. "Female School Attendance in Indonesia." Unpublished paper prepared for the World Bank, Jakarta, 1989.

Ou, Yung-Sheng. "Kuo min hsueh hsiao chiao ke shu chung te hsing pie yi shih hsing tai" (Gender ideology in elementary school textbooks). *Hsin-Chu Shih-Yuan*

Hsueh-Pao (Bulletin of Hsin-Chu Normal College) 12 (1985), pp. 91–124.
Pakistan, Government of. Planning Commission. *Sixth Five Year Plan, 1983–88*. Islamabad: Planning Commission, 1984.
———, Government of. *Report of the Pakistan Commission on the Status of Women*. Islamabad: Pakistan Commission on the Status of Women, 1984.
———, Government of. *Report of the Expert Group on Women's Development During Seventh Five-Year Plan*. Government of Pakistan, 1988.
———, Government of. *Seventh Five-Year Plan, 1988–1993*, and *Perspective Plan, 1988–2003*. Islamabad, Planning Commission, 1988.
———, Government of. Women's Division (Cabinet Secretariat). *World Conference of the United Nations Decade for Women: 1975–85, Equality, Development and Peace, Pakistan Country Paper*. Nairobi, Kenya, July 15–26, 1985.
———, Ministry of Education. *Review of Education Policies and Corresponding Five-Year Plans (1947–1986)*, by M. A. Aziz. Pakistan: Government of Pakistan, Ministry of Education, Planning Wing, APEID, 1986.
Pangestu, Mari and Mayling Oey-Gardiner. "Indonesia," in: Wong Poh Kam and Ng Chee Yuen, eds., *Human Resource Development and Utilization in the Asia-Pacific: A Social Absorption Capacity Approach*. Singapore: Institute of Southeast Asian Studies, 1991, pp. 61–79.
People's Educational Press. *Jiaoyu shinian* (Ten years of education). Beijing: Renmin jiaoyu chubanshe, 1960.
Perera, Iranganie. "Teachers' Classroom Practices—Is there Gender Discrimination?" in: *Gender and Education In Sri Lanka*. Colombo: CENWOR, 1991, pp. 56–72.
Pharr, Susan J. "Japan: Historical and Contemporary Perspectives," in: Janet Z. Giele and Audrey C. Smock, eds., *Women: Roles and Status in Eight Countries*. New York: John Wiley, 1977.
———. "The Japanese Women: Evolving Views of Life and Role," in: Sylvia A. Chipp and Justin, J Green, eds., *Asian Women in Transition*. University Park: Pennsylvania State University Press, 1980.
———. "Women in Contemporary Japan," in: *Kodansha Encyclopedia of Japan*. Tokyo: Kodansha, 1983.
———. *Political Women: The Search for a Place in Political Life*. Berkeley: University of California Press, 1981.
Pryosusilo, Mari. "Schooling in A Javanese Village: Some Observations." *PRISMA* 38 (December, 1985): 91–99.
Raj, Maithreyi Krishna. "Women, Work and Science in India," in: G. P. Kelly and C. M. Elliott, eds., *Women's Education in the Third World: Comparative Perspectives*. Albany: State Universiry of New York Press, 1982.
Randhawa, Aesha, et al. "Rural Female Education: A Neglected Sector." *Pakistan and Gulf Economist* (November 17–23, 1990): 22–25.
Rawjee, Mariam. "Beyond the Chardiwari." *Herald (Pakistan)* 20 (May 1989): 73–91.
Reddy, Rita. "Women and the Legal Sector." Paper presented at the Conference on ASEAN Professional Women. Universiti Teknologi Malaysia, Johor, Sept. 1992.
Renmin ribao (People's Daily). Beijing, China. Overseas edition. May 23, 1993; May 24, 1993.
Republik Indonesia. *Nota Keuangan dan Rancangan Anggaran Pendapatan dan Belanja Negara Tahun Anggaran 1993/94*. 1993/94 National Annual Budget. Jakarta, 1993.
Research Institute of All-China Women's Federation, et al. *Statistics on Chinese Women, 1949–1989*. Beijing: Zhongguo tongji chubanshe, 1993.
Richman, Barry. *Industrial Society in Communist China*. New York: Random House, 1969.
Risseeuw, Carla. *The Fish Don't Talk about Water*. Leiden: E. J. Brill, 1988.
Robin-Mowry, Dorothy. *The Hidden Sun: Women in Modern Japan*. Boulder, CO: Westview Press, 1983.

Ronnas, Per. *Human Resources Development in Pakistan*. Research Reports, No. 11. Sweden: Studies in International Economics and Geography (1990): 1–42.

Rostow, W. W. *The Stages of Economic Growth*. Cambridge, UK: Cambridge University Press, 1960.

Rupasinghe, S. "Gender Differences in Achievement at Secondary School Level in Sri Lanka: Apparent or Real," in: *Gender and Education in Sri Lanka*. Colombo: CENWOR, 1991, pp. 23–35.

———. "Gender Differences in the Career Aspirations of Students in GCE (OL) grades in Sri Lanka," in: *Gender and Education in Sri Lanka*. Colombo: CENWOR, 1991, pp. 97–106.

———. "Social Environment and its Relationship with Factors Associated with Schooling in Sri Lanka." *University of Colombo Review* 5 (1986): 82–95.

Samarasinghe, Vidyamali. "Women and Geographic Space: A Regional Analysis of Women's Well Being and Productive Work in Sri Lanka," in: *The Hidden Face of Development*. Colombo: CENWOR, 1989, pp. 17–40.

Sathar, Zeba A. "Does Female Education Affect Fertility Behaviour in Pakistan?" *Pakistan Development Review* 23, no. 4 (Winter 1984): 573–594.

Sathar, Zeba A. and Shahnaz Kazi. "Women, Work and Reproduction in Karachi." *International Family Planning Perspectives* 16 (June 1990): 66–69, 80.

Schonberger, R. J. "Inflexible Working Conditions Keep Women Unliberated." *Personnel Journal*, 50 (1971): 834–837.

Schultz, Theodore W. *Education and Economic Growth*. Chicago: University of Chicago Press, 1961.

———. "Investment in Human Capital," *American Economic Review* 51, no. 1 (March 1961): 1–17; also in: Mark Blaug, ed., *Economics of Education*, vol.1. Harmondsworth, UK: Penguin, 1968.

Schultz, T. P. "Returns to Women's Education," in: E. King and A. Hill, eds., *Women's Education in Developing Countries*. Baltimore: The Johns Hopkins University Press, 1993.

Shah, Nasra M., ed. *Pakistani Women: A Socioeconomic and Demographic Profile*. Islamabad: Pakistan Institute of Development Economics, 1986.

Shah, Nasra M. and M. Anwar. *Basic Needs, Women, and Development: A Survey of Squatters in Lahore, Pakistan*. Honolulu: East-West Population Institute, East-West Center, 1986.

Sharp, I. *Singapore Trade and Industry*. Singapore: Womenpower in Singapore.

Shih, Ming. *Tai-Wan-Jen Ssu-Pai-Nien Shih* (Four hundred years of the history of the Taiwanese people). San Jose, CA: Paradise Culture Associates, 1980.

Sidel, Ruth. *Women and Child Care in China*. New York: Hill and Wang, 1972.

Sievers, Sharon. *Flowers in Salt: The Beginning of Feminist Consciousness in Modern Japan*. Stanford, CA: Stanford University Press, 1983.

Singapore, Department of Statistics. Census of population 1990 Advance data release. Published 1991.

———, Department of Statistics. Census of population 1970, Singapore.

———, Department of Statistics. Economic and Social Statistics Singapore 1960–1982.

———, Department of Statistics. *Yearbook of Statistics Singapore 1974/75*.

———, Department of Statistics. *Yearbook of Statistics Singapore 1980*.

———, Department of Statistics. *Yearbook of Statistics Singapore 1991*.

———, Department of Statistics. *Yearbook of Statistics Singapore 1981/82*.

———, Government of. *Singapore: the Next Lap*. Times editions, 1991.

———, Government Printing Office. *Annual report of the Department of Education for the Year 1946*.

———, Government Printing Office. *Annual report of the Department of Education for the Year 1952*.

———, Industrial Training Board. *Key Statistics on Vocational Training 1983–84*.

———, Institute of Technical Education. *Key Statistics on Technical Education and Training 1991.*

———, Research and Statistics Department, Ministry of Labour. *Singapore Yearbook of Labour Statistics 1980.* Published 1981.

———, Research and Statistics Department, Ministry of Labour. *Singapore Yearbook of Labour Statistics 1991.* Published 1992.

Singh, Prabhash P. *Women in India: A Statistical Panorama.* New Delhi: Inter-India Publications, 1991.

Smelser, Neil J. " Toward a Theory of Modernization," in: Eva and Amitai Etzioni, *Social Change.* New York: Basic Books, 1964.

Smith, Robert J. and Ella L. Wiswell. *The Women in Suye Mura.* Chicago: University of Chicago Press, 1982.

Smock, A. C. *Women's Education in Developing Countries: Opportunities and Outcomes.* New York: Praeger, 1981.

Sri Lanka, Department of Census and Statistics. *Census 1946, 1953, 1963, 1971, 1981.*

Sri Lanka Federation of University Women. *Report on the Study of Unemployment among Women Arts Graduates.* Colombo, 1980.

Sri Lanka, Ministry of Education. A Study on Educational Opportunity and Employment *Opportunity in Sri Lanka.* UNESCO, 1973.

Standing, Guy and Glen Sheehan. *Labor Force Participation in Low Income Countries.* Geneva: ILO, 1978.

Strauss, Murray. "Family Characteristics and Occupational Choice of University Entrants." *University of Ceylon Review* no. 2 (1951).

Subbamma, Malladi. *Women: Tradition and Culture.* New Delhi: Sterling Publishers, 1985.

Subbarao, K. and L. Raney. *Social Gains from Female Education: A Cross-National Study.* World Bank Discussion Paper No. 194. Washington, DC, The World Bank, 1993.

Sudaryanti. "Persepsi Akuntan Publik Wanita Terhadap Penggunaan Jadwal Kerja Alternatif" (Perception of female public accountants on alternative work schedules). Unpublished thesis, Jakarta: University of Indonesia, 1992.

Sugimoto, Etsu. *Daughter of Samurai.* First published in 1932; reprint, London: Hutchinson, 1960.

Summers, Lawrence H. "Investing in All People: Educating Women in Developing Countries." Speech delivered on Development Economics Seminar at the 1992 World Bank Annual Meetings.

Taiwan, Executive Yuan. *Report on Fertility and Employment of Married Women, Taiwan Area, Republic of China.* Directorate-General of Budget, Accounting and Statistics, 1990.

———. *Yearbook of Manpower Statistics, Taiwan Area, R.O.C.* Directorate-General of Budget, Accounting and Statistics 1990.

———. *Social Indicators in Taiwan Area of the Republic of China.* Directorate-General of Budget, Accounting, and Statistics, 1990.

Taiwan, ROC, Ministry of Education. *Educational Statistics of the Republic of China, 1992.* Taipei: Ministry of Education, 1992.

———, Ministry of Education. *Educational Indicators of the ROC,* Taipei: Ministry of Education, 1992, p. 362.

Tan, Renjiu. *Zhougguo de lihun yanjiu* (A study of divorce in China). Shanghai: Zhonghua jidujiao nu qingnianhui quanguo xiehui, 1932.

Thogersen, Stig. "China's Senior Middle Schools in a Social Perspective: A Survey of Yantai District, Shandong Province." *China Quarterly* no. 109 (March 1987): 72–100.

Tilak, J. B. G. "Inequality in Education by Sex in India," in: Chetana Kalbagh, ed., *Women and Development,* vol. 5. New Delhi: Discovery Publishing House, 1991.

Tsai, Shu-ling. "Occupational Segregation and Differential Educational Achievement: A Comparison between Men and Women." *Chung Kuo She Hui Hsueh K'an* (Chinese Journal of Sociology) 11 (1987): 61–91.
Tsui, Elaine Yi-Lan. *"Are Married Daughters Spilt Water? A Study of Working Women in Urban Taiwan."* Monograph 4. Women's Research Program, Population Studies Center, National Taiwan University, 1987.
Tsurumi, Patricia. "Women's Education," in: *Kodansha Encyclopedia of Japan* V.8. Tokyo: Kodansha, 1983.
Underwood, Horace G. "Report of Education in South Korea." Records of the U. S. Department of War, June 1947.
UNESCO. *UNESCO Statistical Yearbook.* Paris: 1974, 1975, 1980, 1985, 1991.
UNESCO. *Universal Primary Education for Girls: Pakistan.* Bangkok: UNESCO, 1987.
UNICEF and Pakistan. *Situation Analysis of Children and Women in Pakistan.* Islamabad: n.p., 1987.
Universiti Pertanian Malaysia/Ministry of Education. *National Workshop on Technical and Vocational Education for Women in Malaysia.* Report of the Proceedings of the Workshop Universiti Pertanian Malaysia, March 1992.
University Grants Commission. *About Higher Education in India: Some Statistics Relating to Women's Education.* New Delhi: University Grants Commission, 1981.
University Grants Commission. *Annual Report, 1988–89.* Delhi: University Grants Commission, 1989.
Uswatte Aratchi, G. "University Admissions in Ceylon. Their Economic and Social Background and Employment Expectations." *Modern Asian Studies* 8 no. 1 (1974).
Wang, Mengmei. *Kangzhan shiqi de funu gongzuo* (Women work during the Resistance War). Master's thesis. Taiwan: Donghai University, 1987.
Wheeler, Helen R. "Women's Studies, Higher Education, and Feminist Educators in Japan Today." *Journal of the National Association of Women Deans, Administrators, and Counselors* 48 (Summer 1985): 31–36.
White, Merry. *The Japanese Educational Challenge: A Commitment to Children.* New York: Free Press, 1988.
Wilson, R. *Learning to Be Chinese: The Political Socialization of Children in Taiwan.* Cambridge: The M.I.T. Press, 1970.
Wolf, Margery. *Revolution Postponed: Women in Contemporary China.* Stanford, CA: Stanford University Press, 1985.
Woolf, V. *A Room of One's Own.* New York: Harcourt and Brace, 1929.
World Bank. *Indonesia: Adjustment, Growth and Sustainable Development.* Report No. 7222–IND, 1988.
World Bank. *Islamic Republic of Pakistan, Staff Appraisal Report: Balochistan Primary Education Program.* Washington, DC: The World Bank, 1993.
———. *The East Asian Miracle, Economic Growth and Public Policy.* World Bank Policy Research Report. Published for the World Bank by Oxford University Press, New York, 1993.
———. *Women in Pakistan: An Economic and Social Strategy.* Washington, DC: The World Bank, 1989.
———. *World Development Report (WDR) 1993: Investing in Health.* Oxford: The World Bank, 1993.
———. *World Tables.* Baltimore: Johns Hopkins University Press/The World Bank, 1993.
Yasmeen, Mohiuddin. "Discrimination in the Pakistan Labour Market: Myth and Reality." *Pakistan Development Review* (Winter 1991): 965–76.
———. "Economic Role of Women: A Case of Occupational Dependency." *Pakistan and Gulf Economist* (Pakistan) 4 (February 2, 1985): 12–15.

Yeh, C. H. *Nu-Hsing Lao-Kung Pao-Hu Cheng-Tse Chih T'an-T'ao: Lao-Tung Chi-Chun-Fa Chih Shih-Cheng Fen-Hsi* (A study on labor policies protecting female workers—Empirical analysis of the Labor Standards Law of R.O.C.). Taipei: Graduate Institute of Public Policy, National Chung-Hsing University, 1990.

Yeon, Hacheong. *Productivity, Labor Quality Indexes and Labor Structure in Industry: 1962–76.* Seoul: Korea Development Institute, 1980.

You, Chien-ming. *Tai-Wan Jih-Chih-Shih-Tai te Fu-Nu Chiao-Yu* (Taiwanese women's education under the Japanese reign). Department of History, National Taiwan Normal University, 1988.

Young, Yi-Rong. "Chiao-yu yu kuo-chia fa-chan: Tai-wan ching-yen te fan-hsing" (Educational and national development: A reflection upon "the Taiwan experience"), in: Lai, T. H. and C. J. Huang, eds., *Taiwan Chan Hou te Fa Chan Ching Yen* (The development experience of Taiwan since the post-war era). Taipei: Institute of Social Science, Academia Sinica, 1991, pp. 133–179.

———. "Taiwan," in: Wielemans, W. and P. Chan, eds., *Education and Culture in Industrializing Asia.* Leuven: Leuven University Press, 1992, pp. 327–378.

Yu, H. Y. "Tai-wan ti-ch'u lao-tung shih-ch'ang te hsing-pie ch'i-shi" (Sex discrimination in the labor market in Taiwan)." Paper presented at the Conference on Sex Equality at Work Place, Center for Population Studies and Women's Research Center, National Taiwan University, Taipei, 1991.

Yu, Y. S. "The Singapore Women," in: Devan Nair, ed. *Socialism That Works: The Singapore Way.* Singapore: Federal Publishing, 1976.

Zeenatunnisa. *Sex Discrimination in Eduction: Content Analysis of Pakistani School Text Books.* Institute of Social Studies, Working Paper. No. 62 (August 1989): 1–61.

Zhongguo funu bao (Journal of women in China). Beijing, China. January 11, 1988; March 15, 1989; June 20, 1990; October 12 and 16, 1992; May 17, July 28, and August 18, 1993.

Contributors

KOWSAR P. CHOWDHURY is a specialist on education, women, and development. She has been working with the World Bank as a consultant since 1991. She was Co-Director for the Graduate Group for Feminist Studies at the State University of New York, and Research Officer for the Second Primary Education Project conducted by the Ministry of Education, Bangladesh. Her areas of specialization are women's education, literacy, and alternative school systems. She conducted the background work on education for the World Bank's policy paper "Enhancing Women's Participation in Economic Development" and is working on a study entitled "Levelling the Playing Fields: What Works to Equalize Access to Education for Girls and Boys."

RATNA GHOSH is Professor of Education at the Department of Administration and Policy Studies, McGill University, where she began her career in 1977. She has published numerous book chapters and journal articles; and has co-authored volumes on education such as *Women in the Family and Economy* (1981), *Education and the Process of Change* (1987), *Social Change and Education in Canada* (1991), *South Asian Canadians: Issues in the Politics of Culture* (1992). She is presently working on a book on intercultural education.

HSIAO-CHIN HSIEH is Associate Professor at National Tsing Hua University, Taiwan. She received her Ph.D. from the Department of Educational Policy Studies, University of Wisconsin-Madison, and has been conducting research in the fields of sociology of education and gender studies.

SWARNA JAYAWEERA received her Master's and doctoral degrees from the University of London and was a Postdoctoral Fellow at Columbia University, New York. She was Professor of Education and Head of the Department of

Social Science Education at the University of Colombo. She was in turn UNESCO Advisor and UNICEF Consultant on the Access of Women to Education in Nepal and has been a consultant to UN agencies and bilateral agencies in Sri Lanka and in the Asian Region on education and on women's issues. She is a co-founder and currently Joint Coordinator of the Centre for Women's Research in Sri Lanka. She has published extensively on women and on education.

OKSOON KIM earned her doctorate from the University of Southern California. She has been a researcher at the Korean Council for University Education and currently teaches sociology of education and international education at Ewha Woman's University and Sangmyung University. She is also Research Director at the Center for Korean Youth Culture.

GUAT TIN LOW is Senior Lecturer in Education with the National Institute of Education, Nanyang Technological University, Singapore. She was trained in Australia and the United States, and holds master's and doctoral degrees in educational psychology and educational administration. Her areas of interests are cognition, teacher job satisfaction, and mentoring for educational administrators. She has co-authored and edited numerous publications, such as *Developing Executive Skills*, *Management Tools for Educational Managers*, and *Successful Women in Singapore*.

GRACE C. L. MAK has a doctorate in comparative education and is Associate Professor in Education at the Chinese University of Hong Kong. She has published on education and development and women's education and labor force participation in China and in Hong Kong. She has also conducted consultancy for World Bank education projects in China.

MACHIKO MATSUI holds a Ph.D. in comparative education from the State University of New York at Buffalo. Currently she is teaching a course on women in East Asia while directing a Japanese program at Southern Methodist University, Dallas. She has been conducting comparative research on feminism and women's education in Japan and the United States.

MAYLING OEY-GARDINER received her Ph.D. in demography from the Australian National University in 1982. After returning to Indonesia, she resumed her teaching duties at the Faculty of Economics, University of Indonesia. She has been active in various aspects of social science research. It is through Insan Harapan Sejahtera, a private firm specializing in social science research and consultancy where she acts as Managing Director, that she has gained increasing prominence in the area of policy research on women's issues in Indonesia.

ROBIAH SIDIN received her graduate education from the University of Malaya in Kuala Lumpur. She joined the Faculty of Education, Universiti Kebangsaan Malaysia as a lecturer in 1974 and became dean in 1985 and full professor in 1993. She has published five books and many book chapters and journal articles, and is best known for her work on women's education and teacher education. She has often been commissioned to head research projects on educational integration, women's education, teacher education, and Malay values and education. At present she is conducting a study on the impact of economic restructuring on women's education in Malaysia.

RIGA-ADIWOSO SUPRAPTO received her first degree from Rijskuniversiteit Leiden, The Netherlands in Southeast Asian Studies, and her M.Sc. and Ph.D. degrees in sociology and anthropology from Georgetown University, Washington, D.C. She has been a full-time faculty member with the Department of Economics, University of Indonesia, since 1983. Currently she is also Vice-Director for Academic Affairs at the Management School, University of Indonesia. Since 1972 she has been engaged in women's issues both as an activist and as a scholar. Between 1985 and 1991 she worked for the Ministry of Population and Environment with a focus on women and the environment.

ABDULAZIZ TALBANI has a doctorate from McGill University, Montreal, and is Assistant Professor at the University of Saint Thomas in Houston, Texas. He has several chapters in books and articles in journals on education and development, multicultural education, and curriculum studies. Currently he is working on two book projects, one concerning multicultural education and the other on gender role socialization in education.

Index

Page numbers in boldface type refer to main entries.

Asia, 143, 144

Bangladesh, 190, 191
Beldia, 203
bhikkunis, 218
British colonialism, 121, 144, 165, 166, 169, 187, 188, 218-19
Buddhism, 187, 217

caste system, 187, 188
Ceylon, 217. *See* Sri Lanka.
China, People's Republic of, **3-27**, 144
   adult education, 17
   All-China Women's Federation, 7, 12, 23, 24
   birth rates, 14
   Chinese Communist Party, 4
   Confucianism, 4
   Cultural Revolution, 8, 13, 15
   Deng Xiaoping, 14
   development, 3, 7, 8, 9, 11, 14, 15, 16, 21, 24
   economic reform, 19-23
   enrollment statistics, 7-8, 15-16
   family responsibility system, 19
   graduate education, 17
   Great Leap Forward, 8, 12, 13
   Guomindang, 4-6, 13. *See also* Kuomin-tang in Taiwan.
   higher education, 9-11
   history, 4-6
   illiteracy statistics, 15-16
   labor force participation, 11-14, 17-23
      of rural women, 13-14, 19-20
      of urban women, 11-13, 20-23
      the state as employer, 21
      wage differentiation, 21
   marriage and the family, 6-7, 14-15
   political participation, **23-24**
   primary education, 7-8, 15
   secondary education, 8, 15
   structure of education system, 7
   vocational education, 15-16
   women academics, 22, 24
   women's groups, 5
   women's studies, 24
Christian missionary influence in education, 4, 144, 145, 189, 218

Dutch, 65, 218

England, 143

Federated Malay States, 121
female infanticide, 14, 188

Hinduism, 187, 188, 217
Holland, 95
Hong Kong, 237
human capital theory, 35, 38, 51, 58, 60, 61, 217

India, 144, **165-86**, 187
   Aryan expansion, 165
   caste, 168
   Christians, 181
   Committee on the Status of Women, 168
   compulsory education, 169
   constitutional rights for women, **168-69**
   cultural bias in education, 181
   development, 165, 182
      national development, 176
   dropout rates, 170, 172
   elite women, 179

employment, 176–78
  informal and unorganized sector, 176
  labor force participation rates, 176
  organized sector, 176
  sex segregation in, 182
enrollment statistics, 170, 171, 172, 173
First National Policy on Education (1968), 169
Gandhi, Mahatma, 166
government policies toward women, 167–68
history, 166–68
Industrial Training Institutes, 175
literacy rates, 167, 169, 181
National Committee for Women's Education, 180
National Development Plans, 183
national independence (1947), 166, 167, 168, 169
National Policy of Education (1986), 169
Nehru, 166, 183, 184
primary and lower secondary education, 170–171
  rural-urban difference, 170
research programs, 174
Scheduled Castes and Tribes, 180
secondary and higher secondary education, 171–172
  rural-urban difference, 171
sex ration in population, 179
social class, 181
  and education, 170
social outcomes of sexual stratification, 179–82
Status of Women Committee, 168, 181
structure of education, 169
tertiary education, 172–75
  sex-segregation by field of study, 173–74
  urban-rural disparities, 175
women academics, 177–78
women in the civil service, 176–77
women in politics, 178
women in science, 174, 178
International Women's Year (1975), 41, 221
Indonesia, 95–118
  compulsory education, 99
  Constitution of Indonesia, 96
  development, 97, 114, 116
  economic deregulation, 105, 108
  educational expenditure, 96
  enrollment statistics, 98–102
  export-oriented industries, 106, 108
  Five-Year Development Plans:
    Fifth, 97
    Fourth, 97
  illiteracy rates, 96
  labor force participation, **105–16**
    formal sector, 105, 106, 108, 114
    gender-based wage differentiation, 111
    informal sector, 106
    labor force participation rates, 105
      urban-rural difference, 106–108, 109, 111
    impact of vocational vs. general education on, 109
  occupational prospect of education, 97
  primary education, 96, 99, 102, 102
  public vs. private initiatives in education, 96, 97, 103–4
  quality of education, **102–4**
  religious schools, 96, 97
  secondary education, 98, 100, 102, 103
  structure of education system, 95–96
  tertiary education, 101, 103
  unemployment, open, 105, **112–15**
    rural-urban difference in, 114
  vocational schools, 96, 102, 103, 104, 109
Islam, 95, 121, 193
Israel, 151

Jainism, 187
Japan, 29–49, 66, 67, 144
  birth rates, 34
  childcare facilities, 45
  Confucianism, 29
  development, 29, 30, 41, 42, 46
  "education mom," 41
  educational expansion, **32–37**
    private initiatives in, 32, 36–37
  elementary education, 30–31, 33
  enrollment statistics, 30, 34, 43
  Equal Employment Opportunity Law (1986), 30, 43–44
  feminist movement, 32, 43
  higher education, **32–37**
    imperial universities, 32, 36
    segregation by fields of study, 32, 35–37, 44–45
  labor force participation, **37–41**
    labor force participation rates, 37, 38
    marginalization of female labor, 45
    part-time employment, 39, 45
    women in nontraditional employment, 45

maternity leave, 43
Meiji Period (1868–1912), 29–30
missionary influence on girl's education, 31
Mori Arinori, 29
National Women's Center, 41, 42, 45
nonformal education, 41–42
prewar women's education, 30–33
ryosai kenbo, 29–31, 38, 39, 42, 45
secondary education, 34
   gender-streaming in, 43
Tsuda Umeko, 32
vocational schools, 35
women's studies, 42, 43, 45
Yoshioka Yayoi, 32

king of England, 122
Koran, 121, 193
Korea, South, **51–63**
   development, 51, 55, 62
   economic growth, 55–61
   educational expansion, 52–55, 58–61
      private initiatives in, 53–55
   educational expenditure, 53
   enrollment statistics, 52, 54
   export-oriented industrialization strategy, 56, 58, 62
   higher education, 55
      sex segregation by field of study, 55
   Korean War, 51
   labor force participation of women, 56–58
      wage differentiation, 57, 60
   labor migration, 58
   labor productivity, 59–61
   parental expectations for children's education, 54
   population growth rates, 52

Malayan Union, 122
Malaysia, 96, **119–41**, 144
   Bahasa Malay, 119, 124, 129
   Dato' Napsiah Omar, 138
   Dato' Seri Rafidah Aziz, 138
   development, 119, **125–27**
      economic, 119, 126
      national, 119, 120, 135
      social, **136–37**
   Educational Act (1961), 124
   educational attainment of female employees, 130
   enrollment statistics, 121, 123, 124–25, 128–29, 132, 134
   ethnicity and education, 119, 121, 122, 123, 125, 126, 127
   history, **121–25**
   labor force participation:
      horizontal segregation, 135
      labor force participation rates, 119
      labor share of women, 135
      vertical segregation, 135
   labor migration, 138
   missionary influence in education, 121, 124
   National Advisory Council for the Integration of Women in Development, 126
   National Council for Women Organizations, 137
   National Development Policy, 125
   national independence (1957), 121
   National Policy for Women (1989), 127, 135
   New Economic Policy, 125
   nonformal education, 123, 126–27, 129, 137
   primary and secondary education, 127–29
      subject streaming in secondary education, 133
   Second Malaysia Plan (1971–75), 125
   Sixth Malaysia Plan (1991–95), 126
   tertiary education, **132–34**
      sex segregation by field of study, 132–33
      women faculty, 134, 136
   United Malays National Organization, 123
   vocational and technical education, **129–32**
      sex segregation by field of study, 130–31
   women in the civil service, 120
   women in politics, 120, **137–38**
   women in professions, 135–36, 138
   working-class women, 138
M-shape labor force participation profile, 22, 40, 45, 80
Manu's Code, 188
The Middle East, 237
Mohammad Tughlaq, 188
Mughal rule (A.D. 1200–1800), 188
Muslim rule, 187
Muslims, 180, 187, 188, 222

Nairobi, 126

Pakistan, **187–215**
   barriers to female education, **199–203**
   birth rates, 191

coeducation, 192, 199
Commission on the Status of Women, 205
development, 189–90, 202
economic and social returns to women's education, 191
education and fertility, 208
educational expenditure, 194
educational wastage, 196
enrollment statistics, 195, 196, 197
First Five Year Plan, 193
government policy on women's education, 193–94
history, 187–89
household income, 189
infant mortality rates, 191, 208
labor force participation, 203–208
    affirmative action plan, 208
    distribution of women across occupations, 205
    formal sector, 205, 208
    informal and unorganized sector, 204, 205
    labor force participation rates, 203–204, 205
        influence of marital status on, 207
    women in teaching, 205
literacy rate, 194, 195
maternal mortality rates, 191, 208
maternity leave, 208
mothers' influence on daughters' education, 202
nonformal education, 193, 203
Pakistan Education Conference, 193
population growth rate, 191
poverty line, 190
primary education, 196
secondary education, 196–98
Seventh Five Year Plan, 190, 194
sex ration in population, 191
Sixth Five Year Plan, 193, 194
structure of education system, 192
tertiary education, 198–99
    gender streaming in, 199
vocational education, 197, 203
women in politics, 209–10
Women's Division, 192, 203
women's status, 190–92
Portuguese, 65, 218
purdah (seclusion), 167, 222

Raffles, Stamford, 144

sati, 188, 222

Singapore, 96, 143–61, 237
adult and nonformal education, 152–53
childcare facilities, 154, 158
development, 144, 154
educational expenditure, 153
education structure, 145
enrollment statistics, 145, 150, 151
ethnicity and education, 144
family-planning policy, 150, 154
foreign maids, 154
history, 143, 144–45
illiteracy rates, 147
labor force participation, 153–58
    age-specific labor force participation, 158
    labor force participation rates, 154
    labor share of women, 153, 154, 156
    sex segregation by occupation, 156
    wage differentiation, 158
Lee Kuan Yew, 147, 160
literacy rates, 145
male-female ration in population, 143
primary and secondary education, 145–47
tertiary education, 147–51
    sex segregation by field of study, 150–51
Spaniards, 65
Sri Lanka, 217–44
compulsory education, 222
Constitution of Sri Lanka, 222
curriculum, 221, 225
development, 217, 220, 221, 233, 236, 237, 241
domestic violence, 240–41
dropout rates, 223
economic liberalization, 220
enrollment statistics, 221, 223, 228
ethnicity and education, 241
family roles, 239–41
GDP growth rate, 220
higher education, 228
    sex segregation by field of study, 231–32
    social composition of, 221
history, 217–22
labor force participation, 233–38
    informal sector, 238
    labor force participation rates, 234, 236
        and educational attainment, 234–35
        of professional women, 235
    sex segregation in, 236, 238

literacy rates, 219, 221
nonformal education, 225
parental aspirations of children, 222
population growth rates, 220
pre-schools, 232
rural-urban difference
    in education, 224–25, 228
    in employment, 240
single-sex schools, 222
social class and education, 225
structure of education system, 223
unemployment rates, 221, 234
vocational and technical education, 223
Straits Settlement, 121

Taiwan, Republic of China, 65–91
    birth rates, 66
    Cheng Ch'eng-kung, 66
    compulsory education, 67, 68
    development, 65, 68, 79, 80, 83, 84, 85, 86
    divorce, 84
    education structure, 68
    educational expansion, 67–75
        gendered aspect of, 70–72
        uneven rates across fields of study, 70
    enrollment statistics, 67, 71
    ethnicity and women, 84
    Eugenic Protection Law (1984), 85
    Factory-School Cooperative Education, 82
    Family Law (1985), 83
    gender inequality in the family, 74
    gender segregation in education, 72, 73–74
        by field of study, 72
        gender-role stereotypes in textbooks, 73
        in schooling processes, 73
    graduate education, 71
    history, 65–67
    Japanese occupation, 66, 67, 79
    Kuo-min-tang, 66, 67, 68, 79. *See also* Guomindang in China.
    labor market participation, **76–83**
        horizontal job segregation, 77
        informal employment, 81
        labor participation rates, 76
        the role of education in, 76
        student-workers, 82
        vertical job segregation, 78
        wage differentiation, 76, 77
        women as reserve labor, 76, 80
        young female factory workers, 82
    per capita gross national product, 66
    political ideology, 68
    population growth rates, 66
    public vs. private schools, 68–70
    sexual violence, 83
    Social Change Survey (1991), 74, 86
    vocational schools, 67, 70
    women's groups, 85
    women's status, 83
Thailand, 96, 222

United Nations, 168
United Nations Convention on the Elimination of All Forms of Discrimination, 43, 221
United Nations Convention on the Rights of the Child (1989), 222
United Nations Decade of Women (1976–85), 126, 221
United Nations Declaration of Human Rights (1960), 124
United States, 151
University Grants Commission, 177, 231, 232

Vedic period (2000–1500 B.C.), 165, 187
Victorian womanhood, 29, 166, 219

Woolf, Virginia, 143
World Bank, 116, 205, 220, 222, 237
World Declaration on Education for All (1990), 222
World War II, 33, 51, 66, 121

Zenana Schools, 189